FREE TRADE
UNDER FIRE

Princeton University Press   *Princeton and Oxford*

FREE TRADE
UNDER FIRE

THIRD EDITION

DOUGLAS A. IRWIN

Copyright © 2009 by Princeton University Press

Published by Princeton University Press, 41 William Street, Princeton, New Jersey 08540

In the United Kingdom: Princeton University Press, 6 Oxford Street, Woodstock, Oxfordshire OX20 1TW

All Rights Reserved

Library of Congress Cataloging-in-Publication Data

Irwin, Douglas A., 1962-

    Free trade under fire / Douglas A. Irwin.—3rd ed.

      p. cm.

    Includes bibliographical references and index.

    ISBN 978-0-691-14315-6 (pbk. : alk. paper) 1. Free trade—United States. 2. United States—Commercial policy. 3. Globalization. I. Title.

    HF1756.I68 2009

    382′.710973—dc22   2009002285

British Library Cataloging-in-Publication Data is available

This book has been composed in

Printed on acid-free paper. ∞

press.princeton.edu

Printed in the United States of America

1 3 5 7 9 10 8 6 4 2

10 9 8 7 6 5 4 3 2 1

FOR JAGDISH BHAGWATI, CHAMPION OF THE MULTILATERAL TRADING SYSTEM

Contents

Figures

Tables

Dartmouth student who helped with fact checking and the index. Thanks also go to Peter Dougherty and Seth Ditchik at Princeton University Press for their support of this project. Finally, this edition is dedicated to Jagdish Bhagwati, whose friendship and encouragement over many years has been, and will always be, deeply appreciated.

Free trade, one of the greatest blessings which a government can confer on a people, is in almost every country unpopular.
—*Thomas Babington Macaulay (1824)*

Introduction

Nearly two centuries after Macaulay made it, this observation by one of Britain's great historians still rings true. Growing world trade has helped lift standards of living around the world, and yet today, as in Macaulay's time, free trade does not win many popularity contests. Indeed, public opinion surveys in the United States and Europe reveal increasing skepticism about the benefits of international trade and trade agreements. Trade policy remains a highly controversial subject, a source of never-ending public debate.

In almost every country, international trade brings out anxieties and insecurities. With each passing decade, some of the old fears about trade recede and new ones take their place. In the 1980s, many Americans were convinced that Japan would achieve economic dominance by wiping out industry after industry in the United States, from automobiles to semiconductors to supercomputers, and thereby diminish America's position in the world. In the 1990s, many feared that the North American Free Trade Agreement (NAFTA) would result in a "giant sucking sound" of jobs lost to Mexico due to its low wages. Others protested in the streets of Seattle in late 1999 against the World Trade Organization (WTO) for its promotion of free trade and alleged indifference to the world's workers and environment. Now, in the first decade of the twenty-first century, concern has shifted to China and India. China has become a goliath in the production of manufactured goods, and—it is often argued—responsible for stagnant wages in the United States. Meanwhile the offshoring of white-collar jobs (from call centers to software programming) to India has sparked new worries of a "service sector sucking sound."[1]

Fears of trade exist in good times and in bad. The 1990s were a period of robust economic growth and the lowest U.S. unemployment in thirty years, yet NAFTA and the WTO generated heated debates. And economic downturns invariably bring out cries that foreign countries are stealing our jobs and therefore protectionist trade policies are required. Furthermore, the trade agreements of the past are still very controversial. NAFTA was signed long ago, in 1993, but during the 2008 Democratic primaries, Hillary Clinton called NAFTA a mistake and proposed a "time out" on further trade agreements. Meanwhile, to the consternation of Canada and Mexico, candidate Barack Obama promised to renegotiate the agreement. Yet the NAFTA-bashing is puzzling because U.S. tariffs on imports from Mexico had been at very low levels for many decades prior to NAFTA; what NAFTA really did was abolish Mexico's high tariffs on U.S. exports to that country.

The many vociferous critics of free trade believe that it brings pervasive harm. A wide range of groups, from environmentalists to religious organizations to human rights activists, have joined in protesting against free trade. These groups rail against trade agreements and the WTO as benefiting corporations, harming workers, decimating manufacturing industries, sweeping aside environmental regulations, and undermining America's sovereignty.

In his recent book, *Myths of Free Trade*, Senator Sherrod Brown, an Ohio Democrat who has opposed trade agreements, writes: "An unregulated global economy is a threat to us all—to the child in Avon Lake, Ohio, who eats raspberries grown in Guatemala by poorly paid farmers who use pesticides banned in the United States; the unskilled, minimum wage worker in Los Angeles who loses her job to an unskilled, five-dollar-a-day worker in Yucatan; the machinist in New York who takes a wage cut because of his company's threat to move to China; the Chinese prison camp laborer; the tomato grower in Florida who has to sell his farm; and the peasant in Chiapas who must fell the native village where

---

[1] Perhaps not surprisingly, many people in Japan, Mexico, China, India, and the rest of the world have seen things very differently. They fear economic domination by the United States and wonder how local producers can ever compete against large, wealthy, and technologically sophisticated American companies.

his family had made its home for dozens of generations. But our national leaders—particularly Republican congressional leaders and Presidents Clinton and Bush, economists and newspaper editors, business executives and tenured economics professors—continue to ignore the uncomfortable consequences of free trade, hoping the American public will not take notice."[2]

Opponents of free trade are not confined to one segment of the political spectrum. From Patrick Buchanan on the right to Ralph Nader on the left, trade skeptics can be found everywhere. And the litany of complaints placed on the doorstep of free trade goes well beyond the perennial objection—emphasized almost every night by CNN's Lou Dobbs—that trade forces painful economic adjustments such as plant closings and layoffs of workers. Ralph Nader charges that "the Fortune 200's GATT and NAFTA agenda would make the air you breathe dirtier, and the water you drink more polluted. It would cost jobs, depress wage levels, and make workplaces less safe. It would destroy family farms and undermine consumer protections." Patrick Buchanan chimes in with the claim that "broken homes, uprooted families, vanished dreams, delinquency, vandalism, crime—these are the hidden costs of free trade."[3] The organization Public Citizen says that "the real-life devastation being caused by the implementation of the WTO's terms—and the growing social and political backlash this pain is generating worldwide—is the reason the WTO is wracked by the severe crisis that burst into view in Seattle and Cancún."[4]

Why is such hostility directed at free trade policies and the World Trade Organization? The rapid increase in international trade in recent decades may have unleashed a "globalization backlash." In this view, increased global integration has accelerated the pace of economic change and has brought with it painful economic adjustments. Meanwhile, the reach of world trade rules has gone beyond trade barriers to encompass internal regulatory policies regarding health, safety, and the environment. As a result, groups disturbed by these changes, whether directly in terms of their jobs or indirectly in terms of the community values they believe are at stake, have questioned the effects of integration and the institutions associated with it. These groups have raised legitimate concerns

[2] Brown 2006, 4.
[3] Nader 1993, 1. Buchanan 1998, 286.
[4] Wallach and Woodall 2004, 283.

about commerce and the community and about whether sovereignty has shifted from elected representatives at home to faceless and unaccountable bureaucrats abroad.

Clearly, the debate over trade policy is intense and shows little prospect of abating. The debate has raised many fundamental questions. Why is free trade considered to be a desirable policy? Do the most frequently made criticisms of free trade, such as its adverse impact on employment and the environment, have merit? Do the economic circumstances of developing countries qualify the case for free trade in any way? What is the World Trade Organization, and do world trade rules erode a country's sovereignty and undermine its health and environmental regulations?

This book aims to address these basic questions and demystify some of the complex issues that arise in discussions of trade policy. These questions will be examined mainly through the lens of economics. Despite widespread skepticism about free trade among the public at large, economists generally take a positive view of international trade and believe that reducing government-imposed trade barriers is desirable. In the eyes of economists, trade between countries is mutually beneficial, just like the exchange of goods within a country, even though the goods happen to cross national boundaries. While some groups lose from trade, people around the world are generally much better off with trade than they would be without it.

Trade skeptics often accuse economists of having a religious faith in free trade, of blindly clinging to the doctrine in the face of contrary evidence. In fact, the economic case for free trade is based not on faith, but on logic and evidence. As Paul Krugman has written, "The logic that says that tariffs and import quotas almost always reduce real income is deep and has survived a century and a half of often vitriolic criticism nearly intact. And experience teaches that governments that imagine or pretend that their interventionist strategies are a sophisticated improvement on free trade nearly always turn out, on closer examination, to be engaged in largely irrational policies—or worse, in policies that are rational only in the sense that they benefit key interest groups at the expense of everyone else."[5]

[5] Krugman 1995, 31.

Still, the logic and evidence behind the case for free trade deserve to be put under searching scrutiny, as do the logic and evidence behind alternative policies. Even advocates of free trade need to be reminded of the case, lest they simply restate stale arguments that fail to persuade. As John Stuart Mill argued, "even if the received opinion be not only true, but the whole truth; unless it is suffered to be, and actually is, vigorously and earnestly contested, it will, by most of those who receive it, be held in the manner of a prejudice, with little comprehension or feeling of its rational grounds." Consequently, "however true [a proposition] may be, if it is not fully, frequently, and fearlessly discussed, it will be held as a dead dogma, not a living truth."[6]

So the views of economists deserve critical scrutiny, but first they deserve a fair hearing. Economists have studied trade for a very long time and have noticed that the same worries and fears about trade tend to get repeated generation after generation. "With America's high standard of living, we cannot successfully compete against foreign producers because of lower foreign wages and a lower cost of production." This claim is heard today, but this particular quote comes from President Herbert Hoover in 1928 as he urged Congress to pass what became known as the Hawley-Smoot tariff. (Such statements can be found in abundance in the nineteenth century as well.) Among the claims heard yesterday and today are that trade will destroy jobs and lead to unemployment and falling incomes, and that trade deficits will siphon away a country's wealth. To economists, these are economic fallacies that history and experience have refuted time and again. One observer has quipped that "free traders are trapped in a public policy version of [the movie] *Groundhog Day*, forced to refute the same fallacious arguments over and over again, decade after decade."[7]

Chapter 1 in this book, "The United States in a New Global Economy?" sets out basic facts about international trade and the U.S. economy. World trade has expanded rapidly in recent years, and this development provides the context in which to consider questions of trade policy. This chapter discusses the reasons for the increase in trade and the state of public opinion on the question of globalization.

[6] Mill [1859] 1982, 116, 97.
[7] Sanchez 2003.

Chapter 2, "The Case for Free Trade: Old Theories, New Evidence," examines the economic logic of free trade and recent empirical evidence reinforcing the case for it. Ever since Adam Smith and David Ricardo described the gains from trade in a systematic way, economists have stressed the higher income that results from improved resource allocation as the main advantage of trade. But economists have found mounting evidence that trade not only helps to allocate existing resources properly, but also makes those resources more productive. These productivity gains from trade, overlooked in the standard calculations, appear to be substantial. The welfare benefits of a greater variety of products as a result of trade have also been ignored until recently, and yet mounting evidence suggests that they are also quite important.

Chapter 3, "Protectionism: Economic Costs, Political Benefits?" considers the flip side of the case for free trade—that trade interventions are usually misguided and often costly. Tariffs and quotas on imports redistribute income from consumers to producers, but do so inefficiently. That is, trade barriers produce a net economic loss because the costs to consumers far exceed the benefits to producers. In addition, trade barriers reduce exports and harm downstream user industries. The chapter also raises the question of why, despite its costs, trade protectionism is often politically attractive. Finally, the chapter examines situations in which protection may be justified in theory, even if governments are often ill equipped to take advantage of those situations.

Chapter 4, "Trade, Jobs, and Income Distribution," focuses on the most frequent argument in favor of limiting trade—that jobs will be saved in industries that compete against imports. As we shall see, reducing trade saves those jobs only by destroying jobs elsewhere in the economy. Opponents of free trade have also argued that imports have replaced good, high-wage jobs with bad, low-wage jobs. The truth turns out to be quite the opposite: jobs in industries that compete against imports are mainly low-skill and consequently low-wage jobs. This chapter also examines the extent to which trade with low-wage developing countries can be held responsible for the rise in economic inequality within the United States.

Chapter 5, "Relief from Foreign Competition: Antidumping and the Escape Clause," describes the legal framework that allow firms to petition the government for the imposition of tariffs on competing imports.

The antidumping law is the most commonly used measure to block so-called unfair imports. The government's definition of "dumping" is a lower price charged in the United States than in a foreign exporter's home market, but it is not clear that this is a problem requiring trade restrictions, or that the government calculates the dumping margin in a fair manner. This chapter also examines the case for providing domestic industries with temporary relief from imports so that they can adjust to the competition.

Chapter 6, "Developing Countries and Open Markets," takes a look at the special circumstances of developing countries. Is free trade always beneficial in the case of poor countries? What type of trade policy is most likely to promote economic development? Did countries such as Japan and Korea grow rich by rejecting free trade and instead pursuing closed markets and industrial policies? The chapter also addresses how rich-country agricultural subsidies and import tariffs harm developing countries, as well as how developing countries harm themselves with their own antitrade policies.

Chapter 7, "The World Trading System: The WTO, Trade Disputes, and Regional Agreements," focuses on the current controversies about the multilateral trading system, particularly the World Trade Organization. Since its inception, the WTO has come under intense criticism from nongovernmental organizations (NGOs), which attack it as an antidemocratic institution that has struck down domestic environmental regulations by ruling them inconsistent with world trade laws. This chapter examines the WTO's rules and dispute settlement system, as well as the environmental cases that have come before it. Finally, it considers the Doha Round of trade negotiations and the rise of regional trade arrangements such as NAFTA.

As Macaulay so aptly noted long ago, there is a fundamental incongruity about free trade: despite its palpable benefits, it is frequently the object of condemnation rather than approbation. That condemnation is often the result of misconceptions about the benefits of international trade, the impact of trade policies, and the role and function of the WTO. This book seeks to dispel these misconceptions and is offered in the modest hope that it may improve our understanding of the issues of trade policy that confront us.

1

The United States in a New Global Economy?

International trade has become an integral part of the U.S. economy over the past few decades. The United States imports electronics from China, apparel from Mexico, oil from Saudi Arabia, and steel from Korea, and exports aircraft from Washington, wheat from Kansas, software from California, and machinery from Illinois. The United States sells financial and information-technology services to customers around the world and buys data entry, software programming, and call center services from India. There is hardly a sector of the economy or a region of the country that is unaffected by international markets. As the twenty-first century begins, the United States may even have achieved a historically unprecedented degree of economic integration with the rest of the world. Perhaps it is not surprising, therefore, that the rapid growth of trade has been accompanied by an intensified debate over U.S. trade policy. To establish a context in which we can later examine current trade policy, this chapter briefly looks at the role of trade in the U.S. economy.

_____The Increasing Importance of Trade

How important is trade in merchandise goods to the U.S. economy? The simplest way to answer this question is to look at its share in gross domestic product (GDP). In 2008, for example, merchandise exports amounted to roughly $1,291 billion, about 9.1 percent of GDP. At the same time, merchandise imports were almost $2,112 billion, about 14.8 percent of GDP.[1]

[1] Council of Economic Advisers, *Economic Indicators*, March 2009.

Figure 1.1

U.S. Merchandise Exports and Imports as a Percentage of GDP, 1869–2008. Source: For 1929 to 2007, from U.S. Bureau of Economic Analysis (http://www .bea.gov). For GDP from 1869 to 1928, Balke and Gordon 1989 and merchandise trade from U.S. Bureau of the Census 1975.

By looking at these numbers in a historical perspective, we can determine whether they are large or small. Figure 1.1 presents U.S. merchandise exports and imports as a share of GDP from 1869 to 2007. As the figure shows, merchandise trade was fairly stable at about 7 percent of GDP in the period just after the Civil War until the outbreak of World War I in 1914. Exports surged during the war, but the trade shares declined sharply during the period from 1919 to 1939 and on through World War II. Between the world wars, many countries pursued inward-looking economic policies, including protectionist trade policies, restrictions on international labor migration, and limitations on international capital flows. These policies substantially reduced world economic integration.[2] Since the end of World War II, many of these restrictions have been relaxed, and trade has slowly responded. For about a quarter century after 1945, exports and imports remained lower than they had been prior to World War I, but both began to rise in the early 1970s. Thus, in

[2] Estevadeordal, Frantz, and Taylor (2003) examine the reasons for the rise and fall of world trade over this period.

some sense, the United States has gone back to the future, returning to—and, more recently, exceeding—the degree of integration that prevailed before World War I.

Economists have interpreted these data in two conflicting ways. One interpretation—the "fin de siècle déjà vu" view—is that trade is about as important now as it was a century ago. This view points out that merchandise exports stood at about 7 percent of GDP in the late nineteenth century and are about the same today, although the share of merchandise imports is now much higher. A second interpretation—the "new global economy" view—stresses that the rapid rise in trade's share of GDP since the mid-1970s has put trade at a level unprecedented in recent history.[3] Evidence discussed below suggests that this second interpretation is a more accurate description of the current state of trade.

Will the current trend toward a higher trade share continue? There is certainly no law in economics that dictates an inexorable rise in the ratio of trade to GDP over time. In fact, many economists, from Robert Torrens in the early nineteenth century to Dennis Robertson in the mid-twentieth century, have expounded a "law of diminishing international trade." They believed that the spread of industrial technology around the world would result in smaller differences in industrial efficiency across countries. Each country would eventually come to produce manufactured goods just as efficiently as any other, and so international trade would diminish. But this theory has been proven false: over time, the division of labor in manufacturing and in other sectors has become more refined, increasing trade even between those countries with comparable technology. For example, the spread of industrial technology has enabled an increasing number of countries to produce automobiles. Rather than reducing international trade in cars, this development has stimulated a large amount of trade in automobile products, especially parts and components.

A more plausible version of the idea of diminishing international trade is that the trade share would fall as countries grew richer because the composition of demand would shift away from traded goods (such as food, clothing, and manufactures) toward nontraded goods (such as housing, health care, education, and other services). And to some extent,

[3] Bordo, Eichengreen, and Irwin (1999) compare global integration now and a century ago and conclude that, despite similarities, the current period exhibits much greater integration.

this has taken place in the United States: the share of personal consumption expenditures devoted to services has risen steadily in recent decades at the expense of expenditures on durable and nondurable goods. This shift in demand has contributed to a change in the U.S. economy away from the production of merchandise goods and toward the production of services. (The more rapid productivity growth in goods-producing sectors, which has reduced the prices of goods relative to those of services, has also contributed to this result.) As a result, the traded-goods sectors of the economy—agriculture, mining, and manufacturing—have declined from 33.5 percent of current-dollar GDP in 1960 to 14.8 percent in 2007.[4] The service sectors of the economy, comprising transportation and public utilities; wholesale and retail trade; finance, insurance, and real estate; and government have grown more rapidly than the traded-goods sectors. Although in the past most of these service activities could not be traded internationally, an increasing number of them are now tradable, as will be discussed shortly.

Even though the merchandise-goods share of the economy has fallen significantly, the overall merchandise trade share has not. The gradual rise in the share of merchandise trade to GDP therefore masks the vastly increased importance of trade within the traded-goods sector. This is seen most strikingly by comparing merchandise exports to merchandise production rather than to total GDP. As figure 1.2 indicates, merchandise exports as a share of merchandise production soared from about 15 percent in 1970 to nearly 60 percent in 2007, while relative to GDP it has changed only modestly. This implies that the increase in the size of the nontraded sector can sharpen the degree to which countries specialize in the traded-goods sector and therefore increase trade.[5] Thus, a close analysis of the merchandise trade figures indicates that trade is substantially more important now than in the recent past for those sectors engaged in trade.

The rise in trade relative to production is also evident in the case of specific commodities. Both the share of domestic production shipped to other markets and the ratio of imports to domestic consumption are much more pronounced today than just a few decades ago, especially for

---

[4] Council of Economic Advisers 2009, table B-12.
[5] This is precisely what the analysis by Flam (1985) predicted.

Figure 1.2
U.S. Merchandise Exports as a Share of GDP and Merchandise Production,
Selected Years.
Source: Council of Economic Advisers 2009, tables B-12 and B-103.

Table 1.1
Commodity Composition of U.S. Trade, 1960, 1980, 2007

	1960		1980		2007	
	Exports	Imports	Exports	Imports	Exports	Imports
Food, Animals, etc.	16	23	14	8	6	4
Crude Materials	16	20	12	5	6	2
Mineral Fuels	2	11	4	33	4	19
Chemicals and Manufactured Goods	32	36	31	30	24	20
Machinery and Transport Equipment	35	10	39	25	60	55

Sources: By SITC category. United Nations 1962, 574–75. Updated with OECD, *Monthly Statistics of International Trade.*

perishable products, such as fruits, flowers, and vegetables, which only
recently have become widely traded across countries.

Two final points should be made about U.S. merchandise trade.
First, the composition of both exports and imports has shifted toward
manufactured goods over the past few decades. Table 1.1 presents the
commodity composition of these exports and imports. The United States
is a net exporter of agricultural commodities and a net importer of fuels.
But manufactured goods constitute the overwhelming majority—over 70
percent—of both exports and imports. Many of these manufactured
goods fall in the same general categories; the value of both exports and

_____Table 1.2
U.S. Imports by Principal End-Use Categories (percent distribution)

	Consumer Goods	Industrial Materials and Supplies	Capital Goods	Automotive Goods
1960	36	55	4	5
1980	22	53	13	12
2000	28	26	30	17
2008	28	38	22	11

Source: Bureau of Economic Analysis, _Survey of Current Business_, http://www.bea.gov.

Definitions: Consumer goods include consumer durables and non-durable goods (except automobiles), and foods, feeds, and beverages; industrial supplies and materials include crude and processed materials such as fuels and lubricants, paper, building materials, and the like; and capital goods include machinery, equipment, apparatuses, instruments, as well as parts, components, and accessories. Automotive goods includes assembled automobiles, automobile engines and parts.

imports is large in the case of machinery (electrical, general industrial, power generating, and scientific), motor vehicles, and office equipment. In other categories, there is less overlap in trade: leading manufactured exports also include airplanes and parts and a variety of chemicals, while leading manufactured imports include televisions and consumer electronics, clothing and footwear, iron and steel mill products, and toys and sporting goods.

Second, most of this trade in manufactured goods is not in final consumer goods, but in intermediate components and parts. Table 1.2 classifies imports based on their final actual use in several categories: consumer goods, industrial supplies and materials, capital goods, and automotive products. The most striking change since 1980 is the rise of capital goods as a share of U.S. imports. Capital goods include machinery, equipment, instruments, parts, and various other components to production. (Many imports categorized under automotive products are also capital goods, such as engines and parts.) About half of all imports are either intermediate components or raw materials. These imports are sold as inputs to domestic businesses rather than as goods consumed directly by households. As chapter 3 will explain, this fact has important implications for trade policy: protectionist policies will directly harm employment in domestic industries by raising their production costs, in addition to forcing consumers to pay a higher price for the products they buy.

Though trade is more important than ever for the merchandise-producing sector, this is not necessarily the case for the overall economy. Production and employment have shifted toward the service sector, in which international trade does not play as large a role. In fact, only about 12 percent of American workers are directly exposed to international competition by being employed in the goods-producing sectors of the economy (agriculture, mining, and manufacturing). In contrast, about 40 percent of workers were employed in those sectors in 1960.[6] This means that a smaller part of the U.S. economy, in terms of output and employment, is directly affected by fluctuations in merchandise trade.

While this view may have been true in the past, it is increasingly misleading today. Many previously nontraded services are now becoming more tradable. In 2008, the value of these U.S. service exports (excluded from the merchandise trade figures considered so far) amounted to about $544 billion, more than 40 percent of the value of merchandise exports. The United States is a large net exporter of services, having imported just $404 billion in that year. The major categories of services trade include shipping and tourism, royalties and fees (receipts from intellectual property rights, such as trademarks, patents, and copyrights), and military transfers.

The addition of trade in services has raised the overall economic significance of trade. In 2008, exports of goods and services were 12.8 percent of GDP, of which merchandise exports were 9.0 percent and service exports were 3.8 percent. (In 1970, by contrast, service exports were only about 1 percent of GDP.) Also in that year, imports of goods and services stood at 17.6 percent of GDP, of which merchandise imports were 14.8 percent and service imports were 2.8 percent.[7] Figure 1.3 provides a closer look at exports and imports of goods and services as a percentage of GDP since 1970. (The trade deficit will be discussed in chapter 4.)

The most rapidly growing category of U.S. service exports are those listed as "other private services," which include education, finance, insurance, telecommunications, and business, professional, and technical services. Despite recent fears that "offshoring" will harm the employment prospects of white-collar workers, the United States continues to export more than it imports in these "other private services." In 2008, U.S. exports of "other private services," including legal work, computer programming,

---

[6] Council of Economic Advisers 2009, tables B-46 and B-100.

[7] From the Bureau of Economic Analysis, Department of Commerce (www.bea.gov).

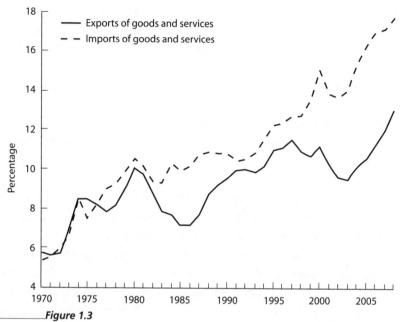

Figure 1.3

U.S. Trade in Goods and Services as a Percentage of GDP, 1960–2008.
Source: Bureau of Economic Analysis, http://bea.gov.

engineering, management consulting, and more, was $238 billion. U.S. imports of such services was $153 billion. This is true even in the narrower category of "business, professional, and technical services," which includes computer and information services, management and consulting services, etc. In this category, the United States exported over $107.7 billion and imported just over $68.8 billion in 2007.[8]

Unlike the case of merchandise, trade in services tends to be a small part of total service production, although the share is rising. In 1960, the ratio of service exports to services value-added was 1.7 percent, but by 2007 that ratio had risen to 4.8 percent.[9] While small in comparison to the merchandise sector, this ratio has been rising slowly even though everyone expects greater trade in services in the future.

Yet even services that cannot be traded are increasingly subject to international competition. This is because direct investments enable

[8] *Survey of Current Business,* October 2008.
[9] Council of Economic Advisers 2009, table B-12.

U.S. firms to enter foreign markets and allow foreign service providers to compete in the U.S. market. U.S. direct investments abroad increased from 6 percent of GDP in 1960 to 24 percent in 2007, and many of these investments were in the service sector. For example, Google has set up its European Union headquarters in Ireland and maintains many offices and labs around the world. The University of Chicago's Graduate School of Business maintains small campuses in London and Singapore to bring education services directly to Europeans and Asians who are not able to travel to Chicago.

Similarly, the value of foreign direct investment in the United States increased from 1 percent of GDP in 1960 to 18 percent in 2007. Many foreign banks have established a presence in the U.S. market to provide financial services, and foreign automobile firms (such as Honda, Toyota, BMW, Mercedes, and Volkswagen) have set up plants to produce in the U.S. market. In addition, domestic service firms are increasingly the target of mergers and acquisitions as foreign firms seek entry into the U.S. market. As an indication of the increased foreign presence in the U.S. economy, the foreign-owned affiliates' share of value added originating in private industry in the United States increased from 3.8 percent in 1988 to 6.1 percent in 2006. In addition, the foreign-owned affiliates' share of private industry employment rose from 3.5 percent to 4.6 percent over the same period.[10]

As a result, firms have a choice in how they can sell products to foreign residents: either by exporting domestically produced goods, or by producing and selling directly in the foreign country. This gives us another way to look at international commerce—based on company ownership rather than production location. In 2007, U.S. companies sold $1,646 billion worth of goods and services to foreign consumers through exports and earned $368 billion in net income from sales to foreign consumers through their foreign affiliates. Meanwhile, foreign companies sold $2,480 billion to U.S. consumers through exports to the United States and earned nearly $134 billion in net income through sales by their U.S. affiliates. The resulting U.S. deficit in goods, services, and net receipts from sales by affiliates in 2007 was almost $234 billion less than the deficit in

---

[10] Anderson 2008. Direct investment figures are from the Bureau of Economic Analysis (www.bea.gov).

goods and services in the conventional international accounts based solely on location of production. The ownership-based deficit was smaller because U.S. companies earned more in net income from sales to foreign consumers through their foreign affiliates than foreign companies earned in net income selling through their U.S. affiliates.[11]

Trade and the Fragmentation of Production

Yet could the recent rise in the trade share be misleading? The increased trade in intermediate components requires that we ask this question. Every time a component is shipped across a border, it gets recorded by customs officials as an export or an import. When components are repeatedly shipped across the border at different stages of production, the official recorded value of trade rises with each crossing, but there may be no more final goods output than before. Thus, the value of trade relative to production may be inflated if intermediate products cross national borders multiple times during the production process. For example, there is substantial two-way trade between the United States and Canada in automobiles and parts. About 60 percent of U.S. auto exports to Canada are engines and parts, whereas 75 percent of U.S. auto imports from Canada are finished cars and trucks.[12] The increase in automobile trade between the United States, Canada, and other countries does not itself indicate that more and more cars are being built; rather, various parts and components that used to be produced domestically are now produced in other countries and traded multiple times across international borders.

This phenomenon is known as _vertical specialization._ Vertical specialization refers to the fragmentation of the production process as

[11] Bureau of Economic Analysis, _Survey of Current Business_, January 2009, 62–64.

[12] Hummels, Rapoport, and Yi 1998, 84. The coordination involved in this cross-border movement of auto parts is mind-boggling. To keep a Ford factory in Toronto producing 1,500 Windstar minivans a day, a logistics subcontractor "organizes 800 deliveries a day from 300 different parts makers. . . . Loads have to arrive at 12 different points along the assembly lines without ever being more than 10 minutes late. Parts must be loaded into trucks in a pre-arranged sequence to speed unloading at the assembly line. To make all this run like clockwork takes a team of ten computer-wielding operations planners and 200 unskilled workers, who make up the loads in the right sequence at a warehouse down the road." _Economist_, December 5, 2002.

intermediate goods and components become a greater part of world trade. According to some estimates, vertical specialization accounts for about half of the growth in U.S. trade since the 1960s and about a third of the increase in world trade since 1970.[13] As the Canada auto trade example suggests, a non-negligible portion of the value of U.S. imports is simply the value of U.S. exports of domestically produced components that are shipped abroad for further processing or assembly and then returned to the United States for additional work before sale or export.

Such vertical specialization, or production sharing, means that the origin of any particular manufactured product cannot be attributed to a single country. The new Boeing 787 aircraft may be assembled at the company's production facility near Seattle, Washington, but the center fuselage is made in Italy, the engines in the United Kingdom, the wings in Japan, the passenger doors in France, the cargo doors in Sweden, the wing tips in South Korea, and the landing gear doors in Canada. For one particular car produced by an American manufacturer, 30 percent of the car's value is due to assembly in Korea, 17.5 percent due to components from Japan, 7.5 percent due to design from Germany, 4 percent due to parts from Taiwan and Singapore, 2.5 percent due to advertising and marketing services from Britain, and 1.5 percent due to data processing in Ireland. In the end, 37 percent of the production value of this American car came from the United States even though the car was imported.[14] Similarly, one type of Barbie doll is manufactured with $0.35 in labor from China; $0.65 in materials from Taiwan, Japan, the United States, and China; $1.00 in overhead and management from Hong Kong. The export value from Hong Kong is $2.00, and, after shipping, ground transportation, marketing, and wholesale and retail profit, the doll is sold in American stores at $9.99.[15] Most of the cost is incurred in the United States.

This phenomenon can make U.S. import statistics quite misleading as to the true origin of a product. For example, a 30-gigabyte Apple video iPod, which sold for $300 in late 2005, is assembled in China. Although counted in U.S. trade statistics as a $150 import from China, only about half of that cost was incurred in China, mainly the $73 hard drive (made in a Toshiba plant) and $4 for assembly and testing. The rest of

---

[13] See Yi 2003 and Hummels, Ishii, and Yi 2001.
[14] World Trade Organization 1998, 36.
[15] Tempest 1996.

the iPod's material inputs came from Japan, Korea, Taiwan, and the United States, and most of the margin was captured by retail, distributor, and Apple profits in the United States. Of the $300 that a consumer would spend on this product imported from China, only a quarter of that price was actually incurred in China.[16]

In fact, a sizable fraction of China's exports are processed goods that require many foreign inputs and components. One recent study found that the overall level of foreign content in China's exports was about 50 percent. Of course, there was a great deal of heterogeneity across sectors: sophisticated or high-technology goods such as computers and telecommunication equipment have a high fraction of foreign content, while labor-intensive goods such as apparel have a high fraction of domestic content.[17]

A small snapshot of this vertical specialization is also captured by looking at an obscure provision of the U.S. tariff code. Imports that incorporate U.S.-made components are often given duty-free or reduced-duty treatment under the "production-sharing" provision of the tariff code (chapter 98 of the Harmonized Tariff Schedule). In 2002, imports entering the United States under the production-sharing provision amounted to $54 billion, or almost 6 percent of total merchandise imports. The value of U.S.-produced components in these imports was about $9 billion, or 16 percent of the total value of imports entered under this provision. In other words, a significant portion of the value of U.S. imports actually represents the value of domestic products that have been exported and then returned to the United States.[18]

This phenomenon is a particularly striking aspect of U.S. trade with Mexico. In 2002, the United States imported $134 billion in goods from Mexico. Of this, $11 billion (9 percent) entered under the production-sharing provision, and $5 billion represented the U.S. content of these imports. Thus, nearly half (47 percent) of the value of Mexican goods that entered the United States under the production-sharing provision actually reflects the value of U.S.-made components.

These official figures grossly understate the magnitude of production sharing in U.S. trade. A majority of imports from Canada and

---

[16] Linden, Kraemer, and Dedrick 2007.
[17] Koopman, Wang, and Wei 2008.
[18] These statistics come from Watkins 2003, table B-2.

Mexico incorporate U.S.-made parts but no longer enter the United States under the production-sharing provisions of the tariff code because they are already eligible for duty-free treatment under the North American Free Trade Agreement (NAFTA). Nearly a third of U.S. imports from Canada, Mexico, and the Caribbean Basin consisted of motor vehicles, televisions, and apparel, the sectors in which production-sharing or off-shoring arrangements are extensive. This tariff provision, along with communication and transportation technology, has significantly deepened cross-border integration in North America and the Caribbean Basin, enabling firms to subcontract some operations to neighboring countries. For example, most apparel imported from Mexico and the Caribbean Basin is sewn from U.S.-made fabrics, whereas apparel imports from Asia are not.

Such specialization in the production process may account for the fact that world trade has grown much more rapidly than world output. It is also related to the role that multinational firms play in international trade. Indeed, a sizable part of U.S. trade is simply the exchange of goods between affiliated units of a multinational company: in 2006, 20 percent of U.S. exports of goods and 14 percent of U.S. imports of goods were "intrafirm" transactions between affiliated companies.[19]

Thus, by simply looking at the sheer volume of goods leaving and entering the country, one can say that the United States engages in significantly more international trade today than in the recent or distant past. But the statistics on trade can also be misleading for two reasons: a final good may be produced with inputs that cross national borders multiple times, each time getting recorded as an export or an import, and imports may actually have a significant degree of U.S. content.

_____Why Is Commercial Integration Greater Today?

International trade has increased rapidly during the postwar period, particularly in the last two decades. What accounts for this growth in trade? One simple answer is that the costs previously inhibiting trade, and preventing exchanges from taking place, are now lower than before. These

[19] Mataloni 2008, Table 3.

impediments to trade include transportation costs, transactions costs, and government policies.

Although the expansion of international trade in the late nineteenth century was propelled by a significant decline in shipping costs, the postwar period has apparently not experienced a comparable reduction in the costs of moving goods between markets. Yet such costs have remained low and have changed in qualitative ways. Technological innovations have expanded the array of delivery mechanisms. Containerization, bulk shipping, and other innovations have cut loading times and resulted in more efficient transportation. The rise of air transport as a means of moving goods between countries has cut delivery times in ways that have brought an ever-increasing variety of perishable goods (cut flowers from Central America, lobsters from Maine) into world commerce. According to one estimate, each day saved of shipping time is worth 0.5 percent of the value of the products. Trade in intermediate goods is the most time-sensitive, and according to one calculation faster methods of transport over the past fifty years have been equivalent to reducing tariffs from 20 percent to 5 percent.[20]

Other transactions costs are harder to quantify, but are lower in potentially important ways. These transactions costs are any expense that must be incurred to bring about exchange. The costs of acquiring information, for example, can limit the extent of market integration. A century ago, before the age of mass communications, obtaining information about distant markets was more difficult than today. Producers are now more likely to have better information about local tastes and demands than they did in the past, which makes them able to service demand in those markets more efficiently. In addition, consumers used to have good information only about the attributes of locally produced goods, but now they are likely to be equally well informed about the products of foreign firms.

Trade has also expanded because government trade restrictions have been reduced. Tariffs, import quotas, and exchange controls that originated in the 1920s and 1930s have been gradually relaxed in the decades after World War II. Average tariffs on manufactured goods have

[20] See Jacks, Meissner, and Novy 2008 for a discussion of trade costs over time and Hummels 2007 for an overview of recent research on trade and transportation costs.

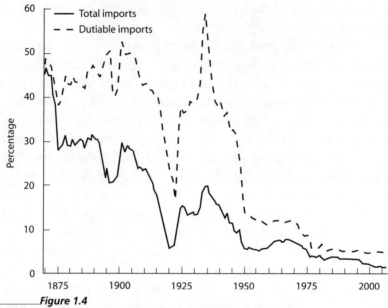

Figure 1.4
Average U.S. Tariff on Total and Dutiable Imports, 1869–2007.
Source: U.S. Bureau of the Census 1975, updated with the U.S. International
Trade Commission's dataweb (http://www.usitc.gov).

dropped to less than 5 percent in most developing countries over the
postwar period. Figure 1.4 illustrates that high U.S. tariffs were the norm
prior to the 1940s, but that taxes on imports have fallen to very low levels
in recent decades.

Furthermore, whole geographic areas, such as western Europe
and North America, have abolished customs duties and become free
trade areas. In recent years, many developing countries have undertaken
unilateral trade policy reforms or have changed their import regimes as
they have joined the World Trade Organization. Although some nontariff
measures have been adopted to protect domestic producers from import
competition, it is nonetheless true that trade barriers have fallen substantially over the postwar period.

Quantifying the precise contribution of these factors to the rapid
growth in world trade is difficult. One study finds that about two-thirds
of the postwar growth in the trade of countries belonging to the Organization for Economic Cooperation and Development (OECD) is due to income growth, a quarter to tariff reductions, and about 10 percent to

transportation cost reductions.[21] This calculation, however, does not take into account production sharing or vertical specialization.

Even though world economic integration has increased rapidly in recent decades, the world remains far from fully integrated. Within-country trade dominates between-country trade by an order of magnitude, suggesting that there is a strong "home bias" in the pattern of trade. The United States is more integrated with the rest of the world than in the recent past, but we are far from the point at which trade between New York and Rio de Janeiro is carried on as easily as trade between New York and Los Angeles. It remains the case that about 85 percent of what the United States consumes is produced in the United States.

One economist has used the following analogy to illustrate how far we are from perfect trade integration: if Americans were just as likely to purchase goods and services from foreign producers as from domestic producers, then the U.S. import-to-GDP ratio should equal the non-U.S. share of world GDP. In other words, the United States would spend as much on foreign products as the average foreign resident, or roughly 75 percent, which is about the non-U.S. share of world GDP. Since the current trade share is about 15 percent, while that hypothetical trade share would be 75 percent, one can conclude that we are only about one-sixth of the way to the point at which "it would literally be true that Americans did business as easily across the globe as across the country."[22]

Empirical models of bilateral trade (the so-called gravity equations) show that there are numerous factors that shape international trade: distance between countries; geographic location; language, currency, and political ties; and so on. In these empirical models, the mere presence of a national border acts as a powerful impediment to trade. The implication is that even when countries share a common language and a common border, similar institutions and a similar culture, the mere existence of a national border creates a significant bias in favor of intranational trade as opposed to international trade, even if trade barriers are low.[23]

[21] Baier and Bergstrand 2001.

[22] Frankel 2000.

[23] Anderson and van Wincoop (2003) find that the border effect (the difference between intranational and international trade) implies a 45 percent reduction in trade, after controlling for other factors affecting trade, such as size, distance, language, and currency. On the issue of trade costs, see Anderson and van Wincoop 2004.

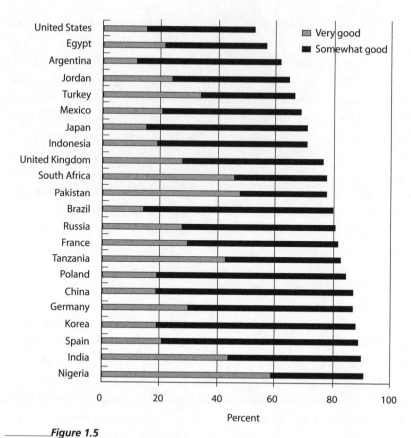

_____Figure 1.5

World Opinion on International Trade.

Source: Pew Global Attitude Project, June 12, 2008 (www.pewglobal.org).

_____Public Views on Globalization: The Trade Policy Controversy

What are the public's views about international trade? A survey of public
opinion in twenty-four countries in 2008 by the Pew Research Center
found widespread support for international trade. As figure 1.5 shows,
nearly half of those polled in Nigeria, Pakistan, South Africa, and India
believe that growing trade is "very good" for their country, while a majority in all countries believe trade is "very good" or "somewhat good." It
appears that people in the least globalized parts of the world want more
trade.

In contrast, Americans are the least supportive of international trade. Just 53 percent of American said that trade was good for the United States, down sharply from 78 percent in 2002. The American public's views also vary by age and income: younger people are more likely to believe that trade has a positive impact, as are individuals with higher incomes. Another Pew poll found that more Americans believe that free trade leads to job losses rather than gains and lowers wages rather than raises them.[24]

There is also growing skepticism of trade agreements. In a July 2004 poll, 47 percent of Americans said that free trade agreements were a good thing for the country and 34 percent said they were bad. In April 2008, however, only 35 percent said such agreements were a good thing and 48 percent said they were bad.[25] The public remains divided over NAFTA because of the perception that businesses benefit more than workers from these trade agreements, leading to an increasing gap between rich and poor in the United States. There is also overwhelming support for including environment and labor standards in trade agreements, and for helping workers adjust to import competition through government programs for education and worker retraining.

More dated polls revealed that these general findings were consistent across almost all demographic and socioeconomic categories. The greatest variation in responses was linked to years of formal education: individuals with at least some college education were much more likely to have positive attitudes about globalization and trade than those with a high school degree only.[26] As we will see in chapter 4, this association could arise because individuals with less education are more likely to be employed in sectors that compete against imports and have greater

---

[24] Hiscox (2007) warns that the responses to such public opinion polls may suffer from framing effects. He finds that respondents who were given an antitrade introduction to the survey question, such as linking trade to the possibility of job losses, were 17 percent less likely to favor increasing trade with other countries than were those asked the same question without any introduction at all. The response of individuals with less education was more sensitive to the framing of the question. He also reports on an experiment in which knowledge of the endorsement of trade openness by economists mitigates framing effects and raises the overall support for trade liberalization by a substantial degree.

[25] Pew Research Center, "Public Support for Free Trade Declines," released May 1, 2008. www.people-press.org.

[26] Kull 2000. Scheve and Slaughter 2001a, 2001b.

_____Figure 1.6

Partisan Division in Congressional Trade Votes, U.S. House of Representatives, 1890–2007 (Share of party voting for trade liberalization).
Source: Compiled by the author.

difficulty becoming reemployed once displaced than those with a higher level of education.

Public opinion polls suggest a willingness to accept increased international trade driven by the anonymous force of technology, but a hesitation to support integration driven by specific policy initiatives. Even though economists have not untangled the precise degree to which recent trade integration has been technology-driven or policy-driven, the public appears to view this distinction as important. This is consistent with the finding that the public appears to care about jobs destroyed because of imports, but does not care as much about jobs destroyed due to the invisible hand of technological change or a change in market prices.

The American public's increasing concerns about trade have filtered into the political arena, where recent congressional voting over trade legislation has become quite contentious. Figure 1.6 shows the share of each party's vote in the House of Representative for trade liberalization (for bills that reduced tariffs or against bills that raised tariffs). Prior to World War II, the Democrats supported freer trade while the Republicans supported high tariffs. By the 1950s, the Republicans had begun to support trade agreements to reduce tariffs for foreign policy reasons and due to the support of big business. For many years thereafter, a bipartisan consensus favored reducing tariffs in trade agreements.

However, particularly since the NAFTA vote in 1993, Democrats have become more opposed to free trade agreements. The switch in the Democrats' position, which first became evident in the early 1970s, is largely due to the opposition of organized labor to more trade. The increased polarization of trade voting in Congress reflects the heightened political conflict over the issue in recent years. For example, in 2008, Democrats in the House of Representatives indefinitely postponed consideration of the U.S.-Colombia Free Trade Agreement submitted by the Bush administration. The Obama administration has avoided taking a strong stand on the issue for fear that it will divide the party.

The public support for trade in the abstract and skepticism about trade policy in the particular is a key aspect of the controversy over free trade. Trade policy has always been contentious, but it has come to involve complex economic, political, and legal factors, making it increasingly difficult to understand. This book aims to examine how these factors affect U.S. trade policy. The appropriate place to begin is the economic case for free trade.

2

The Case for Free Trade: Old Theories, New Evidence

For more than two centuries, economists have pointed out the benefits of free trade and the costs of trade restrictions. As Adam Smith argued more than two centuries ago, "All commerce that is carried on betwixt any two countries must necessarily be advantageous to both," and therefore "all duties, customs, and excise [on imports] should be abolished, and free commerce and liberty of exchange should be allowed with all nations."[1] The economic case for free trade, however, is not based on outdated theories in musty old books. The classic insights into the nature of economic exchange between countries have been refined and updated over the years to retain their relevance to today's circumstances. More important, over the past decade economists have gathered extensive empirical evidence that contributes appreciably to our understanding of the advantages of free trade. This chapter reviews the classic theories and examines the new evidence, noting as well the qualifications to the case for free trade.

Specialization and Trade

The traditional case for free trade is based on the gains from specialization and exchange. These gains are easily understood at the level of the individual. Most people do not produce for themselves even a fraction of the goods they consume. Rather, we earn an income by specializing in certain activities and then using our earnings to purchase various goods and services—food, clothing, housing, health care—produced by others.

[1] Smith 1978, 511, 514.

In essence, we "export" the goods and services that we produce with our own labor and "import" the goods and services produced by others that we wish to consume. This division of labor enables us to increase our consumption beyond that which would be possible if we tried to be self-sufficient and produce everything for ourselves. Specialization allows us to enjoy a much higher standard of living than otherwise and gives us access to a greater variety of goods and services.

Trade between nations is simply the international extension of this division of labor. For example, the United States has specialized in the production of aircraft, industrial machinery, and agricultural commodities (particularly corn, soybeans, and wheat). In exchange for exports of these products, the United States purchases, among other things, imports of crude oil, clothing, and iron and steel mill products. Like individuals, countries benefit immensely from this division of labor and enjoy higher real incomes than they would by forgoing such trade. Just as there seems no obvious reason to limit the free exchange of goods within a country without a specific justification, there is no obvious reason why trade between countries should be limited in the absence of a compelling reason for doing so. (Popular arguments for limiting trade will be examined in subsequent chapters to see if they are persuasive.)

Adam Smith, whose magnificent work *The Wealth of Nations* was first published in 1776, set out a case for free trade with a persuasive flair that still resonates today. Smith advocated the "obvious and simple system of natural liberty" in which individuals would be free to pursue their own interests, while the government provided the legal framework within which commerce would take place. With the government enforcing a system of justice and providing certain public goods (such as roads, in Smith's view), the private interests of individuals could be turned toward productive activities, namely, meeting the demands of the public as expressed in the marketplace. Smith envisioned a system that would give people the incentive to better themselves through economic activities, where they would create wealth by serving others through market exchange rather than through political activities, where they might seek to redistribute existing wealth through brute force or legal restraints on competition. Under such a system, the powerful motivation of self-interest could be channeled toward socially beneficial activities that would serve the general interest rather than toward socially unproductive activities that might advance the interests of a select few but would come at the expense of society as a whole.[2]

Free trade is an important component of this system of economic liberty. Under a system of natural liberty in which domestic commerce is largely free from restraints on competition, though not necessarily free from government regulation, commerce would also be permitted to operate freely between countries. According to Smith, free trade would increase competition in the home market and curtail the power of domestic firms by checking their ability to exploit consumers through high prices and poor service. Moreover, the country would gain by exchanging exports of goods that are dear on the world market for imports of goods that are cheap on the world market. As Smith put it:

> What is prudence in the conduct of every family can scarce be folly in that of a great kingdom. If a foreign country can supply us with a commodity cheaper than we ourselves can make it, better buy it of them with some part of the produce of our own industry, employed in a way in which we have some advantage. The general industry of the country . . . will not thereby be diminished . . . but only left to find out the way in which it can be employed with the greatest advantage. It is certainly not employed to the greatest advantage, when it is thus directed towards an object which it can buy cheaper than it can make.[3]

Smith believed that the benefits of trade went well beyond this simple arbitrage exchange of what is abundant in the home market for what is abundant in the world market. The wealth of any society depends upon the division of labor. The division of labor, the degree to which individuals specialize in certain tasks, enhances productivity. And productivity, the ability to produce more goods with the same resources, is the basis for rising living standards. But, as he put it, the division of

[2] Rosenberg (1960) provides an excellent discussion of this aspect of Smith's work.

[3] Smith 1976, 457. Free trade made this possible: "The interest of a nation in its commercial relations to foreign nations is, like that of a merchant with regard to the different people with whom he deals, to buy as cheap and to sell as dear as possible. But it will be most likely to buy cheap, when by the most perfect freedom of trade it encourages all nations to bring to it the goods which it has occasion to purchase" (464).

labor is limited by the extent of the market. Smaller, more isolated markets cannot support a high degree of specialization among their work force and therefore tend to be relatively poor. Free trade enables all countries, but particularly small countries, to extend the effective size of their market. Trade allows such countries to achieve a more refined division of labor, and therefore reap a higher real income, than if international exchange were artificially limited by government policies.[4]

Comparative Advantage

In 1799, a successful London stockbroker named David Ricardo came across a copy of *The Wealth of Nations* while on vacation and quickly became engrossed in the book. Ricardo admired Smith's great achievement, but thought that many of the topics deserved further investigation. For example, Smith seemed to believe that a country would export goods that it produces most efficiently and import goods that other countries produce most efficiently. In this way, trade is a mutually beneficial way of increasing total world output and thus the consumption of every country. But, Ricardo asked, what if one country was the most efficient at producing everything? Would that country still benefit from trade? Would disadvantaged countries find themselves unable to trade at all?

To answer these questions, Ricardo arrived at a brilliant deduction that became known as the theory of comparative advantage.[5] Comparative advantage implies that a country could find it advantageous to *import* some goods even if it could produce them more efficiently than other countries. Conversely, a country is able to export some goods even if other countries could produce them more efficiently. In either case, countries stand to benefit from trade. Ricardo's conclusions about the benefits of trade were similar to Smith's, but his approach contains a deeper insight.

At first, the principle of comparative advantage seems counterintuitive.[6] Why would a country ever import a good that it could produce

---

[4] For a more complete discussion of Smith's ideas about trade and trade policy, see Irwin 1996a.

[5] For speculation on how Ricardo discovered the theory, see Ruffin (2002).

[6] When challenged by a distinguished mathematician to name "one proposition in all of the social sciences which is both true and non-trivial," the Nobel laureate economist

To take another example, Lee Iacocca, the charismatic chief of Chrysler in the 1980s, once admitted that American automakers had fallen behind their Japanese rivals in the past, but proudly proclaimed that the U.S. auto industry had met the competitive challenge and had finally matched the efficiency of Japanese producers. (This claim may stretch the truth, but let us accept it for the sake of argument.) Unfortunately, the theory of comparative advantage indicates that Iacocca has a problem: it may not be enough for an industry that competes with imports merely to match or even to exceed the productive efficiency of foreign producers to overcome that competition and recapture market share. The reason is that Chrysler and other U.S. automakers were not really competing against Japanese automakers as much as they were against other American industries that enjoyed an even greater productive superiority over their counterparts in Japan. U.S. auto producers might be able to match the productive efficiency of Japanese auto producers, but if American farmers and telecommunications equipment producers remain vastly more efficient than their Japanese counterparts, the United States will continue to export agricultural and telecom products to Japan in exchange for imports of automobiles.

For developing countries, the theory of comparative advantage is good news in terms of their ability to trade profitably with advanced countries. Even if a developing country lacks an absolute productive advantage in any field, it will always have a comparative advantage in the production of some goods. Most countries, from Argentina to Zambia, are unable to match the productive efficiency of any U.S. industry, and yet still they are able to export some goods to the United States. Such countries will export goods where their relative disadvantage is least and use those export revenues to improve their standard of living by purchasing other foreign-produced goods, from fuel to capital equipment to medicine. There is no country whose economic circumstances prevent it from engaging in mutually beneficial trade with other countries. (Chapter 6 examines developing countries in more detail.)

What determines a country's comparative advantage? There is no single answer to this question. Sometimes specialization is based on climate or natural resources, sometimes on accumulated skills and capital, sometimes on an abundance of cheap labor, sometimes on government promotion of a particular industry. Some sources of comparative advantage are relatively immutable, while others—based on technology, education, and worker skills—can evolve over time. Entrepreneurship and the business environment can be critical factors. A country could have an ideal climate for producing wine, but unless someone invests in the capital and skills necessary for production, that climatic advantage will remain latent and unexploited. Whatever the underlying reasons, these differences across countries are the primary driving force behind trade.

Critics of free trade sometimes insist that the theory of comparative advantage is obsolete because Ricardo did not consider capital mobility or technology transfer between countries. But modern economists have altered many of the assumptions underlying Ricardo's analysis, and the main result—that international exchange is mutually advantageous—remains intact.[9]

Figure 2.1 illustrates the concepts of comparative and absolute advantage by comparing industry-level labor productivity in the United States and China in 1980 and 1997. Not surprisingly, the United States has an absolute productivity advantage in every industry and China has an absolute disadvantage in every industry. In every industry, China's labor productivity is significantly lower than the United States', although it closed the gap in many industries between 1980 and 1997. Yet, despite the productivity gap, China has a comparative advantage in some industries. In 1997, the four industries in which China came closest to achieving U.S. levels of productivity were apparel (72 percent of U.S. level), textile mill products (38 percent), rubber and plastics (37 percent), and leather and footwear (21 percent). It should come as no surprise that China's export success has been greatest in these industries. (China also exports a lot of consumer electronics, where its labor productivity appears to be low, but as the iPod example in chapter 1 suggests, many of these exports simply involve the final assembly of imported components.)

How can China export clothing and footwear when its industries are significantly less efficient than their U.S. counterparts, even if that is

---

[9] In fact, the United States is a large free trade area with labor and capital mobility and transferable technology across regions. Yet despite lower wages in the South for much of the late nineteenth and early twentieth centuries, high-wage regions of the country did not suffer from a "race to the bottom," and the South did not get rich at the expense of the North, but rather a slow process of convergence to higher incomes occurred across regions. See McLean and Mitchener 1999.

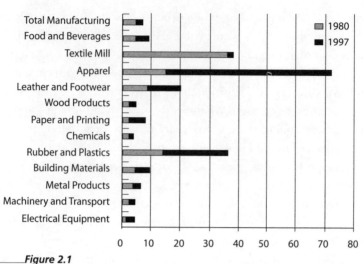

_____*Figure 2.1*
China's Labor Productivity, Relative to the United States, by Industry, 1980 and 1997 (U.S. = 100).
Source: Wu 2001, table 6.

where its comparative advantage lies? The answer is that wages in China are significantly lower than in the United States. In 2004, average hourly compensation in Chinese manufacturing was about $1.19 per hour in city manufacturing and $0.45 in rural town and village enterprises, in contrast to $22.87 in average hourly earnings for workers in U.S. manufacturing. Thus, urban workers in China earn about 5 percent of what American workers earn.[10] Therefore, China can easily export apparel because its productivity is 72 percent of the U.S. level while its wages are only about 5 percent of the U.S. level. This means that its unit labor costs—the costs of labor relative to its productivity—in these goods are very low compared to the United States.

Given that China's wages are only about 5 percent of U.S. wages, on average, why doesn't China export everything to the United States? That is because its productivity in other industries is less than 5 percent of the U.S. level, meaning that it does not have a unit labor cost advantage over U.S. producers. For example, China cannot easily export chemicals and machinery because its productivity level is only 3 to 4 percent

[10] Lett and Banister 2006. Rural workers have lower wages, but the transport costs of delivering their goods to the coastal ports is high.

of the U.S. level, whereas it must pay wages that are 5 percent of the U.S. level. (This link between wages and productivity will be examined further in chapters 4 and 6.) Thus, even though its wages are a small fraction of those in the United States, China's unit labor costs in this industry are high by international standards.[11] Furthermore, labor costs are only one component of the total costs of production.

It may be surprising to learn that China is actually losing its export advantage in low-cost, labor-intensive industries such as apparel and footwear. Not only are Chinese wages rising very fast, but domestic inflation and the appreciation of its currency (the renimbi) against the dollar have made its goods increasingly expensive in world markets.[12] In addition, other countries, such as Vietnam and Cambodia, have wage rates less than half of those in China and can come close to matching its productivity in those labor-intensive industries.[13] The apparel and footwear industries are slowly beginning to migrate from China to Vietnam and Cambodia. This is a natural cycle of economic development: just like the United States, Japan, Taiwan, and Korea before it, China will lose its textile, apparel, and footwear industries as it begins to produce more sophisticated goods and its wages and productivity level rise.

Thus, the United States has an absolute productivity advantage in producing apparel, but still imports almost all of its apparel consumption. So what good is having high labor productivity? Simply put, a country that has an absolute productivity advantage over other countries will be richer than other countries. An absolute advantage in productivity does not

[11] Ceglowski and Golub (2007) find that, in 2002, China's productivity was about 8 percent of the United States while its wages were about 2 to 4 percent of the United States, making its unit labor costs about 30 to 40 percent of those in the United States.

[12] China's exchange rate policy has been very controversial and will be discussed in the context of trade deficits in chapter 4.

[13] As Bradsher (2008) reports: "In coastal provinces [of China] with ready access to ports, even unskilled workers now earn $120 a month for a 40-hour workweek, and often considerably more; wages in inland provinces, where transport is costlier, are somewhat lower but also rising fast. While Chinese wages are still less than $1 an hour, factory workers in Vietnam earn as little as $50 per month for a 48-hour workweek, including Saturdays. . . . When those increases are combined with a currency rising against the dollar at an annual pace of up to 10 percent, labor costs in China are now climbing at 25 percent a year or more. . . A popular saying among Western investors is that Vietnam is the next China. Cambodia, with even lower wages attracting garment manufacturers, is called the next Vietnam."

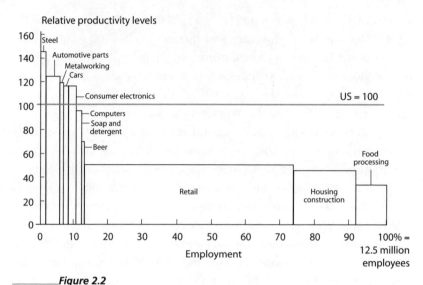

_____Figure 2.2
Employment-Weighted Relative Productivity Level, United States and Japan, 1990.
Source: Lewis 2004, 25.

determine the pattern of trade, but it does translate into higher per capita income. In other words, the reason Americans enjoy one of the highest per capita incomes in the world is that the labor force is highly productive. Conversely, the reason China's per capita income is low is that its overall labor productivity is low. According to figure 2.1, China's overall labor productivity in manufacturing is about 8 percent of the U.S. level, and its relative labor productivity is even lower in agriculture and services. As a result, China's per capita income was only about 4 percent of the U.S. level in 2002.[14] China will only become rich by improving its labor productivity, as Japan and Korea did before it. As Paul Krugman (1990, 9) has put it: "Productivity isn't everything, but in the long run it is almost everything. A country's ability to improve its standard of living over time depends almost entirely on its ability to raise its output per worker."

Figure 2.2 illustrates this point by comparing labor productivity in the United States and Japan across industries. Even though the productivity of several Japanese manufacturing industries exceeds that of the United States, such as steel, automobiles, and consumer electronics, this

[14] This is based on current exchange rates, rather than purchasing power parity.

absolute advantage did not make Japan a richer country than the United States. In fact, per capita income in Japan was only about 80 percent of that in the United States in 1990, more or less where it remains today. This can be explained by looking at the employment-weighted average of Japanese productivity. Japan's weighted average productivity was only about 80 percent of that in the United States because it was dragged down by low productivity in the retail service sector, construction, and food processing.

For example, food processing employs 11 percent of manufacturing workers in Japan, but their total factor productivity was just 40 percent of that in the United States. This low productivity is due to the small scale of Japanese firms in this sector; Japan has six times more food-processing firms per capita than the United States. Insufficient domestic competition in this sector means that there has not been enough pressure to consolidate production and improve efficiency. Trade protection limits competition and encourages this inefficiency. Japan's vegetable oil sector is protected by just a 5 percent tariff and its level of productivity is 85 percent of that of the United States, whereas the dairy industry is protected by a stiff 227 percent tariff and its level of efficiency is less than half of that in the United States.[15]

Thus, Japanese steel and automobile producers may be significantly more efficient than their American counterparts, but that advantage alone does not make Japan a rich country because those sectors are a small part of the overall economy. Japan will match U.S. per capita income only when the average productivity of its overall workforce matches that of the United States.

_____The Gains from Trade

While the idea that all countries can benefit from international trade goes back to Smith and Ricardo, subsequent research has described the gains from trade in much greater detail. In his book, *Principles of Political Economy* (1848), John Stuart Mill, one of the leading economists of the nineteenth century, pointed to three principal gains from trade. First, there

[15] These data are from a 1990 McKinsey study; see "Rotten," *Economist*, August 17, 2000. See also Lewis 2004.

are what Mill called the "direct economical advantages of foreign trade." Second, there are "indirect effects" of trade, "which must be counted as benefits of a high order." Finally, Mill argued that "the economical benefits of commerce are surpassed in importance by those of its effects which are intellectual and moral."[16] What, specifically, are these three advantages of trade?

The "direct economical advantages" of trade are the standard gains that arise from specialization, as described by Smith and Ricardo. By exporting some of its domestically produced goods in exchange for imports, a country engages in mutually advantageous trade that enables it to use its limited productive resources (such as land, labor, and capital) more efficiently and therefore achieve a higher real national income than it could in the absence of trade. A higher real income translates into an ability to afford more of all goods and services than would be possible without trade.

Economists suspect that these static gains from specialization are sizable. But it is difficult to measure the overall gains from trade because most countries have always been open to world trade to some extent. We usually do not observe countries moving abruptly from situations of no trade to trade, or vice versa, so that we can calculate the benefits of trade. Fortunately, history provides a few examples of such changes that allow us to get a glimpse of the total static gains from trade.

The classic illustration of the direct gains from trade comes from Japan's opening to the world economy. In 1859, as a result of American pressure, Japan opened its ports to international trade after two centuries of self-imposed economic isolation (autarky). The gains from trade can be estimated by examining the prices of goods in Japan before and after the opening of trade. For example, the price of silk and tea was much higher on world markets than in Japan prior to the opening of trade, while the price of cotton and woolen goods was much lower on world markets. With the introduction of trade, prices of those goods in Japan converged to the prices on the world market. As a result, Japan began exporting silk and tea in exchange for imports of clothing and other goods. According to one calculation, Japan's national income was 4 percent higher as a result of the static reallocation of resources in response to the

[16] Mill 1909, 580ff.

opportunity to trade.[17] (Of course, the long-run dynamic gains from acquiring better technology and improving its productivity were many multiples of this, and will be discussed shortly.)

The early United States provides another example, this time of a country that was open to trade and then deliberately shut its borders for a short period. In 1807, President Thomas Jefferson ordered an economic embargo to prevent the harassment of American shipping by British and French forces that were engaged in a bitter military conflict. While America's ports were closed to international commerce, the domestic price of imported goods rose 33 percent and the domestic price of exported goods fell 27 percent. The static welfare loss from this embargo was about 5 percent of U.S. GDP. It is little wonder that the embargo was highly unpopular and, as a result, abandoned after just fifteen months.[18]

Today, economists use various methods to estimate the gains from increased trade as a result of the reduction in trade barriers.[19] The estimated gains are much smaller than the total gains from trade because existing trade barriers are relatively modest. One study that simulates the effects of removing all barriers to trade in agricultural and manufactured goods finds that the worldwide gains would be about $287 billion, or 0.7 percent of world income.[20] (This does not include liberalization of services trade or improvements in trade facilitation in developing countries.) For the United States, the real income gain would be $16 billion, or 0.1 percent of its GDP. This gain combines the benefits to the United States of reducing its own trade barriers and the benefits of lower foreign trade barriers. However, most of the gains to the United States from lower trade barriers around the world would likely come from opening up trade in services, which is not taken into account in this calculation.

As these examples indicate, the calculated welfare gains that emerge from these simulations are sometimes small as a percentage of

[17] Bernhofen and Brown 2005.

[18] Irwin 2005b.

[19] Computable general equilibrium models, which are complex computational models used to simulate the impact of various trade policies on specific industries and the overall economy, calculate the gains that arise from shifting resources between various sectors of the economy. Specifically, these models examine the shift of labor and capital away from industries that compete against imports toward those in which the country has a comparative advantage as a result of changes in trade policy.

[20] Anderson, Martin, and van der Mensbrugghe 2006.

GDP. Some have interpreted these calculations to mean that trade liberalization is not especially valuable. But the small numbers arise partly because these agreements usually lead to modest policy changes for the United States. For example, what the United States undertook in signing NAFTA or might undertake as a result of the current multilateral trade negotiations, essentially making already low import tariffs somewhat lower, cannot be compared to Japan's move from autarky to free trade or Jefferson's embargo on shipping. These numbers do not reflect the entire gains from trade, just the marginal gains from an additional increase in trade as a consequence of a partial reduction in trade barriers.

More important, the reallocation of resources across industries as calculated in most simulation models does not take into account the other channels by which trade can improve economic performance.[21] What are these other channels? One view is that greater openness to trade allows firms to sell in a potentially larger market, and that firms are able to reduce their average costs of production by expanding the size of their output. The lower production costs resulting from these economies of scale are passed on to consumers and thereby generate additional gains from trade.[22]

However, the importance of scale economies is overstated. Evidence from both developed and developing economies suggests that economies of scale at the plant level for most manufacturing firms tend to be small relative to the size of the market. As a result, most plants have attained their minimum efficient scale. Average costs seem to be relatively unaffected by changes in output, so that a big increase in a firm's output does not lead to lower costs, and a big reduction in output does not lead to higher costs. For example, many firms are forced to reduce output as a result of competition from imports, but these firms' production costs rarely increase very much.[23]

---

[21] Feenstra (2006) also examines these new sources of gains from trade.

[22] In evaluating the impact of NAFTA through general equilibrium simulations, for example, moving from the assumption of constant returns to scale to increasing returns to scale boosted the calculated U.S. welfare gain from 1.67 percent to 2.55 percent of its GDP, Canadian welfare gain from 4.87 percent to 6.75 percent of its GDP, and Mexican welfare gain from 2.28 percent to 3.29 percent of its GDP, according to Roland-Holst, Reinhardt, and Schiells 1992.

[23] As Tybout and Westbook (1995, 134) argue, "the simulation literature has created a mirage of large potential gains from unexploited scale economies by ignoring plant

There is much better, indeed overwhelming, evidence that free trade improves economic performance by increasing competition in the domestic market. This competition diminishes the market power of domestic firms and leads to a more efficient economic outcome. This benefit does not arise because foreign competition changes a domestic firm's costs through changes in the scale of output, as just noted. Rather, it comes through a change in the pricing behavior of imperfectly competitive domestic firms. Firms with market power tend to restrict output and raise prices, thereby harming consumers while increasing their own profits. With international competition, firms cannot get away with such conduct and are forced to behave more competitively. In fact, a survey of several studies concludes: "In *every* country studied, relatively high industry-wide exposure to foreign competition is associated with lower [price-cost] margins, and the effect is concentrated in larger plants."[24] Numerous studies confirm this finding in other countries, providing powerful evidence that trade disciplines domestic firms with market power. Yet the beneficial effects of increasing competition are not always taken into account in simulation models discussed above because they often assume that perfect competition already exists.

Another problem with the standard estimates of the gains from trade is that they largely overlook the benefits to consumers from exposure to a greater variety of goods. This neglect comes from the traditional emphasis on the easily calculated effects of trade on production, whereas the gains to consumers from choice among a wider variety of goods are more difficult to quantify. (Consumer utility is an amorphous concept, and detailed product-level data are difficult to come by.) Yet the few intriguing attempts to explore this benefit have suggested that it is tremendously important. For example, tariffs may affect not just the amount but the range of foreign goods imported. When the selling of a product in a market has a fixed cost, a tariff reduces the size of the market and therefore the potential profits of engaging in trade. Because the smaller size would not allow firms to recoup the fixed costs of selling in that market, some varieties of goods would be excluded from it. In this way,

---

heterogeneity and, in some cases, by using market structure assumptions that lead to implausible adjustments in plant size."

[24] Roberts and Tybout 1996, 196. See Tybout 2000, 2003.

barriers to trade can reduce the range of goods available to an economy and limit the availability of specialized consumer and producer intermediate goods.

When trade restrictions reduce the number of traded goods, the welfare costs of those restrictions are much larger than in the standard analysis, where the number of traded goods is assumed to be fixed. The reason is this: if a tariff eliminates imports of a particular variety of good, then all the consumption benefits are lost with no offsetting gains. Although the standard computable models do not account for this loss, we know that variety is highly valued. For example, consider consumers in East Germany and Poland who, after the collapse of Communism, found exotic and affordable fruits such as bananas and oranges in the marketplace for the first time in their lives. Or consider their newfound ability to purchase apples and cabbages without worms and rot. The effect of such changes on aggregate output and income was negligible, but the welfare gains from the availability of new and improved goods were not insignificant at all.

If a tariff simply reduces the quantity of an imported good, the loss to consumers is a much smaller, second-order loss to overall welfare, because most of what consumers lose is transferred to producers or paid to the government in the form of tariff revenue. If a computable model assumes that a tariff just reduces the quantity of existing goods, when it actually reduces the range of imported goods, the welfare cost is understated—by as much as a factor of ten, according to one calculation.[25]

One study simulated the experience of a small open economy that reduces its import tariff from 20 percent to 10 percent. With constant returns to scale and no product variety, the welfare gain is 0.5 percent of the present value of consumption. With product variety, the welfare gain is about 10 percent of the present value of consumption over the infinite horizon. This is because the tariff reduction induces entry into the production of intermediate goods, and the resulting increase in variety reduces the cost of intermediates to final goods producers.[26]

[25] See Romer 1994.
[26] Rutherford and Tarr 2002.

These welfare effects need not imply an enormous change in national income: domestic output (measured GDP) may not change much as a result of the tariff. But the cost to consumer welfare is substantial when consumers value the consumption of different varieties of goods. To the extent that economists focus only on trade's effect on production or income, they understate the gains from trade.

Is there systematic evidence that tariffs reduce the range of consumer and intermediate varieties available to an economy? Can we be sure that this reduction in variety is costly to economic welfare? A growing body of evidence suggests that the answer is yes. For example, over the past three decades, the number of varieties imported by the United States has increased by a factor of four. The number of countries supplying each imported good has doubled. As a result, according to one study, welfare is about 2.6 percent of GDP higher over this period simply due to the gains from variety.[27]

Furthermore, trade is responsive to tariff reductions, especially on the variety dimension. After trade barriers are reduced, countries do not simply trade more of the same goods, but rather, trade expands most rapidly in goods that were previously not traded or only traded at low levels. In other words, goods on the margin are those that respond most to reduced costs of exchange. The high sensitivity of trade flows to reductions in trade barriers may be due to this factor.[28]

Variety is just as valuable for producers as it is for consumers. Free trade expands the range of intermediate goods available for domestic firms to use as inputs. The availability of different specialized inputs can increase the productive efficiency of the industry that produces the final goods. For example, the use of new inputs by Korean business groups (chaebol) helped to promote total factor productivity growth at the industry level, even after controlling for other factors such as research-and-development expenditures.[29]

[27] Broda and Weinstein 2006. However, Arkolakis, Demidova, Klenow, and Rodríguez-Clare (2008) find that the gains from importing variety were much smaller for Costa Rica.

[28] Hummels and Klenow 2005.

[29] Feenstra, Markusen, and Zeile 1992. See also Kasahara and Rodrigue (2008) for evidence from China.

_____Productivity Gains

Trade improves economic performance not only by allocating a country's resources to their most efficient use, but by making those resources more productive in what they are doing. This is the second of John Stuart Mill's three gains from trade, the one he called "indirect effects." These indirect effects include "the tendency of every extension of the market to improve the processes of production. A country which produces for a larger market than its own can introduce a more extended division of labour, can make greater use of machinery, and is more likely to make inventions and improvements in the processes of production."[30]

In other words, trade promotes productivity growth. The higher is an economy's productivity level, the higher is that country's standard of living. International trade contributes to productivity growth in at least two ways: it serves as a conduit for the transfer of foreign technologies that enhance productivity, and it increases competition in a way that stimulates industries to become more efficient and improve their productivity, often by forcing less productive firms out of business and allowing more productive firms to expand. After neglecting them for many decades, economists are finally beginning to study these productivity gains from trade more systematically.

The first channel, trade as a conduit for the transfer of foreign technologies, operates in several ways.[31] One is through the importation of capital goods. Imported capital goods that embody technological advances can greatly enhance an economy's productivity. For example, the South Carolina textile magnate Roger Milliken (an active financier of anti-free-trade political groups) has bought textile machinery from Switzerland and Germany because domestically produced equipment is more costly and less sophisticated.[32] This imported machinery has enabled his firms to increase productivity significantly. Between a quarter and half of growth in U.S. total factor productivity may be attributed to new technology embodied in capital equipment. To the extent that trade barriers raise the price of imported capital goods, countries are hindering their ability to benefit from technologies that could raise productivity. In fact,

[30] Mill 1909, 581.
[31] Keller 2004.
[32] Lizza 2000.

one study finds that about a quarter of the differences in productivity across countries can be attributed to differences in the price of capital equipment.[33]

Advances in productivity are usually the result of investment in research and development (R&D), and the importation of foreign ideas can be a spur to productivity. Sometimes foreign research can be imported directly. For example, China has long been struggling against a devastating disease known as rice blast, which in the past destroyed millions of tons of rice a year, costing farmers billions of dollars. Under the direction of an international team of scientists, farmers in China's Yunnan province started planting a mixture of two different types of rice in the same paddy. By this simple technique of biodiversity, farmers nearly eliminated rice blast and doubled their yield. Foreign R&D enabled the Chinese farmers to increase yields of a staple commodity and to abandon the chemical fungicides they had previously used to fight the disease.[34]

At other times, the benefits of foreign R&D are secured by importing goods that embody it. Countries more open to trade gain more from foreign R&D expenditures because trade in goods serves as a conduit for the spillovers of productive knowledge generated by that R&D. Several studies have found that a country's total factor productivity depends not only on its own R&D, but also on how much R&D is conducted in the countries that it trades with. Imports of specialized intermediate goods that embody new technologies, as well as reverse-engineering of such goods, are sources of R&D spillovers. Thus, developing countries that do not conduct much R&D themselves can benefit from R&D done elsewhere because trade makes the acquisition of new technology less costly.[35] These examples illustrate Mill's observation that "whatever causes a greater quantity of anything to be produced in the same place, tends to the general increase of the productive powers of the world."

The second channel by which trade contributes to productivity is by forcing domestic industries to become more efficient. We have already seen that trade increases competition in the domestic market, diminishing

---

[33] Eaton and Kortum 2001. Lee (1995) finds that the ratio of imported to domestically produced capital goods is significantly related to growth in per capita income, particularly in developing countries, and Mazumdar (2001) reaches similar conclusions.

[34] Yoon 2000.

[35] See Madsen 2007 and Acharyat and Keller 2007.

the market power of any firm and forcing them to behave more competitively. Competition also stimulates firms to improve their efficiency; otherwise they risk going out of business. Over the past decade, study after study has documented this phenomenon. After the Côte d'Ivoire reformed its trade policies in 1985, overall productivity growth tripled, growing four times more rapidly in industries that became less sheltered from foreign competition. Industry productivity in Mexico increased significantly after its trade liberalization in 1985, especially in traded-goods sectors. Detailed studies of Korea's trade liberalization in 1980s, Brazil's during 1988–90, and India's in 1991 reached essentially the same conclusion: trade not only disciplines domestic firms and forces them to behave more like a competitive industry, but helps increase their productivity.[36]

Competition can force individual firms to adopt more efficient production techniques. But international competition also affects the entry and exit decisions of firms in a way that helps raise the aggregate productivity of an industry. In any given industry, productivity is quite heterogeneous among firms: not all firms are equally efficient. Trade promotes high-productivity firms and demotes low-productivity firms. On the export side, exposure to trade allows more productive firms to become exporters and thereby expand their output. In the United States, plants with higher labor productivity within an industry tend to be the plants that export; in other words, more efficient firms are the ones that become exporters.[37] The opportunity to trade, therefore, allows more efficient firms to grow.

On the import side, competition forces the least productive firms to reduce their output or shut down. For example, when Chile began opening up its economy to the world market in the 1970s, exiting plants were, on average, 8 percent less productive than plants that continued to produce. The productivity of plants in industries competing against imports grew 3 to 10 percent more than in non-traded-goods sectors. Protection had insulated less productive firms from foreign competition and allowed them to drag down overall productivity within an industry,

[36] Harrison 1994; Tybout and Westbrook 1995; Kim 2000; Ferreira and Rossi 2003; Krishna and Mitra 1998; and Sivadasan 2003.
[37] See Bernard, Jensen, Redding, and Schott 2007 for a survey of this large literature.

whereas open trade weeded out inefficient firms and allowed more efficient firms to expand.[38] Thus, trade brings about certain firm-level adjustments that increase average industry productivity in both export-oriented and import-competing industries.

The impact of the U.S.-Canada Free Trade Agreement on Canadian manufacturing is suggestive. Tariff reductions helped boost labor productivity by a compounded rate of 0.6 percent per year in manufacturing as a whole and by 2.1 percent per year in the most affected (i.e., high-tariff) industries. These are astoundingly large effects. This amounts to a 17 percent increase in productivity in the post-FTA period in the highly affected sectors, and a 5 percent increase for manufacturing overall. These productivity effects were not achieved through scale effects or capital investment, but rather due to a mix of plant turnover and rising technical efficiency within plants. By raising productivity, the FTA also helped increase the annual earnings of production workers, particularly in the most protected industries.[39]

Recent work has highlighted the important distinction between tariffs on final goods (output) and tariffs on intermediate goods (capital goods and material inputs). Tariffs on final goods may harm consumers, but trade policies that increase the price of imported capital goods may be more damaging because they can affect the productivity of domestic firms. Tariffs and other trade barriers that raise the cost of capital goods mean that each investment dollar buys less capital. This reduces the efficiency of investment spending and can reduce overall investment and growth.[40] For example, a study of Indonesia found that a 10 percent reduction in input tariffs increased industry productivity by 3 percent, whereas a similar reduction in final goods tariffs increased industry productivity by less than 1 percent.[41] The reason for the difference is the channel by which the lower tariffs increase productivity: in the case of final goods, the gain comes from intensifying domestic competition, whereas with intermediate tariffs the gains arise more directly from importing higher quality or different varieties of inputs. Indeed, the firms that actually imported intermediate inputs saw an 11 percent rise in productivity.

[38] Pavcnik 2002. Similarly for Colombia, see Fernandes 2007.
[39] Trefler 2004.
[40] Lee 1995.
[41] Amiti and Konings 2007.

To sum up, traditional calculations of the gains from trade stress the benefits of shifting resources from protected industries to those with an international comparative advantage. But trade may affect the allocation of resources among firms within an industry as much as, if not more than, it affects the allocation of resources between different industries. New evidence shows that large productivity differences exist between plants within any given industry, and therefore shifting resources between firms within an industry may be even more important than shifting resources between industries. In addition, allowing domestic firms to import the best and cheapest capital goods and intermediate products in the world allows those firms to improve their performance. In doing so, trade helps improve productivity.

While difficult to quantify, these productivity effects of trade may be an order of magnitude more important than the standard gains. Countries that have embarked upon the course of trade liberalization over the past few decades, such as Chile, New Zealand, and Spain, have experienced more rapid growth in productivity than before. Free trade contributes to a process by which a country can adopt better technology and exposes domestic industries to new competition that forces them to improve their productivity. As a consequence, trade helps raise per capita income and economic well-being more generally.

_____Can We Measure the Gains from Trade?

We have seen that there are gains from trade and that trade raises productivity through a variety of mechanisms. But is there a payoff in terms of higher income? Is it true that countries that engage in more trade, or reduce their trade barriers, will have a higher per capita income as a result? Can this be empirically verified in studies using cross-country data?

These questions may seem straightforward, but they are deceptively difficult. Until recently, empirical analysis of these issues was unsatisfactory. The usual approach was to examine the statistical relationship between trade (typically measured by the ratio of exports to GDP) and income across many countries. Although studies usually uncovered a positive correlation between trade and income, the meaning of this result is uncertain. Perhaps countries that trade more have higher incomes, or perhaps countries with higher incomes engage in more trade, because they have better ports and other infrastructure that support trade or because they have better economic policies in general.

Fortunately, creative research by Jeffrey Frankel and David Romer has overcome this ambiguity. They demonstrated that the reason higher incomes are associated with more trade is not simply because high-income countries trade more.[42] Indeed, they find that the effect of trade on income is strikingly higher once the part of trade that is not driven by income is isolated: the standard estimates suggest that a 1 percent increase in the trade share increases per capita income by about 0.8 percent, but using only geographic determinants of trade raises the estimated effect to about 2 percent (although this is imprecisely estimated). Frankel and Romer find that the effect of trade on income works mainly through higher productivity, but also by increasing the capital stock.

The Frankel-Romer approach has been extended and improved by subsequent researchers. One recent study introduces time-varying distance instruments that allow for the inclusion of country-specific effects.[43] This allows the researcher to control for all time-invariant factors that may be correlated with income, such as distance from the equator, the disease environment, and colonial history. The study finds a smaller impact of trade on income than Frankel and Romer—a 10 percent increase in trade leads to a 5 percent increase in per capita income—but it is much more robust. Furthermore, almost all of the effect of trade on income comes from higher productivity, not more physical or human capital.

Although differences in trade resulting from policy may not affect income the same way as differences resulting from geography, these results are suggestive for trade policy. One study therefore used dozens of statistical specifications to examine the link between various indicators of a country's trade policy and its per capita income. Almost invariably, more open trade policies are associated with higher per capita income,

[42] The fundamental problem is that trade affects income and income affects trade. To isolate the effect of trade on income, a measure of trade that is unrelated to income must be found. Noting that distance from trade partners is a key determinant of trade but is unrelated to income, Frankel and Romer (1999) used a country's geographic attributes to identify the relationship between trade and income. Frankel and Rose (2002) later controlled for other variables and estimated somewhat lower coefficients of trade on income. Using the geographic determinants of trade produced an impact estimate of 0.43, and a long-run estimate of 1.6, lower than the earlier estimate of 2.

[43] Feyrer 2008.

although the magnitude and significance of the relationship varied considerably depending upon the indicator used.[44]

According to the theories discussed earlier in this chapter, freer trade can be expected to lead to higher levels of income or consumer welfare, but not necessarily a higher rate of economic growth. Yet in the transition from a lower to a higher level of income, the growth rate should increase. What sort of growth effect from trade liberalization is plausible? Suppose trade barriers are reduced such that the share of imports in GDP rises from 10 percent to 14 percent. This move to free trade allows the economy to purchase an additional 4 percent of GDP's worth of imports. If we assume that the average surplus gain from these imports is half the export cost, then the real value of consumption rises 2 percent. If the reduction in trade barriers is phased in over a decade, this corresponds to an increase in growth of about 0.2 percent annually.[45]

In this case, the trade policy change would not have a decisive, or even noticeable, impact on the overall rate of economic growth in any given year. But the magnitude of the impact on growth does not need to be large to generate substantial welfare benefits over time. A permanent increase in the steady state growth rate of an economy of just 0.2 percent can yield a welfare gain equivalent to a 5 percent increase in the present value of consumption over a long horizon.[46]

What is the empirical link between trade liberalization and economic growth? While several studies have found a positive relationship between lower trade barriers and more rapid economic growth in the postwar period, others have questioned these results.[47] One obstacle that hampers these empirical studies is the absence of a single variable that accurately measures trade policy.[48] The relationship between trade policy

[44] Jones 2001. However, Rodríguez and Rodrik (2001) have countered that reverse causality precludes this conclusion because richer countries have chosen to have lower trade barriers.

[45] I owe this example to Brad DeLong.

[46] Rutherford and Tarr 2002, 268.

[47] Rodríguez and Rodrik (2001) dissect many of the studies and question the robustness of their results and whether changes in trade barriers are responsible for the observed growth performance. Rodríguez (2007) provides further skeptical analyses of the empirical work on trade liberalization and growth.

[48] There is no single metric that ideally describes the stance of a country's trade policy. Import tariffs can be measured imperfectly, but they are not necessarily the most

and economic growth may be hard to pin down in the context of cross-country growth comparisons, partly because trade policy is poorly measured, and partly because the effects of trade policy may be swamped by other factors that are difficult to measure.

Recent studies have addressed many of the flaws that have plagued previous research. Most previous studies estimated the growth effects of trade liberalization by examining a cross-section of countries, that is, by comparing country X's experience with country Y's. But the difference in these countries' growth rates could be due to a host of reasons that economists cannot adequately control for. Instead, one study used a panel of data from 1950 to 1998 to estimate the *within*-country response of per capita income, investment, and trade share to the date of major trade policy changes.[49] After controlling for time-invariant country characteristics, the average within country growth rate is 1.5 percentage points higher after periods of trade liberalization in comparison to the no-reform period.[50] However, there is considerable heterogeneity in the growth effect—although the average effect is positive and statistically significant, in about half of the countries growth was zero or negative in the post-liberalization period. The within-country effect of trade reform on the investment rate is also positive and around 1.5 to 2.0 percentage points.[51] And the ratio of exports and imports to GDP is found to rise about 5 percentage points as a result of trade liberalization.

Yet another recent study of liberalizing and nonliberalizing countries during the 1990s finds that countries that reduced import duties on capital goods and intermediate inputs grew about 1 percentage point faster.[52] Relative to their baseline growth experience from 1975 to 1989, the liberalizing countries saw their GDP per worker rise 15–20 percent relative to nonliberalizers, consistent with an extra 1 percentage point of

---

important feature of trade policy today. Nontariff barriers can be an even more important impediment to trade in many countries, but they cannot be measured precisely. See the World Bank (2008a) for an attempt to provide benchmark indicators of trade policy across the world.

[49] Wacziarg and Welch 2008.

[50] They are also able to control for the fact that many reforms are undertaken during periods of economic crisis and therefore growth may rebound after a stabilization that includes trade reform.

[51] See also Wacziarg 2001.

[52] Estevadeordal and Taylor 2008.

growth per year. Reducing tariffs on final consumption goods did not have such a strong impact on economic growth. This reinforces the point that trade barriers on capital goods and intermediate products are especially harmful to economic performance.

What should be concluded from this research? While there is no guarantee that trade liberalization will increase the level of income or the rate of economic growth under all circumstances, the repeated finding of a positive relationship between them is more than just coincidence. Despite shortcomings in method and measurement, cross-country and within-country studies support the conclusion that economies with more open trade policies tend to perform better than those with more restrictive trade policies. Additional, striking evidence comes from individual country experiences. These event studies clearly dramatize the benefits of deregulating imports, and the experience of countries such as China, Chile, South Korea, India, and Vietnam will be considered in chapter 6.

Additional Benefits of Trade

The economic gains from trade are substantial, but they are not the only benefits that come to countries with a policy of open trade. John Stuart Mill's third and final claim was that "the economical advantages of commerce are surpassed in importance by those of its effects which are intellectual and moral."[53] Mill did not elaborate, but he may have been referring to the idea of _deux commerce_, exemplified by Montesquieu's observation in _The Spirit of the Laws_ (1748) that "commerce cures destructive prejudices."[54] Trade brings people into contact with one another and, according to this view, breaks down the narrow prejudices that come with insularity. Commerce can also force merchants to be more responsive to customers, as greater competition gives consumers a wider choice. This may be a quality margin on which producers compete for the patronage of consumers.

---

[53] "It is hardly possible to overrate the value . . . of placing human beings in contact with persons dissimilar to themselves, and with modes of thought and action unlike those with which they are familiar," Mill continues, because "there is no nation which does not need to borrow from others, not merely particular arts or practices, but essential points of character in which its own type is inferior" (1909, 581).

[54] Montesquieu 1989, 338.

For example, a study on the effects of fast-food restaurant chain McDonald's on Asian culture noted that restrooms in Hong Kong previously had the reputation for being unspeakably filthy. When McDonald's opened in the mid-1970s, it redefined standards, setting a new, higher benchmark for cleanliness that other restaurants were forced to emulate. In Korea, McDonald's established the practice of lining up on a first-come, first-serve basis to purchase food, rather than the rugby scrum that had been the norm. When McDonald's first opened in Moscow, a young woman with a bullhorn stood outside its doors to explain to the crowd that the servers smiled not because they were laughing at customers but because they were happy to serve them. Sanitation, queuing, and friendly service have their advantages and surely make for more pleasant living, whatever your opinion of McDonald's food.[55]

There is also a long-standing idea that trade promotes peace among nations. Many Enlightenment philosophers in the eighteenth century and classical liberals in the nineteenth century endorsed this view. Montesquieu argued that "the natural effect of commerce is to lead to peace" because "two nations that trade with each other become reciprocally dependent." John Stuart Mill endorsed this view: "It is commerce which is rapidly rendering war obsolete, by strengthening and multiplying the personal interests which are in natural opposition to it. And it may be said without exaggeration that the great extent and rapid increase of international trade, in being the principal guarantee of the peace of the world, is the great permanent security for the uninterrupted progress of the ideas, the institutions, and the character of the human race."

A burgeoning political science literature has examined whether economic interdependence mitigates conflict between nations. Most empirical studies have tended to support the idea that there is a positive link between trade and peace; a recent survey concludes that "most such studies support the liberal hypothesis that heightened economic

---

[55] See Watson 1997. Some globalization critics revile McDonald's for destroying local cuisine and foisting homogeneous, unhealthy, processed food on the public. Yet Watson (1997) points out that McDonald's restaurants located in foreign countries are locally owned and highly attuned to local culture and tastes. One recent survey indicated that nearly half of all Chinese children under the age of twelve identified McDonald's as a domestic brand. See Rosenthal 2002.

exchange inhibits conflict, although some research challenges these findings."[56]

While the link between trade and peace is intriguing, there are also reasons for being skeptical of any attempt to establish a statistical relationship between them. The methodological obstacles include making political concepts operational and representing them numerically, as well as establishing causal relationships. For example, countries that are at peace with one another are also more likely to be trading partners; which is the cause and which is the effect? Countries that are less aggressive are probably more likely to join international institutions, raising the same question. One must avoid reading too much into these findings. After all, on the eve of World War I, Norman Angell proclaimed that, in view of the extensive trade that existed between Germany and Britain and France, economic interdependence had rendered war unprofitable and therefore obsolete. War may be a costly and unproductive activity in many instances, but the age-old struggle for power between nations has not allowed it to disappear.

If the trade-peace link is plausible though uncertain, a stronger finding is that democracies are more peaceful than autocratic countries. While we do not know whether democratic regimes are inherently more peaceful than other types of government, overwhelming evidence shows that democracies rarely go to war against one another. Does increasing trade contribute to peace indirectly, by promoting political reform and democratization? Untangling the links between trade and democratization is difficult because each is related to the other. Trade may indeed promote democracy, but democracies are also more likely to pursue open trade policies and therefore trade more.[57]

But new work suggests that, after accounting for this effect, trade does indeed promote democracy. Examining the period after 1870, this study detects a positive impact of openness on democracy from about 1895 onward. Late nineteenth-century globalization may have helped to generate the "first wave" of democratization. Between 1920 and 1938,

---

[56] Mansfield and Pollins 2003, 837. In his essay "Perpetual Peace," Immanuel Kant suggested that durable peace could be built upon the tripod of representative democracy, international organizations, and economic interdependence, a proposition for which Oneal and Russett (2000) find much support.

[57] Mansfield, Milner, and Rosendorff (2000) examine this relationship.

countries more exposed to international trade were less likely to become authoritarian. These results hold for the post–World War II period as well. However, there is some variation in the impact of openness by region, and commodity exporters and petroleum producers do not seem to become more democratic by exporting more of such goods.[58]

This view of nineteenth-century classical liberals appears to have gained new support in recent years as well: as Chile, Taiwan, South Korea, and Mexico have been integrated into the world economy, they have also moved toward more democratic political systems. Those opposed to U.S. economic sanctions against Cuba believe that greater trade with that country would increase the prospects of political reform there too.

The big question today is whether China will move away from its authoritarian political regime and toward a more pluralistic political system that includes improvements in human rights. The link between trade liberalization and political liberalization was a contentious issue in the debate over extending Permanent Normalized Trade Relations (PNTR) to China in early 2000. Proponents of normalized trade argued that expanding commerce would enhance the power and influence of the private sector in China at the expense of the government. Opponents disagreed, arguing that more trade would simply enrich and strengthen the Chinese government. Although greater openness has operated very slowly in the case of China, there is some evidence of potentially important political changes at local levels.[59]

Even if trade fails to generate a movement toward democracy, it can still promote better performance in other domestic institutions. For example, countries that are more open also tend to be less corrupt, a finding that holds even after accounting for the fact that less corrupt countries may engage in more trade.[60]

While the statistical relationships between trade, peace, and democracy are difficult to sort out, the existing evidence suggests that there are beneficial links between them. In sum, Mill's observations about the

[58] Lopez-Cordova and Meissner 2004.

[59] See Thorton (2008) for a recent assessment of the prospect for democracy in China.

[60] Ades and Di Tella 1999. This finding makes sense for several reasons. Trade restrictions can breed corruption, particularly when bureaucrats are responsible for allocating valuable import licenses.

noneconomic benefits of trade—including peace and political reform—appear to be broadly valid, although they may not hold in every case.

_____Free Trade and the Environment

Among the most vocal of free trade's many critics are those who worry about its impact on the environment. Some environmentalists believe that freer international trade will lead to more economic activity, and more economic activity will lead to greater environmental degradation. In other words, with trade comes more logging, more fishing, more soil erosion, more industrial pollution, and so on. But what, in fact, is the relationship between trade and the environment? Must trade lead to environmental damage, or might it in some ways actually benefit the environment? And do restrictions on trade improve the environment?

To answer these questions, we must recognize that the link between trade and the environment is indirect. Some of the greatest environmental disasters in recent years have taken place in Eastern Europe and the former Soviet Union. The horrible air pollution caused by state-run, coal-burning, capital-intensive industries and the destruction of lakes and streams with toxic chemicals owed nothing to free trade but resulted from a system of centralized decision-making that valued resources less wisely than a system of decentralized markets with well-established property rights and prudent government regulation. In other countries as well, trade is not the underlying cause of environmental damage. The burning of the Amazon rain forests is largely motivated by local inhabitants clearing land for their own use, not international trade. And simple observation demonstrates that more trade and commerce does not always create more pollution: air quality in Delhi and Mexico City prior to economic liberalization was much worse than in most industrialized countries, even though those cities had fewer cars and generated less electricity.

Environmental damage results from poor environmental policies, not poor trade policies. Environmental damage arises from the inappropriate use of our natural resources in the land, sea, and air. The overuse of these resources is commonly related to the lack of well-defined property rights. When property rights are not well established, that is, when no one has ownership rights and control over a resource, then open access to the resource frequently leads to its exploitation beyond the socially optimal level. For example, if ownership of a forest is not well defined, then anyone can chop down trees for his or her own use without paying the costs associated with utilizing the resource.[61] If control of the forest were established through property rights, then the owners would regulate and charge for the use of the timber. Obviously, the ownership and overuse problems are particularly acute for the air and ocean, where government regulation of the right to use the resource, reflecting public ownership of it, may be called for.

In many such cases, because environmental problems stem from the failure to clearly establish and enforce private or public property rights, trade policy is not the first-best means by which to achieve environmental objectives. Trade is only indirectly related to environmental problems, and therefore trade policy is an indirect, inefficient, and often inefficacious way of addressing environmental problems.

Fortunately, the objectives of free trade and a cleaner environment often work together. For example, numerous studies have traced the relationship between pollution emissions and a country's per capita income. They have generally found a relationship shaped like an inverted U: as per capita incomes rise from low levels, pollution increases, but beyond a certain point (about $5,000), further increases in income tend to diminish pollution.[62] The initial increase in pollution is due to industrialization, while the decrease is due to cleaner production technologies and more effective environmental regulation that come with higher incomes. Both Delhi and New York City have traffic jams, for example, but the locally made cars and scooters in developing countries tend to belch out worse fumes than the cleaner exhaust systems in the United States.

Beyond the threshold, higher incomes do not mean more pollution and lower incomes do not mean less pollution. To the extent that trade increases a country's income beyond the turning point in the inverted U relationship, it helps indirectly to improve the environment.

---

[61] Ferreira (2004) finds that openness to trade alone does not promote deforestation, but that it can do so in countries with poor government institutions that fail to define and protect property rights.

[62] This is also known as the environmental Kuznets curve; see Dasgupta, Laplante, Wang, and Wheeler 2002.

More directly, new technology is cleaner technology and trade facilitates the diffusion of new technology. Furthermore, the "dirty industry migration" hypothesis, that polluting industries will move to developing countries where environmental regulations are lax, has received no empirical support. There is no "race to the bottom" in environmental standards because the costs of abating pollution are not a significant determinant of industries' location, and consequently not a significant determinant of trade flows.[63]

A recent study examined three channels by which trade can affect sulfur dioxide (SO_2) emissions: the scale effect (increases in economic activity increase SO_2 emissions), the technique effect (increases in income lead to cleaner production methods and reduce emissions), and the composition effect (trade alters the composition of activity and hence the average pollution intensity of national output). The authors were surprised to conclude that free trade is good for the environment because, as an empirical matter, the technique effect outweighs the scale and composition effects.[64] The effect of income growth on pollution depends largely on the underlying source of growth: growth achieved through capital accumulation tends to raise pollutants, while growth achieved by trade and technological change appears to reduce pollutants. This could also account for the inverted-U-shaped relationship of pollution to income—developing countries initially tend to achieve growth through (dirtier) capital accumulation, whereas growth in developed countries is based on human capital accumulation and technology (cleaner methods).

Another study focused on the issue of causality in estimating the effect of trade on the environment for a given level of income.[65] This study looked at the links between trade and seven measures of environmental quality and found that trade had a strongly beneficial impact in reducing SO_2 emissions, and a less significant but still positive impact in reducing in NO_2 emissions and total suspended particulate matter. Trade also reduced energy depletion and increased access to clean water, while

[63] See Jaffe et al. 1995.

[64] Antweiler, Copeland, and Taylor 2001. Their empirical estimates of the scale effect indicate that a 1 percent increase in the scale of economic activity increases SO_2 emissions by 0.3 percent, but that the technique effect suggests that a 1 percent increase in income decreases emissions by 1.4 percent.

[65] Frankel and Rose 2005.

having no impact on deforestation. The one exception was CO_2 emissions, where increased openness was related to greater emissions, perhaps because of the free-rider problem afflicting countries that seek to limit greenhouse gas emissions. But the study found no evidence for a "race to the bottom" in environmental standards or the "pollution haven" hypothesis that trade encourages some countries to specialize in dirtier industries.

In terms of the United States, real manufacturing output has increased by more than 70 percent over the past thirty years, while pollution emissions have fallen significantly (ranging from 30 percent for nitrogen oxides to 66 percent for sulfur dioxides). Most of this decline is due to improved production technology or abatement processes, not importing dirtier products from abroad to avoid regulation. Indeed, the average pollution content of U.S. imports has fallen over time.[66]

Unfortunately, U.S. trade policy sometimes supports special interests at the expense of the environment. For example, to reduce its dependence on imported oil and reduce greenhouse gas emissions, the United States has encouraged the use of ethanol, an agricultural-based product that is blended with gasoline. U.S.-produced ethanol is primarily based on corn, which Congress subsidizes with a fifty-one-cent-per-gallon tax credit (which has been one factor in rising corn prices). But sugar-based ethanol is significantly cheaper and generates eight times more energy per unit of input than corn-based ethanol. Yet Congress imposed a tariff of 2.5 percent plus fifty-four cents per gallon on sugar-based ethanol (which comes primarily from Brazil) in order to protect Midwestern corn farmers and agribusinesses from foreign competition. Using sugar ethanol is energy-efficient and environmentally sustainable, would reduce fuel prices and help friendly nations like Brazil, and limit dependence on imported oil from Venezuela and the Middle East. The Bush administration proposed eliminating the tariff in 2006, but Congress rejected this idea, thereby discouraging the use of sugar ethanol.

The environmental degradation associated with China's trade and economic growth has been a particular concern. The 2008 Olympic Games highlighted the problem of intense smog around Beijing, and there are many stories of lakes and rivers being poisoned by industrial

[66] Levinson 2007; Kahn 2003.

pollution, fertilizer runoff, and algal bloom. Unfortunately, in its push for growth the Chinese government has not valued the environment (which underscores the importance of accountable governance), although this is beginning to change. But has trade per se exacerbated the problem? One recent study shows that industrial emissions have stabilized while rapid growth in trade has continued—a result that can be explained by the declining pollution intensity of output.[67] The study examined the direct emissions of four pollutants for about thirty Chinese industries and found that the pollution intensity of almost all sectors has fallen in terms of water pollution (chemical oxygen demand) and air pollution (measured by SO_2, smoke, or dust). The study also revealed that China's export bundle is shifting toward relatively cleaner sectors over time, such as office and computing machinery and communications equipment as opposed to textiles and apparel. The most polluting sectors, such as paper and nonmetallic minerals, have very low and declining shares in China's manufacturing exports. Furthermore, China's exports are less water pollution intensive and generally less air pollution intensive than Chinese import-competing industries, and both Chinese exports and imports are becoming cleaner over time.

Across the world, governments tend to protect and support heavy industries, such as steel and petrochemicals, which are among the dirtiest and most polluting industries. State-owned enterprises in China, for instance, are much dirtier than their private counterparts because they are much less efficient and technologically up-to-date. Therefore, reducing subsidies and trade barriers can help shut these polluters down and shift production to more efficient producers that use cleaner technologies. In addition, a recent study that examined trade in high-efficiency and clean coal technologies, efficient lighting, solar photovoltaics, and wind power found that tariff and nontariff barriers are significant impediments to the diffusion of clean energy technologies to developing countries.[68]

Furthermore, international negotiators are attempting to limit many government trade policies that are harmful to the environment. Three specific cases provide an illustration of the environmentally damaging effects of trade barriers and subsidies: fisheries, agriculture, and

[67] Dean and Lovely 2008.
[68] World Bank 2008.

forestry trade. Ocean fishing is a classic example of a common resource that is overutilized, and yet fishing is a heavily subsidized activity. The Food and Agriculture Organization estimates that world fishing subsidies are on the order of $54 billion annually, nearly 80 percent of the total value of the world's harvested fish.[69] Many of these subsidies have led to excess capacity in fishing fleets, which in turn promotes overfishing. In this way, such subsidies directly harm efforts to conserve fishing stocks and promote sustainable development. Clearly there is no trade-off in eliminating fishing subsidies and preserving the environment. In fact, the United States, Iceland, Australia, and New Zealand have pressed the membership of the World Trade Organization to discuss an international agreement to limit or abolish fishing subsidies, not just because such subsidies distort trade, but to prevent further depletion of ocean resources.

In the agricultural sector, import restrictions, domestic price supports, and export subsidies are widespread among the industrialized countries. These trade barriers and price subsidies tend to intensify agricultural production in countries that do not have a comparative advantage in such goods. As figure 2.3 indicates, the more a country protects its domestic agricultural producers, the more those producers rely on pesticides and fertilizers. Korea, Japan, Switzerland, and, to a lesser extent, the European Union heavily protect agriculture and must rely on chemicals to boost yields because these regions are not particularly well suited for all types of agricultural production.[70] As a result, trade barriers and production subsidies have "intensified land use, increased applications of agrochemicals, [and caused] adoption of intensive animal production practices and overgrazing, degradation of natural resources, loss of natural wildlife habitats and bio diversity, reduced agricultural diversity, and expansion of agricultural production into marginal and ecologically

[69] Milazzo 1998.

[70] As Anderson (1998, 74) notes, "land-scarce Western Europe and Japan crop twice as much of their total land area as does the rest of the world on average, so the extent of contamination of their soil, water, and air from the use of farm chemicals is even greater [than figure 2.6 suggests]." Thus, "the relocation of crop production from densely populated protectionist countries to the rest of the world would cause a much larger reduction in degradation in the former compared with any increased degradation in the latter, where chemical use would expand from a low base and to still-modest levels."

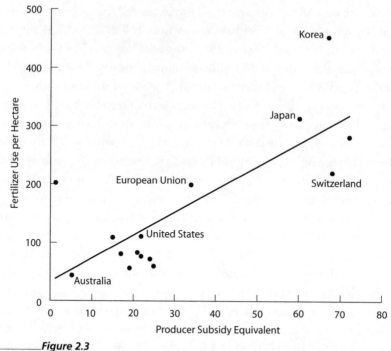

___*Figure 2.3*

Producer Protection and Fertilizer Use in Agriculture, 2000.
Source: OECD 2008, table 3.3, and FAO 2002), table 14.

sensitive areas."[71] Countries that have a comparative advantage in agriculture, whether they are industrialized, such as Canada and Australia, or developing, such as Argentina and Brazil, do not depend as heavily on fertilizers and pesticides to maintain output.

Liberalizing trade in agricultural products would therefore benefit the environment by allowing countries with a comparative advantage in agriculture to expand production and forcing countries with a comparative disadvantage to contract output. One economist has noted that "an international relocation of cropping production from high-priced to low-priced countries would reduce substantially, and quickly, the use of chemicals in world food production."[72] In addition, the relocation of meat and milk production from intensive grain-feeding enterprises in densely populated rich countries to pasture-based enterprises in relatively lightly

[71] Sampson 2000, 55.
[72] Anderson 1992, 163.

populated poorer countries would reduce the use of growth hormones and medicines for animals.

A related issue is the effort to minimize "food miles" (the distance food travels) and to encourage consumers to buy local produce. The goal of reducing greenhouse gas emissions has led many people to conclude, erroneously it turns out, that buying locally produced food is better for the environment than importing food over long distances. As Adrian Williams, an agricultural researcher at Cranfield University in the United Kingdom, explains: "The idea that a product travels a certain distance and is therefore worse than one you raised nearby—well, it's just idiotic. It doesn't take into consideration the land use, the type of transportation, the weather, or even the season," or other factors such as cultivation and harvesting methods, water use, fertilizer use, and packaging.[73]

In fact, greenhouse gas emissions are dominated by the production phase, not the transport. For example, the environmental cost of air-freighting roses from Kenya to Britain is much less than importing them across the English Channel from the Netherlands because heated greenhouses in Europe have a very high carbon footprint, whereas Kenya's natural climate is much less energy- and fertilizer-dependent. Lamb produced in New Zealand and shipped 11,000 miles by boat has one-fourth the CO_2 emissions of British-produced lamb because of New Zealand's greater production efficiency and cleaner production methods (less energy intensive, less fertilizer, etc.). The same applies for production of New Zealand apples, which requires less fertilizer than elsewhere and uses electricity generated from renewable resources.[74] Finally, in terms of environmental impact, New Yorkers might consider consuming more wines from France as opposed to California because the carbon intensity of transporting wine by sea is substantially less (per unit) than transport via truck across the country.

With regard to forest products, the United States sought without success to eliminate all tariffs on such goods in recent multilateral trade negotiations. Environmental critics have charged that liberalizing trade in forest products will merely accelerate an unsustainable rate of deforestation around the world. Yet trade in timber and timber products is a minor

---

[73] Specter 2008.
[74] Saunders, Barber, and Taylor 2006.

cause of deforestation in tropical countries. Almost all the annual logging in developing countries is for the domestic production of fuel and
charcoal—for the simple reason that fuel and charcoal are the cheapest
source of energy for poor people. About 77 percent of forest timber production in Asia, 70 percent in South America, and 89 percent in Africa is
for domestic fuel and charcoal.[75] As with all open-access resources, better forestry management is the key to reducing the rate of deforestation.

In fact, not only are policies that reduce trade in forest products
ineffective in reducing deforestation, limiting trade in forest products may
exacerbate the problem. Without the timber trade, which raises the value
of forests by providing external demand for its products, the investment
value of these forests would fall. This smaller value would give local
users less of an incentive to conserve the resource. In addition, eliminating trade restrictions would directly improve the efficiency of wood use.
For example, Indonesia maintains high export taxes on logs to promote
domestic forest-based industrialization. These export taxes have generated a large but inefficient domestic lumber industry. Every cubic meter
of Indonesian plywood produced requires the cutting of 15 percent more
trees than if plywood mills elsewhere in Asia had processed the logs. Indonesia's policy of protecting plywood mills has not only failed to reduce
total log demand, but gross operational inefficiencies have also led to a
much higher rate of logging than if log exports were allowed.[76] Thus, a
ban on imports of raw tropical forest lumber by developed countries
would not only fail to counter the underlying cause of deforestation, but
might accelerate it due to the inefficiency of local processors.

Despite all of this evidence, critics of free trade are often quick to
oppose trade agreements ostensibly on the basis of their environmental
impact. Controversy about the environmental impact of free trade was
particularly intense during the debate over NAFTA in 1993. Yet there were
reasons to expect that NAFTA would lead to environmental improvements
in Mexico. Aside from increasing income and promoting the adoption of
newer, cleaner production technologies, Mexico has a comparative advantage in unskilled labor-intensive goods rather than in capital-intensive
goods. Hence, freer trade may force dirtier capital-intensive industries in

[75] World Resources Institute 1999, table 11.3.
[76] Barbier et al. 1995, 419.

Mexico to contract as a result of competition. With protective tariffs eliminated, these industries are forced to shut down or adopt better technology
to stay in business.

Furthermore, an environmental side agreement to NAFTA was
negotiated. As a result, environmental groups that represented approximately 80 percent of the membership of the entire environmental community agreed to support the agreement.[77] But more militant organizations, such as the Sierra Club, Friends of the Earth, Greenpeace, and
Public Citizen, continued to oppose NAFTA. These groups generally oppose any growth-oriented trade policy, regardless of its environmental
provisions. Steward Hudson of the National Wildlife Foundation testified
before Congress that "a fair and objective reading of the NAFTA leaves
you with one uncompromising conclusion: the environment is far better
off with this NAFTA than without . . . . those who want to kill NAFTA are
hiding behind the environment. The environmental critics of NAFTA,
those who would forever be holding out for more, even at the expense
of making progress on the environment in dealing with problems that
concern all of us, are out to kill trade . . . . No amount of fine tuning or
renegotiation will satisfy these opponents of NAFTA. The bar will continue to be raised because the goal is to kill NAFTA."[78]

In fact, recent assessments have concluded that NAFTA did not
lead to a deterioration in Mexico's environment, but it has not spurred
many improvements either. A trade agreement itself cannot reverse decades of abuse. Environmental conditions along the U.S.-Mexican border
remain poor despite the institutions and programs created to improve the
situation.[79]

This evidence should not be interpreted as minimizing the importance of taking effective measures to improve the environment. But free

---

[77] These groups included the World Wildlife Fund, the National Wildlife Federa-
tion, the Environmental Defense Fund, the National Audubon Society, and others (Audley
1997, 90).

[78] U.S. House of Representatives 1994, 368–70. In the end, the major congressional critics of NAFTA, such as Richard Gephardt, David Bonior, and Marcy Kaptur, made no
reference to the environment in their floor speeches against the agreement, but rather focused on job loss in the United States (Audley 1997, 106). The more extreme opponents of
NAFTA were prone to exaggeration and hyperbole. The Sierra Club, for instance, said that
NAFTA would be "a major step toward ending democracy" in America.

[79] Hufbauer and Schott 2005.

trade and a cleaner environment are not incompatible. Because trade in itself is not a driving force behind pollution, a policy of free trade rarely detracts from such goals, and in many instances may help. (The link between world trade rules and environmental regulation is also considered in chapter 7.)

_____Free Trade in Perspective

The benefits of free trade appear to be substantial, although precise quantification of those benefits is sometimes difficult. In extreme cases, governments that force their citizens to forgo the advantages of international trade, particularly in developing countries (as discussed in chapter 6), do not sacrifice just a couple of percentage points of national income, but risk impoverishing their people. The higher real income that comes with trade is valuable not just to allow the consumption of more goods for crass material reasons, but to help people afford food and medicine. Free trade and higher incomes give people access to better health care, better education, and better technologies that will help improve the environment. Regrettably, the United States imposes stiff import barriers on agricultural products and labor-intensive manufactured goods, such as clothing and leather, in which developing countries have a comparative advantage. This not only harms consumers in the United States, but reduces income in developing countries as well.

But several caveats should be offered. Free trade is beneficial because it allows a country to take advantage of the opportunity to trade, but it is not the only—or even the most important—determinant of whether a country achieves economic prosperity. Free trade is not a "magic bullet" that can solve all economic problems. The real and substantial gains from free trade should not be exaggerated when other fundamental economic problems are pressing. Stable macroeconomic policies, the rule of law, and the protection of property rights that enable the market mechanism to function properly are preconditions for reaping the full benefits of international trade.[80] As Thomas Macaulay stated back in

[80] According to Adam Smith, "Commerce and manufactures can seldom flourish long in any state which does not enjoy a regular administration of justice, in which the people do not feel themselves secure in the possession of their property, in which the faith of contracts is not supported by law, and in which the authority of the state is not supposed

1845, "It is not one single cause that makes nations either prosperous or miserable. No friend of free trade is such an idiot as to say that free trade is the only valuable thing in the world; that religion, government, police, education, the administration of justice, public expenditure, foreign relations, have nothing whatever to do with the well-being of nations."[81]

At the same time, restricting trade entails real economic costs. These losses may appear to be abstractions, but they are in fact harmful for real individuals. And yet many protectionist policies are maintained, and new ones are always being proposed. This is because most trade restraints have a superficially plausible justification. These rationales are often more apparent than real, however, and the next two chapters will address them.

---

to be regularly employed in enforcing the payments of debts from all those who are able to pay. Commerce and manufactures, in short, can seldom flourish in any state in which there is not a certain degree of confidence in the justice of the government" (1976, 910).

[81] Macaulay 1900, 89.

3

Protectionism: Economic Costs, Political Benefits?

Economic analysis has long established free trade as a desirable economic policy. This conclusion has been reinforced by mounting empirical evidence on the benefits of trade, and yet protectionism is far from vanquished in the policy arena. Of course, this is nothing new: as Adam Smith observed more than two hundred years ago, "not only the prejudices of the public, but what is much more unconquerable, the private interests of many individuals, irresistibly oppose" free trade.[1] Indeed, interest groups opposed to free trade often have a political influence that is disproportionate to their economic size. This chapter describes the economic costs of trade restrictions and examines why, despite these costs, protectionism is often a seductive and politically attractive policy. The chapter concludes by considering instances in which trade protection might actually be beneficial.

The Costs of Tariffs and Quotas

In *The Wealth of Nations*, Adam Smith not only developed a powerful case for free trade, but he also issued a scathing attack on contemporary mercantilist policies that restricted trade. The ostensible purpose of these government policies was to promote national wealth, but Smith argued that such policies were ill-conceived and detracted from that objective. Smith observed that policymakers too frequently equated the interests of producers with the interests of the nation as a whole. Under mercantilism, almost any policy that helped existing producers expand output,

[1] Smith 1976, 471.

such as limits on imports or restrictions on competition, was deemed beneficial. But Smith pointed out that this approach confused the means with the end:

> Consumption is the sole end and purpose of all production; and the interest of the producer ought to be attended to only so far as it may be necessary for promoting that of the consumer. The maxim is so perfectly self-evident that it would be absurd to attempt to prove it. But in the mercantile system the interest of the consumer is almost constantly sacrificed to that of the producer; and it seems to consider production, and not consumption, as the ultimate end and object of all industry and commerce.[2]

Furthermore, Smith argued that policies such as trade barriers would not expand total output but merely divert resources to less productive uses. As he put it, "No regulation of commerce can increase the quantity of industry in any society beyond what its capital can maintain. It can only divert part of it into a direction into which it might not otherwise have gone; and it is by no means certain that this artificial direction is likely to be more advantageous to the society than that into which it would have gone of its own accord."[3]

While governments often justified trade restrictions as serving the public interest, Smith noted that such restrictions did not benefit the public as much as they served the private interests of influential merchants who had captured government policy for their own advantage. In fact, he believed that trade restrictions "may . . . be demonstrated to be in every case a complete piece of dupery, by which the interests of the State and the nation is constantly sacrificed to that of some particular class of traders."[4]

> In every country it always is and must be the interest of the great body of the people to buy whatever they want of those who sell it cheapest. The proposition is so very manifest that it seems ridiculous to take any pains to prove it; nor could it ever

[2] Smith 1976, 660.
[3] Smith 1976, 453.
[4] Smith 1977, 272.

have been called in question had not the interested sophistry of merchants and manufacturers confounded the common sense of mankind. Their interest is, in this respect, directly opposite to that of the great body of the people. As it is the interest of the freemen of a corporation to hinder the rest of the inhabitants from employing any workmen but themselves, so it is the interest of the merchants and manufacturers of every country to secure to themselves the monopoly of the home market.[5]

Policies that give preferential treatment to domestic producers in the home market still exist today. For example, in rebuilding the San Francisco-Oakland Bay Bridge, the California transit authority found it difficult to hold down costs. "Buy America" rules, which give preference to domestic producers in government procurement contracts, dictate that foreign steel can be used only if it is more than 25 percent cheaper than domestic steel. In this case, a domestic bid came in at 23 percent above the foreign bid, and so the more expensive domestic steel had to be used. Because of the large amount of steel used in the construction project, this preference means that California taxpayers would pay a whopping $400 million more for the bridge.[6] While this may be good for domestic steel firms, it is hard to see the benefit to California taxpayers, who might wish to devote the nearly half a billion dollars to other uses, such as schools or health care, or even fiscal deficit reduction.

Despite the gradual decline in trade barriers over the past half century, the array of protectionist policies around the world is still quite large. The principal means of blocking trade include tariffs (taxes on imports), quotas (quantitative restrictions on imports), and nontariff barriers of various sorts (such as product standards and technical regulations). The easiest policy to measure is tariffs. Table 3.1 shows the average applied tariff on all manufactured and agricultural imports for selected

---

[5] Smith 1976, 493–94. "That this monopoly of the home-market frequently gives great encouragement to that particular species of industry which enjoys it, and frequently turns towards that employment a greater share of both the labour and stock of the society than would otherwise have gone to it, cannot be doubted. But whether it tends either to increase the general industry of the society, or to give it the most advantageous direction, is not, perhaps, altogether so evident" (453).

[6] Renaud 2004. In this case, the California transit authorities managed to work around the "Buy America" provision.

_____*Table 3.1*

Average Applied MFN Tariffs for Selected Countries, 2007 (percent, unweighted average)

	All Goods	Manufactured Goods	Agricultural Goods
Developed Countries			
United States	2.7	2.6	3.5
European Union	1.6	1.5	2.9
Japan	2.8	2.3	7.6
Canada	3.6	3.8	2.4
Australia	2.8	2.9	0.8
Middle Income Countries			
Argentina	10.7	10.9	9.0
Korea	8.3	6.0	37.7
Brazil	12.1	12.3	9.4
Thailand	10.0	8.2	22.1
Egypt	16.7	9.2	66.4
Iran	21.3	21.2	24.3
Russia	8.3	8.3	7.6
Developing Countries			
India	14.0	12.5	39.1
China	8.7	8.3	14.7
South Africa	7.8	7.8	7.7
Tanzania	12.5	12.0	19.1
Bangladesh	14.6	14.4	17.2

Source: World Bank, Trade Research, www.worldbank.org/trade.

countries in 2007. Developed countries have relatively low average tariffs, usually less than 5 percent. (Only certain places, such as Hong Kong and Singapore, have zero tariffs.) Developing countries are much more diverse in their average tariff rates, but they are invariably higher than in most rich countries. And nearly every country imposes higher tariffs on agricultural goods than on manufactured goods.

In the case of the United States, the 2007 Harmonized Tariff Schedule consists of 10,253 tariff lines for itemized imports, each with an associated tariff rate. A simple average of the applied rates is 4.8 percent, with 4.0 for nonagricultural goods and 8.9 for agricultural goods. There are many tariff peaks, including tobacco at 350 percent, sour cream at 177 percent, and peanuts at 164 percent.[7] Yet it is also the case that about

[7]About 15 percent of the lines in the U.S. tariff code exceed 15 percent. World Trade Organization 2008b, 31–32.

70 percent of imports (by value) enter the country without paying any duties, partly because of free trade agreements such as NAFTA, which applies to America's two largest trading partners, Canada and Mexico.

The tariff figures in table 3.1 are simple unweighted averages of each country's tariff code and significantly understate the magnitude of protection. Tariff peaks may apply to only a few lines of imports, but may severely restrict trade. In addition, the indicators ignore other non-tariff forms of protection, such as quotas and quantitative restrictions. A study that looks at the overall trade restrictiveness of a country's import policy, including tariffs, quotas, and nontariff barriers, has calculated the overall tariff average that replicates the anti-import effect of all these policies. This overall tariff is much higher than simple tariff averages. For example, India's average tariff on all goods is about 14 percent, but the restrictiveness of its trade regime is equivalent to a 22 percent across-the-board tariff. Similarly, Japan's average tariff is less than 3 percent but its trade restrictiveness is equivalent to an 11 percent tariff. For the United States and European Union, average tariffs of less than 3 percent yield restrictiveness equivalents just shy of 7 percent.[8]

These anti-import policies reduce trade and tend to distort economic activity, leading to inefficient outcomes. Their effects can be separated into two components. First, import barriers redistribute income from domestic consumers to domestic producers. When imports of a product are restricted, the product becomes more scarce in the domestic market. Scarcity drives up the price, benefiting domestic producers of the product but harming consumers who are forced to pay more for it.

This redistribution is often hard to justify. For example, the United States helps the domestic sugar industry through price supports and import restrictions in the form of a tariff-rate quota. Under a tariff-rate quota, sugar-exporting countries are given a certain (small) quantity that they can bring into the United States at the regular tariff rate, and any exports beyond that specified quantity are subject to a tariff rate of nearly 150 percent. Because of the import restrictions, the price of sugar in the United States has been roughly two to three times that on the world market. Domestic sugar producers reap about $1 billion annually as a result of this policy. However, 42 percent of the total benefits to sugar growers

---

[8]Kee, Nicita, and Olarreaga 2009.

goes to the top 1 percent of all farms.[9] The rationale for rewarding a few large sugar producers with hundreds of millions of dollars every year at the expense of consumers has never been made clear.

Second, and even worse, protectionist policies distort prices and therefore economic incentives. This distortion leads to wasted resources, known as a deadweight loss. As import restrictions push the domestic price of a good above the world price, domestic firms produce more, while consumers reduce their overall purchases and suffer a real income loss as a result of the higher prices. The inefficiency associated with these distortions of incentives imposes a deadweight loss on the overall economy. Trade barriers are like an income transfer in which ten dollars is taken from consumers while giving only eight dollars to producers, resulting in a two-dollar loss to the economy as a whole. The sugar policy benefited producers of sugar to the tune of $1 billion, but it imposed far greater costs—about $1.9 billion, according to the General Accounting Office—on consumers. The result is a deadweight loss to the economy of $900 million.

Economists have made rough estimates of the income transfers and the deadweight losses associated with trade barriers. Although the average tariff on imports is low, the United States has significant restrictions on agricultural imports, particularly beef, canned tuna, dairy products, and sugar and sugar-containing goods. In addition, the average tariff on apparel is 14 percent and on footwear, 11 percent.[10] The U.S. International Trade Commission (ITC) has calculated that the net cost—that is, the deadweight loss—of these trade barriers was about $3.7 billion in 2005.[11] (The overall costs to consumers, and transfers to producers, of course, are much larger than this figure.) Because the average tariff is

[9] U.S. GAO 2000a; 1993, 32–33. See also Beghin et al. 2003.

[10] When it comes to manufactured goods, the United States essentially has a two-tiered tariff system: average tariffs of 10 to 15 percent on light consumer goods (clothes, shoes, suitcases) and 0 to 1 percent on everything else. For example, clothes and shoes account for less than 7 percent of all imports yet bring in nearly half of all tariff revenue. Gresser 2007.

[11] U.S. International Trade Commission 2007a. This figure excludes the cost of antidumping duties, which will be considered in chapter 5. In addition, this figure is based on a highly aggregated view of trade. Because the variance of tariff rates across imports matters for its welfare cost, a more refined study yields a higher welfare loss of $7 billion (Kee, Nicita, and Olarreaga 2008b).

quite low, the elimination of these barriers would increase overall U.S. imports by only 1.2 percent (or $20 billion), although imports of some products might increase substantially.

The net cost of $3.7 billion in 2005 is significantly lower than the $16.4 billion that the ITC calculated in 2002. The reason for the reduction is the expiration of the Multi-Fiber Arrangement (MFA). Until its demise in January 2005, the MFA was the biggest piece of protectionist cholesterol blocking the arteries of world trade.[12] The MFA restricted imports of foreign textiles and apparel through a complex maze of country- and product-specific quotas. Under the MFA, the United States maintained more than three thousand separate quotas on imports from more than forty nations. The narrowly defined quotas include cotton diapers from China, men's and boys' cotton coats from Sri Lanka, women's and girls' wool coats from Czech Republic, women's bras from Mexico, men's trousers from Guatemala, women's and girls' man-made-fiber woven blouses from the United Arab Emirates, and so on. In 1989, the Treasury Department's Customs Service prohibited the import of thirty thousand tennis shoes from Indonesia because the boxes contained an extra pair of shoelaces, which, it was decided, fell in a separate import quota category.[13]

The result was severely distorted trade and significantly higher prices of clothing for U.S. consumers.[14] The combined effect of tariffs and quotas raised domestic prices of apparel by 18 to 24 percent and prices of finished textile products by about 14 percent in 2002.[15] Indeed, according to virtually every study on the matter, the economic benefits to the United States from eliminating the MFA were enormous. The direct consumer cost of this protection amounted to $24.4 billion in 1990, a burden of over $260 per household.[16] The tax is generally believed to have

---

[12] Under the Uruguay Round trade agreement of 1994, the United States and other countries vowed to abolish the MFA by January 2005.

[13] Customs later decided that an extra pair of shoelaces would be permitted so long as they were laced into the shoes and color-coordinated with the shoes; Bovard 1991, 45.

[14] The restrictiveness of the MFA varied considerably across commodity products, ranging from 7 to 12 percent for apparel overall, 12 to 28 percent for women's and girl's cotton knit shirts, 44 to 47 percent for cotton bed sheets, etc. U.S. International Trade Commission 2006, 70.

[15] U.S. International Trade Commission 2006, 71.

[16] Hufbauer and Elliott 1994.

been quite regressive, because lower-income households devote a greater share of their expenditures to clothing than those with higher incomes.

The high costs of the MFA illustrate an important difference between an import tariff and an import quota. When the United States imposes a tax on imports, the government collects as tariff revenue the difference between the world price and the higher, tariff-inclusive domestic price charged to consumers. But when a country limits the quantity of imports with a quota, the difference between the world price and the higher domestic price becomes a scarcity rent rather than tariff revenue. This scarcity (or quota) rent is captured by foreign exporters as a markup if they have obtained the right to export a certain amount under the quota in the import-restricting market, where they get to charge a higher price than on the world market.

The transfer of quota rents is a national loss because money is taken from consumers and handed to foreign exporters (in the form of a higher markup) instead of the government (in the form of tax revenue), as would have happened if a tariff had been imposed. According to most studies, almost all of the roughly $12 billion net cost to the United States of the MFA was due to the transfer of quota rents to foreign exporters and very little due to domestic deadweight efficiency losses.

The transfer of quota rents also distorts the incentives of the exporters, particularly in developing countries. When the United States imposes an import quota, foreign governments are usually responsible for determining which exporters will be allowed to sell in the U.S. market (and thus receive the quota rent) and which exporters will be prohibited from exporting. The allocation of quota rights, except when those rights are auctioned off, is inherently arbitrary and increases the power of government bureaucrats, thereby fostering corruption. The politically well-connected firms, who perhaps are not averse to sharing the quota rents with the bureaucrats, are most likely to obtain export licenses, whereas other firms are shut out. This gives entrepreneurs in developing countries the wrong signal: the way to get rich is to invest in political influence, not to invest in productive efficiency.

As the MFA example indicates, the quota rents can be extremely valuable. In some cases, the quota rent received by foreign producers helps them compete against American firms. For example, when the United States limited the quantity of Japanese black-and-white televisions sold in the U.S. market in the early 1970s, the quota rent transfer is said to have given Japanese producers the financial resources to enter the market for color televisions and videocassette recorders more quickly. When the United States persuaded Japan to limit its automobile exports in 1981, Japan's auto exporters were able to raise the average price of their cars by about $1,000, part of which they invested in product improvements that enabled them to compete even more effectively against their American rivals.[17] When the United States forced Japan to maintain high minimum prices on its semiconductor exports in the late 1980s, some of Japan's electronics producers were pleased that the American government, in order to help domestic semiconductor producers, was also helping them raise their prices in the U.S. market. Japanese companies that produced one-megabyte dynamic random access memories (DRAMs) made an additional $1.2 billion in profits in 1988 because of the U.S. trade intervention.[18]

Yet simply documenting the economic costs of protection often has a limited impact on policy. One reason could be that the calculated welfare gains from additional trade liberalization are quite small as a share of GDP. In the case of the United States, the ITC's estimate of $3.9 billion in gains from unilaterally removing U.S. import restraints in 2005, for example, amounts to only 0.03 percent of that year's GDP. This is the cost of existing trade barriers and should not be confused with the gains from trade. Still, it is almost a trivial sum—it is equivalent to an extra $15 pay for a worker who earns $50,000 a year—even though it is an annual gain that accrues in perpetuity. But the small number reflects the fact that average tariff barriers are low, due in part to free trade agreements with Canada and Mexico, America's largest trade partners, and that the United States has avoided the use of costly import quotas.

However, this understates the true cost of trade barriers for many reasons, such as the failure to consider the productivity and variety benefits of trade. In addition, it does not reflect the gains to the United States from a multilateral trade agreement in which it benefits from greater market access in other countries. And, of course, just because the cost of protection is relatively low for the United States does not mean that it is

[17] Feenstra 1984.
[18] Flamm 1996, 277.

low for other countries, particularly many developing countries. For those whose trade barriers are much more pervasive and restrictive, the potential gains from liberalization are much more substantial.[19] For example, the static deadweight loss due to trade restrictions amounts to 3.1 percent of GDP in Egypt, 2.8 percent of GDP in Ghana, and 2.2 percent of GDP in Tunisia, according to a recent study. Once again, these costs are understated because they ignore the productivity gains from trade and the benefits of international agreements that would give these countries greater access to other markets.[20]

The estimates of the cost of protection are also understated because they do not take into account the resources devoted to political pressure. Expenditures on campaign contributions and legal fees may generate private benefits for those making the expenditures, if they can persuade policymakers to restrict trade on their behalf. Those expenditures are socially unproductive because the goal is to redistribute wealth rather than create it.

Indeed, the impact of trade barriers can be significantly understated when the political determinants of those barriers are not taken into account. A standard statistical method of gauging the effect of trade restraints on imports is to examine the determinants of import demand, such as the relative price of imports, domestic income, and other explanatory variables. But this approach ignores the simultaneity of imports and protection: higher tariffs may reduce imports, but more imports also lead to greater political pressure for higher tariffs. This confounds any attempt to isolate the effect of tariffs on imports and, unless corrected for, leads one to understate the effect of tariffs on imports. When one study confronted this problem by examining the political-economic determinants of trade barriers in the United States and using the results to help explain imports, the statistical coefficient representing the negative impact of nontariff barriers (such as quantitative restrictions) on imports was increased by a factor of ten. The conventional estimate suggests that removing nontariff barriers would increase manufactured imports by $5.5 billion

---

[19] Messerlin (2001) reports that the costs of protection in the European Union are equivalent to about 6–7 percent of the EU's GDP, or about the same as the annual value of output in Spain. The net cost of trade protection in Japan (circa 1989) has been estimated to be anywhere from $8 billion to $17 billion, according to Sazanami, Urata, and Kawai 1995.

[20] Kee, Nicita, and Olarreaga 2008.

(in 1985), whereas after controlling for the political determinants of those barriers, the impact was estimated to be closer to $50 billion.[21]

The numbers assigned to the welfare costs of trade barriers have a surreal feel to them that makes them difficult to grasp. What may be more distressing is the rarely exposed seamier details of the protectionist racket, which allow one to go behind the numbers and see how firms and sectors actually get the government to intervene on their behalf. The sugar program is a classic example. Sugar imports are restricted to maintain domestic price supports for sugar beet and cane producers. The benefits of these restrictions are highly concentrated because Congress has not limited the amount of support that large firms can receive. For example, one farm received over $30 million in benefits from the sugar program in 1991, and just 0.2 percent of all sugarcane farms—thirty-three in total—received 34 percent of the entire program benefits.[22] The family of Alfonso Fanjul single-handedly supplies the United States with about 15 percent of its sugarcane through its land holdings in south Florida and the Dominican Republic, collecting somewhere between $52 to $90 million in benefits from the price supports on U.S. production and the quota rents on Dominican sugar exports.[23] Not surprisingly, the Fanjul family could afford to make nearly $300,000 in campaign contributions in 1988.[24] At the same time, the Fanjul farms were being investigated for chronic violation of U.S. labor laws. Government support for the sugar industry has also harmed the environment because chemical runoff from the intensive farming of sugarcane in south Florida has seeped into the Everglades.

The sugar program is not just an economic, political, and environmental inequity, but it prevents desperately poor sugar-producing countries from exporting to the United States. Countries such as Colombia and Guatemala are deprived of valuable foreign exchange earnings that could be spent on food, fuel, and medicine. Congressional opponents of the sugar policy have suggested that Andean farmers, who have

[21] Trefler 1993.
[22] U.S. General Accounting Office 1993.
[23] Mayer and de Cordoba 1991.
[24] Alfonso Fanjul is so politically powerful that President Bill Clinton interrupted a "meeting" with Monica Lewinsky to take a phone call from him. This is according to Lewinsky's testimony as presented in the Kenneth Starr report.

been prevented from selling their sugar in major markets, have turned their cropland toward the production of coca used in cocaine production and other illegal drugs. The Caribbean and Latin American farmers who find themselves cut out of the American sugar market may be forced to turn to illegal crops as a way to make a living.

When politics and trade meet, the result not only harms consumers, but may even jeopardize national security. Shortly after the tragic events of September 11, 2001, President Pervez Musharraf of Pakistan requested the suspension of tariff and quota on Pakistan's exports of textiles and apparel to the United States in an effort to lift its economy. After debate within the Bush administration, Commerce Department officials informed Pakistan that the United States would be unable to grant trade concessions; pressure from the domestic textile and apparel industry successfully blocked any expansion of imports. In fact, Pakistan's textile exports to the United States actually fell sharply in the months after 9/11 because of a sharp rise in insurance premiums, costing Pakistan over $1 billion in exports and throwing untold numbers of workers out of their jobs at a delicate time in the region.[25]

When examined up close, trade policy is not pretty. Steel industry lobbyists, for example, have induced members of Congress to change U.S. trade laws for the specific benefit of their industry, which has received pension bailouts, loan guarantees, environmental exemptions, decades of trade restrictions—and continues to press for more. When powerful industries push politicians to intervene on their behalf, the picture is often an ugly one.

So far we have examined the direct costs of import barriers. But the indirect effects of import barriers are also important, though not always readily apparent. The indirect consequences of import restrictions include a reduction in exports and lower employment in downstream industries, and we consider each in turn.

[25] According to Foer (2002), the reason for the rejection of Pakistan's request was that Congressional Republicans decided that they wanted to give the president trade negotiating authority without Democratic support to show the business lobbies that pro-trade Democrats were not trustworthy on the issue. To get a majority, Ways and Means Chairman Bill Thomas needed to woo protectionist Republicans to support the bill with promises that key industries in their districts would be protected. House Republican leaders secured the deciding vote of Robin Hayes (R-N.C.) only by promising not to increase quotas on Pakistani textile imports.

Import Barriers Harm Exports

Imagine taking a poll of Americans and asking: "Should the United States impose tariffs on foreign goods to prevent imports from low-wage countries from harming American workers?" A sizable fraction of the respondents would probably answer "yes." If asked to explain their position, they would probably reply that import tariffs would create jobs for Americans and thereby reduce unemployment. (The validity of this opinion will be examined in chapter 4.)

Then suppose you asked the same people: "Should the United States levy an export tax on domestically produced goods such as aircraft, grains, machinery, software, and the like?" The answer would probably be a resounding and unanimous "no!" After all, they would argue, export taxes would destroy jobs and harm important industries.[26]

Yet according to an important proposition known as the Lerner symmetry theorem, these two policies are equivalent in their economic effects.[27] The Lerner symmetry theorem holds that a tax on imports is functionally equivalent to a tax on exports. In other words, any restriction on imports also operates as a restriction on exports. This theorem helps us understand another aspect of import tariffs—how they destroy jobs in export industries.

Some participants in the debate on trade tend to believe that a country's exports and imports are independent of one another, and therefore one can reduce imports without having an adverse effect on exports. In fact, exports and imports are the flip side of the same coin. Exports are the goods a country must give up in order to acquire imports. Exports are necessary to generate the earnings to pay for imports. The past century illustrates the close relationship between exports and imports in the United States. Looking back at figure 1.1, which plots U.S. merchandise exports and imports as a percentage of GDP from 1869 to 2007, we see

---

[26] In addition to being unconstitutional under Article 1, section 9 of the Constitution.

[27] The theorem is named after Abba Lerner, who published a short but brilliant paper on the subject as a graduate student at the London School of Economics in 1936. Lerner's paper established the formal truth of the proposition, but it had been a feature of trade policy debates long before then.

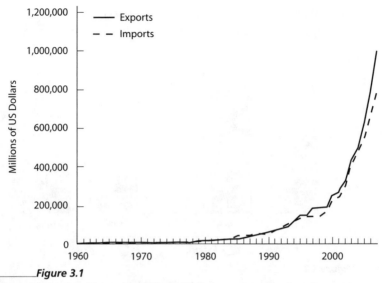

_____*Figure 3.1*
China's Exports and Imports, 1960–2007.
Source: International Monetary Fund, International Financial Statistics Yearbook, 2008.

that exports and imports have been highly correlated, except in recent years. (The trade deficit will be discussed in chapter 4.)

Additional evidence of the Lerner symmetry theorem comes from the recent experience of developing countries. Figure 3.1 depicts China's exports and imports. Most people are well aware that China has become a major exporter. Few realize that China's astounding growth in exports has been matched by astounding growth in imports. This simply demonstrates that trade is indeed a two-way street, not a one-way flow.

As another example, consider two South American countries, Chile and Brazil. These countries have pursued quite different types of commercial policies in recent decades. Chile undertook an extensive liberalization of its trade policy in the 1970s, dramatically cutting its import tariffs. As figure 3.2 indicates, this change in policy helped Chile's imports surge from about 15 percent of GDP in 1970 to 30 percent of GDP in 1998. And yet this period also witnessed a surge in exports on the same order of magnitude: the import expansion was matched by an export expansion. As in the case of other countries, Chile's experience also

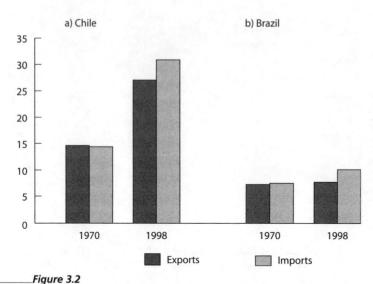

_____*Figure 3.2*

Exports and Imports as a Share of GDP, Chile and Brazil, 1970 and 1998.
Source: International Monetary Fund 2000.

suggests that export diversification is an additional benefit that comes with lifting the implicit export tax that is inherent in import tariffs.[28]

By contrast, Brazil has pursued "import substitution" policies since the 1960s. These policies aimed to promote industrialization by severely restricting imports. In 1970, Brazil's exports and imports amounted to about 7 percent of its GDP. Brazil's trade policy did not change dramatically in the subsequent twenty-eight years, and thus, Brazil's exports and imports remained at 7 percent of GDP in 1998 despite the tremendous growth in world trade over this period. The Brazilian government has made great efforts to expand exports, but substantial import barriers have indirectly constrained exports and undermined those efforts.

At one level, the idea that import restraints will reduce exports is straightforward. If foreign countries are blocked in their ability to sell

[28] By reducing import taxes, a country is lifting an implicit tax on the export sector. This tax relief allows marginal exports, previously squelched by the tax, to become profitable. As a result, countries do not simply export more of the same things, but other goods that were previously unprofitable to export. This implies that trade liberalization allows exports to become more rather than less diversified, thereby reducing the risk of adverse export price shocks. Chile, for example, reduced its export dependence on metals (mainly copper) from 64 percent of exports in 1980 to 46 percent in 1996.

their goods in the United States, they will be unable to earn the dollars they need to purchase U.S. goods. The mechanisms that link a country's exports and imports to one another are complex and not always readily apparent, but can be illustrated by focusing on the foreign exchange market. If the United States unilaterally reduces its tariff on Brazilian goods, for example, one would expect U.S. demand for Brazil's goods to increase. To make these purchases, consumers in the United States will (indirectly) have to sell dollars on the foreign exchange market to purchase Brazil's currency, the *real*. In response to the increased demand for *real* from those holding dollars, the value of the dollar will fall in terms of *real*, or conversely the *real*'s value will rise in terms of dollars. This change tends to raise the price of Brazilian goods in the United States, dampening demand for those goods.

But here is the flip side: although it was the United States that lowered its tariffs while Brazil left its tariffs unchanged, Brazil will now purchase more goods from the United States. This is because the cheaper dollar tends to lower the *real* price of U.S. goods, stimulating Brazilian demand for them. Therefore, the foreign exchange market is one of several mechanisms that link exports and imports, ensuring that a country's exports increase when it unilaterally reduces its own import tariffs.[29]

The pattern of U.S. exports and imports shown in figure 1.3 also illustrates this relationship. The ratio of exports and imports to GDP was fairly stable in the 1950s and 1960s, but in the early 1970s and again in the late 1970s there was a pronounced jump in both of these ratios. These jumps coincide with large increases in world oil prices. (As late as 1980, almost 30 percent of U.S. imports by value were mineral fuels.) The big increase in the import bill is seen in the higher ratio of imports to GDP, but—since those imports must be paid for with something—the export ratio also rose in each case. In both instances the increase in exports was brought about by a depreciation in the value of the dollar.

This link between exports and imports also explains why the employment effects of trade intervention tend to cancel each other out. Throughout U.S. history, large tariff increases have failed to stimulate

[29] A change in the exchange rate is only one of several mechanisms by which symmetry will hold; for example, it still holds for countries with fixed exchange rates or in single currency areas such as the Euro-zone in Europe.

greater employment because any increase in employment in import-competing industries is offset by a decrease in employment in export-oriented industries. The Hawley-Smoot tariff of 1930, for example, significantly reduced imports but failed to create jobs overall because exports fell almost one-for-one with imports, resulting in employment losses in those industries.

Thus, the connection between imports and exports cannot be overlooked when evaluating trade policy. Governments that undertake policies to reduce imports will find themselves also reducing exports. This reduction in imports may expand employment in industries that compete with them, but the reduction in exports contracts employment in those industries dependent upon foreign sales. An appreciation of the Lerner symmetry theorem is particularly important when assessing the claim that import tariffs have a beneficial effect on overall employment.

Import Barriers Harm Downstream Industries

Not only do import restrictions reduce the number of jobs required to produce exports, but they also destroy jobs in downstream industries that use the imports. Recall from table 1.2 that the majority of U.S. imports are not final consumer goods, but intermediate goods used by domestic firms in their production. Any trade restriction that raises the price of an intermediate good directly harms downstream user industries and thus adversely affects employment in those industries. In other words, when domestic firms have to pay a premium on their productive inputs, particularly when they are competing with foreign rivals who do not pay those taxes, employment in those industries suffers.

Restrictions on imported sugar, for example, have produced sour results for those employed in the sugar-refining and candy-making industries. When food manufacturers who produce sugar-intensive products are forced to pay a higher price for sugar than their foreign rivals, their competitive position suffers. In 2002, a LifeSavers candy plant that employed 650 workers in Michigan was closed and relocated to Canada. Before the shutdown, the plant produced about 3 million rolls of LifeSavers per day using 250,000 pounds of sugar. Due to the high price of sugar in the United States, the company will save over $10 million a year in sugar costs just by relocating across the border. Canada is the location of choice for large sugar-using food manufacturers because the country does not have any sugar farmers and hence does not artificially inflate the price of sugar on their behalf.

Limits on sugar imports have had repercussions throughout the American food manufacturing industry. In 1990, Brachs Candy Company announced that because of the high domestic price of sugar, it would close a factory in Chicago that employed three thousand workers, and expand production in Canada. According to Mayor Richard Daley, Chicago's confectionary industry has lost 11 percent of its jobs since 1991. "The continuation of domestic sugar price supports," Daley said, "is a key reason these companies [confectioners] are considering leaving Chicago and relocating their facilities outside of U.S. borders."[30]

After noting that the U.S. price of sugar had been at two to three times the world price for twenty-five years, a Commerce Department report in 2006 concluded that "this price difference results in a significant competitive cost disadvantage for domestic sugar-containing products manufacturers."[31] It reported that employment in the sugar-refining and sugar-containing products industry had fallen by more than eleven thousand between 1997 and 2002, even as employment in the non-sugar-containing food products industry had risen by more than thirty thousand. Of the ten thousand jobs lost, the Commerce Department attributed at least 6,400 to plant closings and relocation related to the high domestic price of sugar. In fact, sugar policy jeopardizes many more workers in sugar-using industries than it protects in the sugar-growing industry: in 2002, employment in sugar-using industries was 987,810, whereas there were only 61,000 workers employed growing and harvesting sugarcane and beets. Trade barriers are thought to protect only 2,260 of those sugar-growing jobs, which means that the consumer cost per job saved is $826,000. As a result, the report noted, "nearly three confectionery manufacturing jobs are lost for every job protected in the sugar-growing sector due to the price gap between U.S. and world refined sugar prices."

There are numerous examples of the adverse effect that trade restrictions have on employment in related industries. In 1991, the United States imposed antidumping duties on imported flat panel displays, used

[30] Groombridge 2001, 5.
[31] U.S. Department of Commerce 2006.

by domestic manufacturers of laptop computers: specifically, 62.67 percent duties on active matrix LCD displays and 7.02 percent duties on electroluminescent displays. Producers of laptops could no longer afford to purchase the expensive displays in the United States and still compete effectively against overseas rivals, who could buy the same displays at much lower prices on the world market and then export their laptops freely to the United States. To avoid the higher domestic prices, several manufacturers decided to shift production abroad. Immediately after the imposition of the antidumping duties, Toshiba announced that it would cease production of laptops in California and shift production to Japan, Sharp announced that it would cease production of laptops in Texas and move production to Canada, and Apple announced that it would relocate its assembly of laptops from California to Ireland or Singapore.[32] Similarly, after the United States imposed price floors on Japanese DRAM semiconductors, computer manufacturers shifted their assembly operations outside of the United States to take advantage of the lower prices for memory chips in other markets. In these and numerous other cases, import restrictions benefiting one industry have only harmed another industry.

When the purchasers of imported intermediate goods organize politically, they can alter the debate over the desirability of protection on employment grounds. In the case just mentioned, firms that used semiconductors (particularly computer manufacturers IBM, Hewlett-Packard, Sun Microsystems, and others) formed a coalition to oppose the renewal of the price floors on Japanese memory chips. As a result of this consumer coalition, U.S. trade officials no longer heard a single voice—that of semiconductor producers—regarding America's trade policy. The government did not know how to deal with the sharply conflicting domestic interests, so it simply let the price floor agreement expire.[33]

The same political process played out in the steel industry. In 1984, the United States negotiated voluntary restraint agreements (VRAs) that limited steel imports from all major foreign suppliers. The VRAs raised the domestic price of steel and helped steel producers, but harmed the production, employment, and exports of the far more numerous domestic users of steel, including the automobile, machine tool, and con-

---

[32] Hart 1993.
[33] Irwin 1996b.

struction industries. To fight the VRAs, these downstream industries formed the Coalition of American Steel-Using Manufacturers (CASUM), led by Caterpillar, the manufacturer of heavy earthmoving equipment, and by the Precision Metalforming Association, a small business group whose members process raw steel for industrial users such as the automobile industry.

As in the case of semiconductors, the VRAs were allowed to expire in 1991 in part because CASUM posed an extremely difficult question to government officials: How are Caterpillar, John Deere, and other domestic steel-using firms supposed to compete at home and abroad against such foreign competitors as Komatsu when they are forced to pay a hefty premium for the steel they must purchase? If Caterpillar laid off workers because higher domestic steel costs led to sales being lost to foreign producers, those workers could justifiably ask whether the government believed that jobs in the steel industry were more important to the economy than jobs in the equipment-manufacturing industry.[34]

The protectionist steel industry used to get its own way when lobbying Washington for import relief. Now it has to battle steel-consuming industries for political influence. When the steel industry filed massive antidumping suits in 1998–99, steel-using groups formed the "40-to-1" coalition, referring to the fact that the fewer than two hundred thousand steelworkers are outnumbered by 8 million employees in steel-using industries, particularly in construction, metal fabrication, heavy machinery, and transportation equipment. The jobs of workers in steel-using industries would be at risk if steel prices were artificially increased. General Motors, which purchases over 7 million tons of steel annually, warned that imposing tariffs on imported steel would make GM's domestic operations "less competitive in the international marketplace to the extent that those operations are subjected to costs not incurred by offshore competition, and to the extent that U.S. import barriers impede access to new products and materials being developed offshore, or remove the competitive incentives to develop new products in the United States."[35]

In 2002, when the Bush administration was considering whether to impose special safeguard tariffs on imported steel, the steel-users

[34] Moore 1996.
[35] Lindsey, Griswold, and Lukas 1999, 7.

coalition—the Consuming Industries Trade Action Coalition, or CITAC—responded once again. According to a study commissioned by CITAC, the proposed import relief would save between four thousand and eight thousand jobs in the steel industry. But, by increasing steel prices and imports of steel-containing products, the import restrictions would reduce employment by thirty-six thousand to seventy-four thousand in other sectors of the economy. The higher prices would force steel consumers to pay between $2 billion and $4 billion in extra costs, would cost the economy eight jobs for every one steel job created, and thus cost consumers about $425,000 per job saved in the steel industry.[36]

A year after the Bush administration imposed tariffs of up to 30 percent on certain steel imports in March 2002, the International Trade Commission surveyed steel consumers about the impact of this action. About half of steel purchasers reported an increase in contract or spot prices after the tariffs were imposed. Based on the survey responses, roughly 8 percent of the decline in employment in steel-consuming firms between 2002 and 2003 was attributed to the safeguard measure.[37] Once again, in deciding whether to limit steel imports, the government faced the choice of protecting jobs in the steel industry or protecting jobs in automobiles, commercial building, wire products, electronic equipment, heavy machinery, oil and gas drilling, and other steel-using industries.

These examples demonstrate the first lesson of economics: there is no such thing as a free lunch. Every government intervention involves a trade-off of some sort. Higher sugar prices increase employment in sugar production, but reduce employment in food-manufacturing industries. Higher semiconductor prices increase employment in the semiconductor industry, but decrease employment in the computer industry. Higher steel prices increase employment in the steel industry, but decrease employment in the steel-using industries. When a domestic industry asks the government to impose trade barriers that would raise the domestic price above the world price, the choice means trading off jobs in one sector of the economy for jobs in another sector, not creating or losing jobs overall.

[36] Francois and Baughman 2001.
[37] U.S. International Trade Commission 2003, 2–50.

Why do policymakers usually fail to see themselves as facing such a trade-off? For one thing, if downstream consumers do not organize politically, the indirect consequences of trade barriers may never be brought to legislators' attention. And the nature of the political process gives members of Congress and officials in the executive agencies responsible for trade policy a strongly biased view of the effects of trade. Constituents who lose their jobs in import-sensitive industries, such as steel, invariably complain to their representatives and government agencies about foreign competition. Legislators and bureaucrats cannot ignore these voters and it is hard to resist the temptation to help by "doing something" about the situation, even if that imposes hardship on others who are often silent. Meanwhile, those who owe their jobs and high wages to exports or to industries that depend upon inexpensive intermediate goods almost invariably fail to express their appreciation to policymakers for not interfering in the process of trade. As a result, those seeking to limit trade tend to be more vocal than those who benefit from open markets.

_____The Politics of Protection

If free trade is so beneficial and protectionism so costly, then what explains the attractiveness and persistence of high trade barriers? One reason why free trade is so controversial is that, in the short run, not everyone stands to benefit from the policy. Changes in trade flows and in trade policy have a ripple effect through the economy and alter the distribution of income. Because some groups are harmed by trade and benefit from trade barriers, it is not clear that free trade policies will always be adopted. The actual policy will depend upon the relative political strength of those supporting and opposing trade restrictions, based on underlying economic interests or any other motivation.

Indeed, specific groups that benefit from protectionist barriers usually exert political influence beyond their numbers. Political influence tends to be skewed in favor of those seeking government assistance because those who stand to gain have more at stake than those who stand to lose. As Vilfredo Pareto pointed out long ago, "a protectionist measure provides large benefits to a small number of people, and causes a very great number of consumers a slight loss."[38] This circumstance makes it easier to enact such measures. Pareto's idea that the benefits of trade protection are highly concentrated, while the costs are widely diffused, has been a central point of departure for explaining the existence and persistence of import restrictions.

The U.S. sugar program, once again, illustrates this imbalance in costs and benefits. Import restrictions have kept domestic sugar prices at roughly twice the world price. The General Accounting Office estimated that domestic sugar producers reaped about $1 billion in 1998 as a result of this policy. However, 42 percent of the total benefits to sugarcane and sugar beet growers went to just 1 percent of all producers; indeed, just seventeen sugarcane farms collected over half of all the cane growers' benefits. Clearly, the owners of these few farms have a powerful incentive to maintain the import restrictions. Although the sugar policy imposes far larger costs on consumers of sweeteners ($1.9 billion according to the GAO) than are distributed to growers, consumers are far more numerous, and these costs are spread widely among them.

This combination of concentrated benefits and dispersed costs leads to an enormous imbalance in the relative size of the political forces opposing and favoring any change in the sugar policy. The incentive for household consumers to oppose the policy is virtually nonexistent: even though the total cost across all consumers is large, the cost to each individual consumer is small: only about seven dollars per person per year. On the other hand, the policy creates large, tangible benefits for a few producers, who are willing to devote substantial resources to defend the policy. In the 2006 election cycle (January 2003 to December 2006), sugarcane and sugar beet political action committees spent $3.3 million in campaign contributions. Since 1990, the sugar industry has made campaign contributions totaling almost $30 million.[39] As a result, such special interests have an influence on policy that is disproportionate to their size.

Another example is wire clothes hangers used by dry cleaners. In 2008, M&B Metal Products Co. of Leeds, Alabama, succeeded in getting the government to impose antidumping tariffs of 15.44 percent and 94.06 percent on two major exporters from China. (Chapter 5 covers an-

---

[38] Pareto 1971, 379.
[39] See data available at http://www.opensecrets.org.

tidumping policy.) The manufacturer argued that the cost to consumers of the additional tariffs would be trivial, only a penny or two per hanger, so that if someone paid $12.95 to have his or her suit cleaned, the price would rise to just $12.96 or $12.97. As a result, it was argued, consumers would not notice the difference. Yet the costs add up. With 30,000 dry cleaners in the United States, each paying an additional $4,000 per year due to the hanger tariff, the annual cost to consumers would be about $120 million. Even though individual consumers might not notice, the tariffs would allow the domestic producer to capture a share of this amount, giving them a powerful financial incentive to press for the duties. (Furthermore, according to the International Trade Commission, U.S. employment in wire hanger manufacturing was just 564 workers in 2004; if each of those 564 jobs were "saved" by the tariff, the cost per job saved would be $212,765 per year in an industry where the typical full-time worker earns about $28,000 per year.[40])

Yet such imbalances in the concentration of costs and benefits are not the whole story. Many small groups could benefit from special government policies, but few actually succeed in organizing and obtaining it. Why are some special interests able to form a political organization or interest group while others are not? And why do only some of those that organize succeed in influencing policy? The formation of interest groups is a critical element of the politics of trade policy. Unfortunately, economists and political scientists have not been hugely successful in revealing much about the organization of economic interests.[41] However, several hypotheses are worth exploring.

One difficulty in forming a successful political interest group is the "free-rider" problem. If a tariff benefits all firms in an industry regardless of whether they contributed to the political effort to get the tariff imposed, then some firms may choose not to contribute. They would prefer that others undertake the burden because, if protection is secured, the shirking firms cannot be excluded from the benefits of higher prices as imports are squeezed out of the market. But at the same time, the fewer firms participating in seeking protection, the lower the probability of obtaining protection.

[40] U.S. International Trade Commission 2007b.
[41] Rodrik (1995) and Gawande and Krishna (2003) survey the economic literature on the political economy of trade policy.

Industries that are relatively concentrated, either economically (a small number of firms) or geographically (the same regional location), are best positioned to overcome the costs of collective action. They can monitor the political contributions of others and attempt to punish or exclude free riders. The free-rider problem also explains the difficulty of mobilizing the dispersed opponents of programs. The numerous but widely dispersed consumers who pay higher prices for sugar have a collective interest in changing the current policy, but there is a strong incentive to shirk from any organized effort to do so.

For other economic interests, however, political organization is not even necessary. For example, wheat farmers in Kansas and Nebraska, tobacco farmers in North Carolina, and citrus producers in Florida do not require much political organization to ensure that their elected representatives take their interests to heart. Legislators represent the preferences of important unorganized constituents in order to raise the probability that they will be reelected. In addition, with the spread of antidumping and other bureaucratic mechanisms for obtaining protection, described in chapter 5, it is not even clear that political contributions by interest groups are the predominant means by which trade policy is affected. The free-rider problem is less of an obstacle in antidumping cases because the definition of an industry is often so narrow that even a single firm has the standing to file a petition.

Thus, because of the conflicting interests of specific groups, there is no reason to believe that free trade will necessarily be adopted as a country's trade policy. But what if citizens could actually vote on trade policy matters? An interesting benchmark to consider is the trade policy that would emerge in a democratic vote under majority rule. While trade policy is rarely determined in this way, this is a useful starting point for thinking about the policy that would arise in a competitive, representative political system.

In a direct democracy, trade policy would be determined by the preferences of the median voter.[42] If free trade raises aggregate income but reduces the income of the median voter, then free trade might not get a majority vote to pass in a referendum. This points to the distribution of

---

[42] See the classic analysis by Mayer (1984). The median voter is the decisive marginal voter whose views determine which side will win under majority rule.

workers' skills across the electorate as a potentially important determinant of the median voter's interests. Suppose workers with a high school education lose one dollar as a result of free trade, while those with a college education gain two dollars. If workers with a college degree constitute at least one-third of all voters, free trade would raise overall income. But if the less-educated workers comprise more than half of the electorate, the median voter would oppose the policy, unless guaranteed a compensatory income transfer.

As noted in chapter 1, educational attainment does appear to be an important factor in shaping the American public's views of trade policy. Several studies have shown that the more education a person receives, the more likely that person is to support open trade policies.[43] This is consistent with the view that economic interests are at stake: the United States exports goods and services that require a highly educated workforce, whereas it imports more labor-intensive goods where, in the competing domestic industry, few years of formal education are required. Because the fraction of the population receiving advanced education has risen in recent decades, support for freer trade might be expected to grow over time.[44]

Other factors affecting the median voter's views on trade include the manner in which voters perceive their economic interests to be related to trade policy. One such factor is the degree to which workers are potentially mobile between different sectors of the economy or different regions of the country. For example, a worker who over time has built up industry-specific skills (such as a blast furnace worker in the steel industry) will probably view trade policy differently from someone whose skills are useful in several different industries (such as a financial accountant who happens to work in the steel industry). A coal miner in West

[43] Scheve and Slaughter 2001a, 2001b. Mayda and Rodrik (2005) examine how various factors (income, education, employment, political views) are correlated with individual trade policy views for many countries around the world.

[44] In 2006, for example, 42 percent of persons aged sixty-five to seventy-four had received some college education or had earned a higher degree, while 58 percent of persons aged twenty-five to thirty-four had reached this level of educational attainment (U.S. Bureau of the Census 2008, table 219). There is also evidence that home ownership is a factor that shapes an individual's preferences on trade policy. Even highly educated individuals tend to express support for protectionist policies if they own a home in a region that is adversely affected by imports. Scheve and Slaughter 2001b.

Virginia who refuses to consider relocating to another part of the country is going to think about economic change differently from someone who is willing to move thousands of miles in search of a new opportunity.

In most developed countries, trade policy is determined by elected representatives in the legislature. In this case, the distribution of economic interests across electoral districts can interact with the rules of the political system (a winner-take-all versus a proportionate representative system) and shape the outcome. If a sizable minority of the electorate is opposed to free trade but is uniformly distributed across districts, then a winner-take-all system might result in the election of few opponents to free trade, whereas their political strength might be greater in a proportional system.

Politicians can be crafty in exploiting the geographic variation in trade interests by using selective promises of protection to win votes. To help get NAFTA passed by the House of Representatives in 1993, President Bill Clinton negotiated a special safeguard agreement for citrus producers just to win the support of Florida's congressional delegation. During the 2000 election campaign, candidate George Bush promised to aid steelworkers in West Virginia, which helped swing the state to the Republicans for the first time in decades and helped him win the election. (The Bush administration followed through on its promise by imposing tariffs on imported steel in 2002.) In the 2008 Democratic primaries, candidates Barack Obama and Hillary Clinton questioned the wisdom of NAFTA in Ohio, where many manufacturing jobs had been lost, but not in Texas, where the agreement is viewed favorably. In general, the states of North Carolina, Alabama, and Idaho have a high concentration of economic activity in commodities that are protected by import restrictions. The state of Washington has a large stake, and many other states have a small stake, in open trade due to the export orientation of local producers.[45]

Finally, trade policy outcomes also depend upon how the conflict between these competing groups is mediated by policymaking institutions in the government. These institutions may be biased in favor of one group over another, either because certain groups have better access to decision makers or because those decision makers are more sensitive to the interests of some groups. This can obviously affect the direction

---

[45] U.S. International Trade Commission 2006, 125.

that trade policy takes. For example, antidumping policy (considered in chapter 5) is essentially nonpolitical and administered in a routine, bureaucratic way by government agencies. Small, narrowly defined industries tend to choose the antidumping route to trade protection, whereas larger industries may have the political clout to secure protection directly from the president and Congress. Because of all these variables, generalizations about the politics of trade policy are difficult to make. So it should not be surprising that political economists have failed to answer basic questions about how firms achieve political influence.

But one generalization seems fairly robust: once policies are in place, they are difficult to change, particularly if change involves taking benefits away from any industry. During the Korean War, Congress introduced support measures for owners of mohair goats, whose wool was useful for making warm army uniforms. These subsidies persisted for forty years after the end of the war because farmers adamantly opposed their withdrawal and politicians did not want to fight them. Although the government program was abolished in 1994, saving $200 million, it was revived just a few years later. Other industries—such as steel, textiles and apparel, and semiconductors—have found that once the government gives you a special program, that program becomes institutionalized at various levels of government and becomes very difficult to take away.

It has been said that voting for freer trade is an unnatural act for a politician because they are taking away tangible benefits for some in exchange for uncertain benefits for others. When imports increase, some groups know with a high degree of certainty that their jobs and incomes are at stake. Yet there is great uncertainty about which individuals and industries stand to gain jobs and income when exports increase. Uncertainty about whether an individual will benefit from or be harmed by trade can lead to a status quo bias in favor of maintaining trade restrictions. Even if the entire electorate recognized that a clear majority would benefit from free trade, a reform in which most voters would benefit might not pass in a popular vote if the majority thinks that it is unlikely to gain from the reform. This uncertainty means that the expected value of reform could be negative for a majority of voters, in which case they would block it. This logic gives the political system a status quo bias.[46]

[46] Fernandez and Rodrik 1991.

The status quo bias is simply reinforced if voters are risk averse (wherein they prefer a lower but certain return over a higher but less certain return) or loss averse (wherein they are more sensitive to losses than to equivalent-sized gains, and thus prefer to avoid any loss). These factors might help explain why countries with trade restrictions find it politically difficult to eliminate them. In such cases, tariffs may be viewed as a social welfare mechanism to prevent substantial reduction of real incomes in certain sections of the community. This function might explain why so many tariffs in the past seem to have had income maintenance as their goal and why they have continued, even when designed to be only temporary. For example, if the goal is to keep real incomes of certain farmers, steelworkers, or textile manufacturers higher than they would be otherwise, there is less of a motivation to reduce trade barriers, even though other income transfer policies would be more efficient than restricting trade.

Despite the forces that favor the imposition and maintenance of trade restrictions, political leaders in many countries have recognized the economy-wide benefits of free trade and have been able to overcome political inertia, throw off existing measures, and adopt more open trade policies. The United Kingdom eliminated virtually all protectionist policies in the mid-nineteenth century when export-oriented cotton textile interests grew powerful enough to defeat import-competing agricultural producers. The United States significantly reduced its tariffs in the mid-twentieth century as it came to dominate world trade in manufactured goods. As chapter 6 discusses, many developing countries—from Korea in the 1960s to Chile in the 1970s to China in the 1980s—have undertaken radical changes in economic policies in the direction of open markets.[47] Often these changes require creative political leaders who respond to a crisis or form new political coalitions in a way that breaks through the inertia of the status quo.

Is Protection Ever Beneficial?

The theory and evidence reviewed thus far have failed to address the idea that, in certain instances, import restrictions might be economically

---

[47] For a set of case studies on unilateral moves to free trade, see Bhagwati 2002.

beneficial.[48] In fact, economists have identified certain conditions under which trade protection can actually improve welfare. Broadly speaking, trade interventions can be beneficial when they are used to improve the terms of trade, to promote industries with positive externalities, or to capture rents in international markets.[49] Although these theoretical cases exist, daunting political problems remain in actually having government implement policies that can capture these benefits. Let us consider each case in turn.

When a country has the ability to influence the prices of its exports and imports on the world market, then trade restrictions can potentially raise national income by improving the ratio at which a country exchanges exports for imports, something known as a country's terms of trade. An improvement in the terms of trade, either through higher export prices or lower import prices, increases the purchasing power of exports in terms of the imports they procure. This translates into higher income because the country can acquire more imports for the same amount of exports. For example, oil exporting countries benefit from a higher price for oil (i.e., their terms of trade improve), whereas oil importing countries suffer from a higher price for oil (i.e., their terms of trade deteriorate).

The power to influence the world market price is usually held by a country or group of countries that dominate production of a certain good, often a natural resource commodity. For example, the United States produced 80 percent of the world's cotton prior to the Civil War. Southern cotton producers collectively had a significant impact on the world price, but each producer alone had no particular influence. The United States might have been better off if producers had formed a cartel to restrict exports or, barring that, if the government had imposed an export tax to force up the world price of cotton. The Organization of Petroleum Exporting Countries (OPEC) has used limits on production to help increase the world price of oil, and its members have reaped billions of dollars in additional revenue as a result. (Of course, it is always difficult

[48] Adam Smith fully conceded that there are sound noneconomic rationales for restricting trade, such as protecting industries essential for national defense.

[49] Corden (1974) provides a good overview of the various cases in which protection might be economically justifiable. Irwin (1996a) explores the debate among economists about these cases.

for such cartels to prevent smaller members from cheating and to prevent nonmembers from increasing production.) Similarly, the number of large exporters of gold, diamonds, and some metals is limited by natural resource endowments, giving some countries the power to influence prices on world markets.

Except in such special cases, the terms-of-trade motive for trade restrictions has little relevance for most countries' policies.[50] Few countries have the clear-cut ability to manipulate their terms of trade to much advantage, except for those commodity examples, and most policymakers probably have little idea what conditions would have to be met for tariffs to be set optimally.[51] Most governments are highly sensitive to domestic political concerns about trade and seek to minimize adjustment costs to producers rather than search out goods in which optimal tariffs might be employed.

To the extent that countries can influence the price of their exports, the appropriate response is an export tax, something that is unlikely to be popular. In addition, any gains from such a policy could evaporate if competing suppliers emerged or if other countries imposed retaliatory duties. Finally, such a trade restriction is not desirable from the standpoint of world welfare and global efficiency. An improvement in the exporting country's terms of trade implies a deterioration in the importing country's terms of trade and actually leaves the world as a whole worse off.

Another situation in which trade interventions can, in principle, yield economic benefits is when they serve as a second-best measure to promote industries that generate positive externalities. In the case of positive externalities, the private costs of production are higher than the social costs of production because producers do not take into account the benefits of their actions for other sectors of the economy. As a result,

---

[50] See Panagariya, Shah, and Mishra (2001) for evidence that developing countries are price-takers on world markets and therefore cannot improve their terms of trade by restricting exports or imports. However, Broda, Limao, and Weinstein (2008) find evidence that countries impose higher tariffs on goods for which foreign export supply is relatively inelastic, which is at least consistent with countries imposing tariffs to reduce import prices (net of tariff) and thereby improve the terms of trade.

[51] If domestic producers are aware of their market power, they can appropriately determine the price of their exports with less need for government interference (Rodrik 1989).

the domestic industry produces less of a good than is socially desirable. These benefits can be captured if the private and social costs of production are properly aligned, which can sometimes be achieved through domestic subsidies. If subsidies cannot be used, there may be a second-best case for promoting the industry through protection. Recent theoretical cases have considered optimal trade policy for industries in which there are static or dynamic external economies, such as learning-by-doing or R&D spillovers, in which the production experience or research of one firm benefits others in the industry, as is alleged to be the case in certain high-technology industries. In theory, circumstances can arise in which some government promotion may be appropriate.

But as a practical matter, using trade policy to correct for such market failures is problematic. Correctly identifying these externalities is, by their very nature, extremely difficult.[52] Even if the externality can be identified, the first-best policy of a subsidy has to be ruled out. Using tariffs to promote a targeted industry has been likened to acupuncture with a fork: the relevant market failure may be corrected, but at the cost of introducing a by-product distortion, such as a higher price for domestic consumers. Finally, the relevant externality must be external to the firm and internal to the country. The R&D or learning benefits could spill over between countries, particularly if foreign firms maintain a presence in the domestic market or have an ownership stake in the domestic firms, or when the knowledge cannot be limited geographically. In this case, any promotion scheme benefits all firms around the world, not just domestic ones, significantly narrowing the cases in which intervention would produce purely a national advantage instead of simply providing an international public good. It is particularly difficult for the United States, where policy is determined largely by lawyers who are responding to self-interested producers, to discern impartially which industries exhibit

[52] Industrial policy advocates propose various criteria for determining which industries are better than others and therefore deserve promotion. One proposed criterion was industries with high value-added per worker, but as Krugman (1994) notes, these are really just capital-intensive industries. This would lead one to support the cigarette industry and the oil pipeline industry. Sometimes it is argued that the presence of external economies of scale is demonstrated by geographically concentrated industries. Just because most U.S.-made carpets come from one county in Georgia, to use a commonly cited example of this phenomenon, does not mean that the carpet industry deserved to be subsidized at its inception or deserves to be subsidized now.

such dynamic externalities and which do not, let alone the degree to which the knowledge spills over to foreign firms.

Many industries that are touted as creating positive externalities fail to do so. For example, in the late 1980s and early 1990s, high-definition television (HDTV) was widely believed to be a "technology driver" for the high-technology industry: if the United States failed to dominate the underlying technology, it would lose its competitive position in commercial applications and in related industries, such as semiconductors and workstations. Whichever country invested in the "right" technology first was expected to have a strategic advantage over latecomers in what was projected to be a lucrative new market. To this end, Europe and Japan moved quickly to subsidize their producers. Japan invested nearly $1.2 billion in HDTV research (much of it from the Ministry of International Trade and Industry and the state broadcaster, NHK), while taxpayers in the European Community spent about $1 billion on HDTV research through 1991.[53]

Fearing the United States would be left behind, in 1989 the American Electronics Association proposed that Congress appropriate $1.35 billion in direct subsidies and loan guarantees to support HDTV research. Congress authorized $30 million in research grants through the Defense Department and promised more, but the first Bush administration opposed the funding. The ensuing stalemate prevented any further spending. Yet gridlock not only saved American taxpayers millions of dollars, it proved to be the best policy. The European and Japanese technologies were developed first, but they settled on an analog standard that was soon viewed as obsolete. Meanwhile, frustrated by the impasse in Washington, American firms set to work themselves on HDTV research and, by entering the field somewhat later, were able to improve upon foreign research. Ultimately, American firms created a digital system that was later selected as the industry standard by the Federal Communications Commission. Moreover, only now has HDTV become commercially available, and it has failed to become the driving or profitable technology that many influential commentators thought it would be twenty years ago.

The final rationale for trade intervention is to capture rents or profits in the international market. To understand this process, consider

---

[53] Hart 1994; and Dai, Cawson, and Holmes 1996.

a firm that is competing against a single foreign rival in an imperfectly competitive market (i.e., one in which there are above-normal profits) in a third country. In this case, a government export subsidy for the firm could induce the foreign rival to cut its output, thereby shifting profits from the foreign to the domestic firm. This practice is known as strategic trade policy, in which the government undertakes a precise, strategic intervention on behalf of domestic firms in a way that increases national welfare.[54] For example, European support for Airbus is commonly believed to be an attempt to shift profits away from Boeing in the lucrative market for wide-body aircraft.[55]

Although there was much enthusiasm for this idea in the 1980s, numerous theoretical and practical objections have diminished its appeal. First, successful intervention depends crucially upon key parameters in the market's structure that make it difficult for governments to determine the best policy. For example, one study showed that if the firms competed by setting prices rather than quantities, then the optimal policy would switch from an export subsidy to an export tax. The introduction of asymmetric information between the firms and the government further increases the range of possible outcomes and makes clear-cut predictions even more difficult. Setting aside theoretical issues, calibrated simulation models of strategic trade policy reveal that the potential gains from implementing the optimal policy are exceedingly small. When the right policy is excruciatingly difficult to determine in the first place and depends upon getting parameters of industry structure and competitive interaction exactly right, the small potential payoff suggests that such interventions are not worthwhile, especially when the potential outlays are high.

Theoretical work on optimal trade interventions is usually developed in the context of an omniscient government that has full information and the capability of setting policy in an optimal manner. In the real world, governments are neither omniscient nor immune to external pressure. Do the theoretical results stand up when the government is confronted with political pressure to use policy on behalf of certain industries? Not surprisingly, the answer is no. Research has shown that the

[54] Brander (1995) provides a comprehensive survey of this literature.

[55] Irwin and Pavcnik (2004) examine the impact of Airbus's A-380 super jumbo on Boeing sales of the 747.

case for such interventions is substantially weakened when government policy is subject to strategic manipulation by politically active firms.[56] Thus, there are many reasons to be skeptical about whether a government can determine where strategic intervention will be worthwhile among the many industries competing for government assistance, especially in a representative democracy, where trade policy is often driven by the interests of politically active domestic producers.[57]

It is sometimes said that free trade is right in theory but wrong in practice. Actually, the opposite is true. Any clever graduate student in economics can quickly come up with half a dozen reasons why free trade fails as a theoretical proposition. Yet in practice, the economic benefits of trade and the costs of protection are tangible.

The three theoretical possibilities for trade intervention discussed here depend upon particular circumstances in special cases and require constant adjustment to changing market conditions. Free trade is a much simpler policy because it does not need changing when the underlying economic conditions change. Furthermore, any government that undertakes large, systematic sectoral interventions creates a great deal of concentrated political and economic power, not just to do good but also to make costly mistakes.

[56]Grossman and Maggi (1998) examine whether a welfare maximizing government should pursue a program of strategic trade intervention or instead commit itself to free trade when domestic firms have the opportunity to manipulate the government's choice of the level of intervention. Domestic firms, for example, may overinvest in physical and knowledge capital in a regime of strategic intervention in order to influence the government's choice of subsidy. They find that this manipulation can make a commitment to free trade desirable even in settings where profit-shifting opportunities are available.

[57]Krueger (1990, 21) argues that "in the real world of scarce information, uncertainty, and pervasive rent-seeking, policy makers will inevitably miss the crucial and subtle distinctions between profits that are high because of rents and those that are high because of risk; between wages that are high because of rents, and those that are high because of skills; and between sectors that provide inputs, and those that result in spillover externalities."

4

Trade, Jobs, and Income Distribution

The argument against free trade that resonates most strongly with the public and with politicians is that imports destroy jobs. Indeed, the greatest fear about international trade in general, and imports in particular, is that it can harm workers, reduce wages, and lead to unemployment. But is this an accurate view of trade as a whole? And if so, are import restrictions the remedy? This chapter addresses the relationship between trade, jobs, and wages, and examines government policies to assist displaced workers. The chapter also considers the underlying causes of trade deficits to see if a country suffers when it imports more than it exports.

Does Free Trade Affect Employment?

The claim that trade should be limited because imports destroy jobs has been around at least since the sixteenth century.[1] And imports do indeed destroy jobs in certain industries: for example, employment in the Maine shoe industry and in the South Carolina apparel industry is much lower because both industries have faced stiff competition from imports. So we can understand why the plant owners and workers and the politicians who represent them would like to change this situation by imposing trade barriers.

But just because imports destroy some jobs does not mean that trade reduces overall employment or harms the economy. (Technology also destroys jobs, such as the replacement of bank tellers with ATM machines, office assistants with computers and voice mail, and manual

[1] See Irwin 1996b, 36ff.

_____Figure 4.1

Civilian Labor Force and Civilian Employment in the United States, 1950–2007.
Source: Council of Economic Advisers 2009, table B-35.

workers with machines, yet these innovations are not viewed as a bad
thing.) As we saw in chapter 3, blocking imports may protect jobs in industries that compete against imports, but it also diminishes employment
in other industries by reducing exports and raising costs for import-using
industries. Therefore, the statement that imports destroy jobs is incomplete because trade also creates jobs in export industries and import-
using industries.

    Since trade both creates and destroys jobs, one question is
whether trade has any effect on overall employment. Unfortunately, just
about every attempt to quantify the overall employment effect of trade is
an exercise in futility.[2] This is because the impact of trade on the total
number of jobs in an economy is best approximated as zero. Total employment is not a function of international trade, but the number of people in the labor force. As figure 4.1 shows, employment in the United
States since 1950 has closely tracked the number of people in the labor
force. For this reason, the former chairman of the Federal Reserve Board,
Alan Greenspan, once remarked, "Over the long sweep of American

---

[2] For one recent attempt, see Groshen, Hobijn, and McConnell 2005.

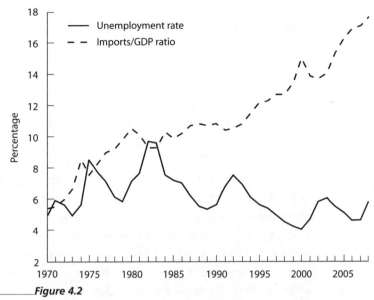

Figure 4.2

Unemployment and Import Penetration in the United States, 1960–2007.
Source: Council of Economic Advisers 2009, tables B-42, B-103, B-1.

generations and waves of economic change, we simply have not experienced a net drain of jobs to advancing technology or to other nations."[3]

And while there is always some unemployment, represented by the gap between the two series in figure 4.1, this is determined more by the business cycle than by changes in trade flows or trade policy. The business cycle has a rhythm of its own and is driven by factors largely independent of trade. To see this more directly, figure 4.2 compares the unemployment rate with the ratio of imports of goods and services to GDP since 1960. Except for the period from 1970 to 1975, higher unemployment rates are not associated with increases in imports as a share of GDP. Since the early 1980s, the unemployment rate has moved lower even as the imports-to-GDP ratio has increased. When unemployment rose in the early 1980s, the early 1990s, the early 2000s, and in 2008–09 because of the recessions in each of those periods, imports were not surging but actually falling off because of declining demand.

As figure 4.1 demonstrates, overall job creation has exceeded job destruction over time. Although the net change in employment is relatively

[3] Greenspan 2004.

small in any given year, a striking feature of the U.S. labor market is that gross rates of job creation and destruction are very high. In a dynamic and rapidly changing economy, jobs are continuously created and eliminated, at a rate of about 4 to 5 million per month. In 2007, for example, there were 62.1 million job separations (36 percent of which were layoffs and discharges, the remainder being quits) and 63.4 million hires. National employment rose by about 1 million between January and December of that year, but the net change in jobs was a small fraction of the gross flows of workers in and out of the labor force and moving between jobs.[4]

How much are imports to blame for the job losses experienced in any given year? Not much. Changes in consumer tastes, domestic competition, productivity growth, and technological innovation, in addition to international trade, all contribute to the churning of the labor market. It is virtually impossible to disentangle all of the reasons for job displacement because they are interdependent; for example, technological change may be stimulated by domestic or foreign competition. Yet to the extent that such attributions are made by the Bureau of Labor Statistics, trade is a tiny factor in the displacement of labor. As table 4.1 shows, import competition and overseas plant relocations accounted for about 3 percent of total employment separations due to mass layoffs in recent years.

Indeed, study after study has confirmed that the trade-induced turnover in U.S. labor markets is small in comparison with the overall turnover.[5] Trade is only slightly related to cross-industry variation in worker displacement rates. Although industries with high displacement rates are often import-sensitive, not all import-sensitive industries have high displacement rates. One respected study concludes that there is "no systematic relationship between the magnitude of gross job flows and exposure to international trade . . . On balance, the evidence is highly unfavorable to the view that international trade exposure systematically reduces job security."[6]

---

[4]Bureau of Labor Statistics, Job Openings and Labor Turnover Survey, January 2009. In 2008, there were 56.5 million hires and 59.3 million separations.

[5]See Addison, Fox, and Ruhm 1995. Kletzer (1998b, 455) also concludes that "increasing foreign competition across industries accounts for a small share of job displacement" across industries because there are "high rates of job loss for industries with little trade."

[6]Davis, Haltiwanger, and Schuh 1995, 48–49. They find that there is a higher rate of gross job destruction in very high import penetration sectors, but that this disappears

_____Table 4.1
Number of Workers Affected by Extended Mass Layoffs, 1996–2008

Year	Total Number of Workers, All Reasons	Due to Import Competition	Due to Overseas Relocation	Percentage of Total Due to Imports and Relocation
1996	948,122	13,476	4,326	1.9
1997	947,843	12,019	10,439	2.4
1998	991,245	18,473	8,797	2.8
1999	901,451	26,234	5,683	3.5
2000	915,962	13,416	9,054	2.5
2001	1,524,832	27,946	15,693	2.9
2002	1,272,331	15,350	17,075	2.5
2003	1,216,886	23,734	13,205	3.0
2004	993,909	8,064	16,197	2.4
2005	884,661	11,112	12,030	2.6
2006	935,805	10,458	13,367	2.5
2007	965,935	11,589	11,526	2.3
2008	1,383,553	9,592	11,147	1.5

Source: Bureau of Labor Statistics (www.bls.gov/mls/#tables).

Note: Displaced workers are those who face involuntary separations due to plant closings, mass layoffs, etc. and do not include those who lose their jobs due to temporary layoffs or voluntary separations.

But how can we be sure that the number of jobs destroyed by imports will be matched by the number of jobs created elsewhere in the economy? One reason is that macroeconomic policy can be adjusted to offset any imbalance in the forces that drive job creation and destruction. If imports begin rolling in and trigger widespread layoffs, for example, the unemployment rate may begin to rise. If the unemployment rate rises, and with it the risks of a recession, the Federal Reserve Board is likely to ease monetary policy and reduce interest rates, other things being equal. This action not only stimulates the economy in the short run, but also leads to a depreciation of the dollar on foreign exchange markets, which in turn makes U.S. exports less expensive to foreign consumers and imports more expensive to U.S. consumers. As a result, employment goes

---

after controlling for industry wages. "This is evidence that import-intensive industries exhibit greater gross job flows because their workers have relatively low levels of specific human capital—not because foreign competition subjects these industries to unusually large and volatile disturbances" (49). Simply put, workers who lack industry-specific skills are more apt to switch jobs and are less apt to remain in any given industry than workers who have industry-specific skills.

back up and returns to its long-run relationship with the labor force. (The trade deficit will be discussed at the end of this chapter.)

Yet the effect of trade on jobs is a politically sensitive issue and one that is prone to exaggeration in political discourse. For example, the debate over the North American Free Trade Agreement in the early 1990s largely consisted of claims and counterclaims about whether the agreement would add to or subtract from total employment. NAFTA opponents claimed that free trade with Mexico would destroy jobs: the Economic Policy Institute put the number at 480,000 workers. NAFTA proponents countered with the claim that it would create jobs: the Institute for International Economics suggested that 170,000 jobs would be created.[7] Those stressing the job losses gave the impression that there would be a permanent reduction in the number of people employed in the economy. Those stressing the positive employment effects gave the impression that more trade would lead to a higher level of employment and that this should be the motivation for pursuing more open trade policies.

Both of these impressions were false because at the end of the day it is virtually impossible to know the precise effect of the trade agreement on employment changes. (Furthermore, as we saw in chapter 2, the reason for pursuing more open trade policies is not to increase employment, but to generate more productive employment that will raise aggregate income.) Every estimate of the medium-term impact of NAFTA on employment was a fraction of the monthly turnover in U.S. labor markets. And as demonstrated by the experience after 1994, when NAFTA went into effect, the fears of massive job losses in the United States as a result of free trade with Mexico proved to be unwarranted. The "giant sucking sound" of jobs being lost to Mexico, as famously predicted by Ross Perot, the Texas billionaire who ran for president in 1992, was never heard. As several analysts noted in 1998, four years after NAFTA went into effect:

> By any reasonable measure, even the gross job turnover
> induced by the agreement has been slight. According to the
> Department of Labor, over the nearly four years from January
> 1994 through mid-August 1997, 220,000 workers had petitioned
> for adjustment assistance (cash and training allowances) under
> the legislation enacted when the trade deal was signed. Of this

[7] Orme 1996, 107.

total, 136,000—an average of about 40,000 workers per year—
were certified as eligible for assistance (under both the more
general trade adjustment assistance program and that created as
part of NAFTA). Even this figure overstates NAFTA's true
impact, because to be eligible under both programs workers
only need to show that "imports" have contributed to their
losses, but not specifically as a result of NAFTA. By way of
comparison, the gross monthly turnover of jobs in the United
States exceeds 2 million. Since NAFTA, overall employment in
the United States has risen by more than 10 million.[8]

Even when judged by the liberal standards of the NAFTA assistance program, only 2.4 percent of displaced workers on permanent layoff required assistance as a result of being harmed by the agreement.[9]

The claims of large employment gains were equally flawed. Analysts at several Washington think tanks (both favorable and unfavorable
to NAFTA) settled upon the rule of thumb that every $1 billion in exports
generates or supports 13,000 jobs (implying conversely that every $1 bil-
lion in imports eliminates the same number of jobs) as a way of evaluating the employment effects of trade agreements. Some NAFTA proponents argued that, because Mexico was to eliminate relatively high tariffs
against U.S. goods while U.S. tariffs against Mexican goods were already
very low, the agreement would generate more exports to, than imports
from, Mexico. Using the rule of thumb, it was therefore reasoned that
NAFTA would result in net job creation. For example, President Clinton's
trade representative, Mickey Kantor, claimed that the agreement would
create 200,000 new jobs within two years.

Such formulaic calculations and predictions were made to fight
the dire forecasts that thousands of jobs would be lost as a result of
NAFTA, but there was never any reason to believe these figures. Even if
tariff reductions are asymmetric, exports may not grow more rapidly than
imports.[10] And it is a further mistake to think that changes in the trade
balance translate into predictable changes in employment; a booming

---

[8] Burtless et al. 1998, 57.

[9] Schoepfle 2000, 115.

[10] Trade agreements themselves have little effect on bilateral trade balance or the
overall trade balance, as we will see later.

economy with low unemployment may be accompanied by a growing trade deficit because people have more money to spend on imports. In any case, these claims for the job-creation benefits of NAFTA soon boomeranged. When the peso collapsed in late 1994, for reasons that had nothing to do with NAFTA, imports from Mexico surged and the U.S. trade surplus evaporated.[11]

More recently, the performance of the U.S. labor market was relatively weak in recovering from the 2001 recession, particularly in comparison to the late 1990s. When juxtaposed with the growth in trade, many have suspected that foreign competition and imports might be responsible for the disappointing outcomes. Yet a study of trade and offshoring in the 2000 to 2003 period concluded that

> weakness in U.S. payroll employment since 2000 has not been caused by a flood of imports of either goods or services. It should certainly not be attributed to any trade agreements the United States has signed. Rather, the weakness of employment is primarily the result of inadequate growth of domestic demand in the presence of strong productivity growth. . . . to the extent that trade did cause a loss of manufacturing jobs, it was the weakness of U.S. exports after 2000 and not the strength of imports that was responsible—the share of imports in the U.S. market actually declined.[12]

The weakness of exports was in part due to the strength of the dollar on foreign exchange markets over this period.

Finally, the sharp, recent rise in the unemployment rate due to the recession that began in December 2007 can be attributed to the financial problems associated with the collapse of housing prices, not a sudden intensification of import competition.

Despite the fact that trade and trade policy have little relationship to a country's overall level of employment, trade policy debates in

---

[11] NAFTA opponents then argued, using the rule-of-thumb formula endorsed by NAFTA proponents, that thousands of jobs had been lost as a result of trade with Mexico because the trade surplus had become a trade deficit. An analyst at the Economic Policy Institute, for example, claimed that the trade deficit with Mexico and Canada destroyed 440,172 American jobs between 1994 and 1998.

[12] Baily and Lawrence 2004, 213.

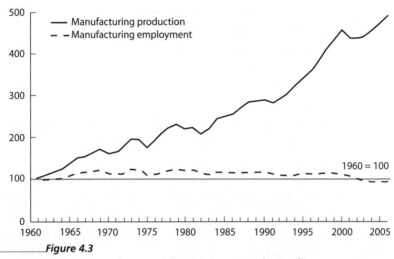

Figure 4.3

U.S. Manufacturing Production and Employment, 1960–2006.
Source: Council of Economic Advisers 2009, tables B-51, B-46.

Washington and elsewhere are often framed through the lens of jobs alone. Yet trade does have important implications for employment in different sectors of the economy and even the wages paid to workers.

Trade and the Manufacturing Sector

Even those who may agree that the effect of trade on total employment is essentially zero may oppose free trade in the belief that it shifts jobs into less desirable sectors. One of the greatest concerns in recent decades has been that trade has led to the "deindustrialization" of the U.S. economy in which good jobs in manufacturing have been sacrificed for bad jobs in services.

It is certainly true that the number of jobs in manufacturing has declined in recent decades. U.S. employment in manufacturing fell from 17.9 million workers in 1970 to 13.9 million in 2007. Manufacturing's share of total employment fell even more sharply, from 25 percent of the nonfarm workforce in 1970 to 10 percent in 2007. At the same time, real manufacturing output has increased significantly, by nearly 40 percent in the 1990s alone, and has declined only slightly as a share of GDP when measured at constant prices. This contrast is shown in figure 4.3, which illustrates the vast increase in domestic manufacturing output while the manufacturing workforce has been unchanged or declining. How is this possible? By rapid increases in labor productivity. Just as U.S. agricultural output has increased steadily even as the number of farmers has declined, manufacturing has been a victim of its own success in increasing labor productivity.

The flip side to these developments is that a growing share of the labor force is employed in the service sector. As consumers have shifted their spending to such services as health care, education, recreation, and personal finance, the economy has responded by devoting more resources to those sectors. Because of the relatively poor productivity performance in these service sectors, a greater share of the labor force has to be devoted to these occupations in order to increase output and meet consumer demands.[13]

Has trade contributed to the shift of employment away from manufacturing? A little, but the strong growth in labor productivity is overwhelmingly responsible for the fact that the number of workers in manufacturing has fallen even as output has increased. The problem with blaming trade for the relative decline in manufacturing employment is that the United States is both a big exporter and a big importer of manufactured goods, as table 1.1 showed. The trade deficit in manufactured goods is smaller than the overall trade deficit, because the United States is a large net importer of mineral fuels (petroleum). The trade deficit in manufactured goods is also a small percentage of GDP. Thus, even if the United States had balanced trade in manufactured goods after 1970, the effect on output and employment in manufacturing would have been modest.

A simple thought experiment illustrates this point. Between 1970 and 2000, the share of nonfarm employment in manufacturing fell twelve percentage points, from 25 percent to 13 percent. If manufacturing productivity remained fixed at its 1970 level, manufacturing's share of employment would have to have risen eight percentage points in order for output to have matched its 2000 level. Alternatively, if the United States had balanced trade after 1970 but labor productivity grew as rapidly as it did, manufacturing's employment share would have been only one

[13] This is not a uniquely American phenomenon, but one that has taken place (sometimes to an even greater extent) in most developed countries. See Burtless et al. 1998, 54.

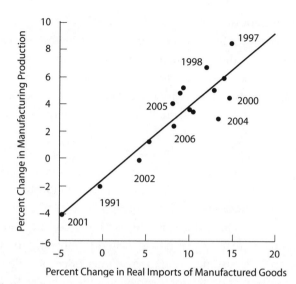

_____*Figure 4.4*

Change in Production and Imports of Manufactured Goods, 1991–2007.
Sources: Federal Reserve Board (manufacturing industrial production) and
Bureau of Economic Analysis (real imports).

percentage point higher than it actually had been—14 percent, instead of
13 percent. Accordingly, "the effect of long-term productivity improvements on the shift to service-providing jobs is far more important than
increased manufactured imports."[14]

But if imports of manufactured goods were lower, wouldn't domestic production of manufactured goods be higher? Not necessarily, because imports and domestic production may be complements rather than
substitutes. As figure 4.4 indicates, annual changes in domestic manufacturing output and in real manufactured imports are positively correlated:
an increase in imports is positively related to an increase in domestic
production. This is because a strong and growing economy brings about
more domestic production and more imports, whereas a weak economy
tends to see a falloff in both.

[14] Council of Economic Advisers 2004, 70–71. The rise in subcontracting of services formerly done within manufacturing firms may explain part of the decline in measured manufacturing employment. If a worker paints a car in a car factory, that job counts
as part of manufacturing. If the assembled car is sent out to a paint company for the work,
then that job counts as a service job.

Even in labor-intensive industries highly affected by trade, job losses come as much from technological change—the substitution of capital for labor and the introduction of new technology—as from imports. Trade protection cannot arrest this process of change. For example, the apparel industry has experienced a secular decline in the number of workers that even relatively high trade barriers have been powerless to stop.

Still, some people justify import restrictions as a way of slowing the movement of workers out of manufacturing industries. Here, two points should be recognized: jobs are "saved" in the industry only by destroying jobs elsewhere, as we have already seen, and protection is a costly and inefficient jobs program. The consumer cost per job saved as a result of trade restrictions can be calculated by dividing the total cost of protection to the consumer (due to the higher prices that they pay) by the number of jobs that protection maintains in the industry. In the textile and apparel industry, for example, trade restrictions cost consumers about $24 billion annually and prevent the loss of roughly 170,000 jobs in the industry. To preserve one job in the textile and apparel industry, therefore, consumers pay $140,000 a year. This is a stiff price for society to pay merely to keep workers employed in relatively low-wage occupations. The cost per job saved is even higher in the industries typically associated with high-paying manufacturing jobs, such as the machine tool industry ($350,000 per job) or the sugar industry ($600,000 per job).[15]

_Offshoring and Trade in Services

Many of the fears about trade and manufacturing employment are now being echoed with respect to the service sector. In the past, most service workers were completely insulated from foreign competition. But, as discussed in chapter 1, many services are now tradable. A growing concern is that white-collar service workers will see their jobs "outsourced" or "offshored" to low-wage countries such as India because of the Internet and other communication technologies. Although many of the offshored jobs involve relatively low-skill work, such as manning phones at call centers, even highly paid professionals, such as architects and

---

[15] Hufbauer and Elliott 1994.

software programmers, have found that their work can be shifted to much lower paid but technically qualified English-speaking workers in India.

Estimates vary widely as to the number of service workers whose jobs are potentially offshorable. One prominent economist, Alan Blinder, has estimated that the jobs performed by 30 to 40 million American workers could be done abroad.[16] Although Blinder fears for the consequences, he notes, "Despite all the political sound and fury, little service-sector offshoring has happened to date." Indeed, the actual number of service sectors jobs lost so far appears to be small. The Bureau of Labor Statistics began asking about the overseas transfer of jobs in collecting data on mass layoffs in the first quarter of 2004. In that quarter, 8.7 percent of all layoffs were due to the movement of work and 2.5 percent (a total of 4,633 jobs) related to the movement of work to another country.[17]

Furthermore, it should be remembered that international trade—in services, as in goods—is not a one-way flow but a two-way street. The estimate of jobs lost due to offshoring mentioned above does not take into account the projected increase in demand for skilled information technology workers in the United States due to work for export. The BLS does not collect statistics on the number of jobs created by work that is offshored from other countries to the United States, otherwise known as "inshoring." As chapter 1 noted, the United States is a major net exporter of services to other countries. In 2007, the value of U.S. exports of business, professional, and technical services was $108 billion. U.S. imports of such services, which included call centers and data entry from developing countries, among other things, was $69 billion. Trade is roughly balanced in the narrower category of "computer and information processing services" in which the United States exported $13 billion and imported $15 billion in 2007.[18] The United States is likely to begin exporting many more services to other countries as a result of technological developments that also allow for more imports of services.

In addition, there are natural equilibrating forces that limit how much work will be offshored. While Indian wages remain much lower

[16] Blinder 2006.
[17] Bureau of Labor Statistics 2004.
[18] *Survey of Current Business*, October 2008.

than American wages, higher demand for skilled Indian workers has put upward pressure on costs that will diminish the advantage of offshoring.[19] Wages in India's software industry, a major center of offshored work from the United States, have been rising at a rate of close to 15 percent per year. When combined with the recent appreciation of the rupee against the dollar, the cost of hiring Indian workers has increased sharply. As a result, the United States has even received "inshoring" contracts from India. For example, in March 2004, IBM won a ten-year, $750 million contract from Bharti Tele-Ventures, India's largest private telecommunications company, which will transfer some jobs from Asia to the United States and France. IBM will service Bharti's hardware and software requirements and take over its customer billing and relations operations. Wipro and other Indian firms are offshoring some work to "underdeveloped" parts of the United States, such as Idaho and Georgia, because they have found it cheaper to do it there.[20]

Thus, the fears about a "service sector sucking sound" have been exaggerated. One analysis concludes that, "similar to manufacturing, it is highly unlikely that a significant share of high-wage, skill-intensive service activities will move to emerging markets in the short term and even in the long term."[21] It is likely that many of the easily offshorable jobs have already been lost, and some have even returned as companies discover that cheaper English speakers abroad ultimately may not be cost-effective or good enough to maintain quality. And some scare stories, such as the offshoring of the work of highly paid radiologists, have turned out to be false.[22]

Trade and Wages

Another concern is that trade puts downward pressure on U.S. wages as firms strive to match lower wages in developing countries, unleashing a "race to the bottom" in cutting labor costs. Such fears overlook the fact that high American wages are based on the high productivity of U.S. workers. And the growth in a country's average wages is determined by

[19] Scheiber 2004.
[20] Giridharadas 2007.
[21] Jensen and Kletzer 2008.
[22] Levy and Goelman 2005.

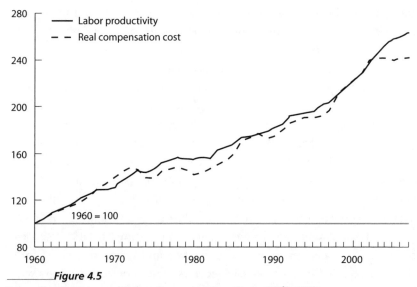

_____*Figure 4.5*

Labor Productivity and Labor Compensation Costs, 1960–2007.
Source: Council of Economic Advisers 2009, table B-49. Productivity is output per hour of all persons in the nonfarm business sector. Real compensation is compensation per hour in the nonfarm business sector divided by producer price index of total finished goods from table B-65.

the growth of a country's productivity. As figure 4.5 shows, the growth of worker compensation (deflated by the producer price index) tracks growth in productivity remarkably well.[23] Foreign competition does not suppress this growth. Rather, as chapter 2 described, trade can foster growth in productivity through several channels. Foreign competition cannot take away the advantages that give rise to this high productivity, namely, the availability of sophisticated technology, the substantial stock of human capital, and the many other advantages of operating in the U.S. market.

Economists have sought to understand why the two series diverged after 2002. Part of the explanation is an increase in the share of profits in national income, a development that is thought to be cyclical,

[23] Thus, workers have been compensated for the growth in output per worker in terms of the revenue received by firms. See Feldstein 2008. When compensation is deflated by the consumer price index, however, the growth in real wages is lower because consumer prices (which include items such as the cost of housing) have risen more rapidly than producer prices. However, it is well known that the consumer price index is biased upward and overstates the rise in the cost of living.

and a disproportionate share of real income gains accruing to the top 1 percent of the income distribution.[24] It remains to be seen whether this trend continues to run counter to historical experience; the two series have deviated in the past only to return to the same level.

Although average wages are determined by the underlying attributes that make American workers productive, trade can affect the *distribution* of wages in an economy. And here, a very basic point must be stressed: the perception that imports destroy good, high-wage jobs in manufacturing is almost completely erroneous. It is closer to the truth to say that imports destroy bad, low-wage jobs in manufacturing. This is because wages in industries that compete against imports are well below average, whereas wages in exporting industries are well above average.

For example, the United States tends to import labor-intensive products, such as apparel, footwear, leather, and goods assembled from components. These labor-intensive sectors tend to employ workers who have a lower than average educational attainment, and who therefore earn a relatively low wage. For example, in 2007 average hourly earnings of Americans working in the apparel industry were 36 percent lower than in manufacturing as a whole. Average hourly earnings were 30 percent lower in the leather industry and 25 percent lower in textile mills than in the average manufacturing industry.[25] Figure 4.6 shows the relationship between the share of imports from low-wage developing countries in a given industry and the average U.S. wage. The United States tends to import more from developing countries in industries that pay relatively low wages.[26] (The category of computers and electronic products is an outlier because these items are assembled in low-wage developing countries from components produced elsewhere, as noted in chapter 1.)

By contrast, the United States tends to export more skill-intensive manufactured products, such as aircraft, construction machinery, engines

[24] See Lawrence 2008 and Dew-Becker and Gordon 2005. The top 1 percent of income earners captured 21 percent of the real income gains between 1997 and 2001, according to the latter study.

[25] U.S. Bureau of the Census 2009, table 612.

[26] Bernard, Jensen, and Schott (2006) examined how U.S. manufacturing plants responded to import competition from low-wage developing countries. They found a variety of adjustments: some labor-intensive operations reduced output or closed, while more capital-intensive plants adjusted their product mix to more sophisticated goods and actually grew.

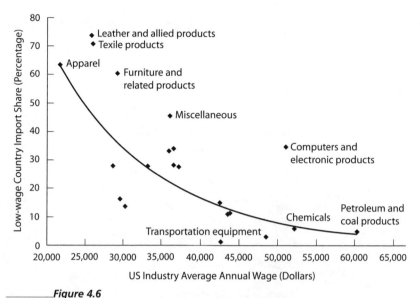

Figure 4.6

U.S. Wages and Import Competition from Low-Wage Countries.
Source: Jensen and Kletzer 2008.

and turbines, and industrial chemicals. Workers in these industries earn relatively high wages. For example, in 2007 average hourly earnings in the aircraft and aerospace industry were 64 percent above the average in manufacturing, 8 percent higher in metalworking machinery, and 18 percent higher in pharmaceuticals.[27] Figure 4.7 shows the positive relationship between exports per worker and the average wage by industry.

Because exports increase the number of workers in relatively more productive, high-wage industries, and imports reduce the number of workers in relatively less productive, low-wage industries, the overall impact of trade in the United States is to raise average wages.[28] Conversely, any policy that limits overall trade and reduces both exports and imports

[27] Katz and Summers (1989, 264) report that even "after being adjusted for skill differences, wages in export-intensive industries are 11 percent above average, whereas wages in import-intensive industries are 15 percent below average."

[28] One often reads that median household income has stagnated in recent decades, but the composition of the median household has changed quite a bit over this time. Fitzgerald (2008) discusses the difficulties in measuring income inequality and shows that real median household income for most household types increased somewhere between 44 percent and 62 percent from 1976 to 2006.

_____*Figure 4.7*
Exports per Worker and U.S. Industry Wages, Manufacturing.
Source: Jensen and Kletzer 2008.

tends to increase employment in low-wage industries and reduce employment in high-wage industries. Restricting trade would shift American workers away from things that they produce relatively well (and hence export and earn relatively high wages in producing) and toward things that they do not produce so well (and hence import and earn relatively low wages in producing) in comparison with other countries. Employment gains for the low-wage textile machine operators in the factory mills would be offset by employment losses for the high-wage engineers in aircraft and pharmaceutical plants.

This raises the concern that trade has contributed to increased income inequality in the United States. In theory, trade can have sharply different effects on the wages of different types of workers. In a classic article, Wolfgang Stolper and Paul Samuelson connected the distribution of wages in an economy to the prices of traded goods that are determined by the world market. They reached the unambiguous conclusion that the real income of some factors of production will rise absolutely as a result of free trade, while the real income of other factors will fall absolutely.[29] This is implicit in what we have discussed: trade creates jobs in high-wage industries in which the United States exports (aircraft, machinery), and reduces jobs in low-wage industries in which the United States imports (apparel, footwear).[30]

In fact, as international trade has increased over the past three decades, the wage premium for college-educated workers relative to workers with less education (high school degree or dropout) has risen substantially since 1979, although there are some indications that this premium has leveled off since about 2000.[31] There is also evidence of an absolute decline in the real wages of workers with very few years of formal education. Has international trade contributed to this increase in wage inequality in the United States, as theory suggests it might?[32]

The consensus among economists seems to be that increased demand for educated workers due to technological changes is mostly responsible for the rising wage premium. By contrast, the role of trade in generating wage inequality appears to be modest. How has this conclusion been reached? If trade had been driving the changes in relative wages in the United States during the 1980s, then theory suggests that the

---

[29] Stolper and Samuelson 1941. For example, if we consider only skilled and unskilled labor, a rise in the relative price of skill-intensive goods increases the real wage of skilled workers and decreases the real wage of unskilled workers. While the precise relationship between product prices and factor rewards depends upon many other factors, such as the degree to which labor can move between sectors, the key conclusion is that trade can have sharp consequences for income distribution.

[30] Revenga (1992) has shown that domestic industries do not adjust to an intensification of import competition by reducing wages, but by reducing employment. This makes sense: if a firm tried to cut wages, the best workers would leave because they have skills that give them opportunities elsewhere in the economy. The least desirable workers would stay because they have no attractive alternatives. Rather than cut wages, firms usually adjust to competition by reducing employment. Then they can choose which workers to keep and which to lay off in an attempt to raise productivity and position the company to survive.

[31] Autor, Katz, and Kearney 2008.

[32] There are various measures of economic inequality, but wage inequality will be the focus here. Income and wealth inequality have also increased substantially in recent years, but are less directly related to international trade. Instead, factors such as asset holdings and capital gains, as well as the "superstar" phenomena in certain industries (hedge funds, CEOs, sports and entertainment), have been driving the income distribution at the very top 1 percent.

price of unskilled labor-intensive goods should have fallen relative to the price of skilled labor-intensive goods. But after closely examining the data, researchers failed to detect such a decline. In addition, they found that manufacturing firms were consistently choosing to employ more skilled labor relative to unskilled labor, despite the rising cost of hiring those skilled workers. This evidence is consistent with an increase in the demand for educated workers.[33]

Another way of looking at the question examines the quantities of imports of labor-intensive goods as a factor that may cause the displacement of less educated workers and reduce their wages. In this case, the volume of traded goods, rather than their prices, is the focus. This approach yields essentially the same conclusion. Examining the period from 1980 to 1995, one study finds that the wages of college graduates rose 21 percent relative to high school graduates. At the same time, trade and immigration accounted for only about two percentage points (or 10 percent) of this change.[34] The relatively small contribution of trade is related to the fact that imports of manufactured goods from developing countries, presumably the primary source of unskilled labor-intensive goods, rose from just 1.0 percent of GDP in 1970 to 3.2 percent in 1990, hardly a dramatic increase in light of the spectacular increase in the labor market returns to education during this period.

Studies are just emerging of the more recent period from the late 1990s in which there was a large increase in imports from low-wage developing countries, such as China and Mexico after NAFTA. Yet the preliminary evidence also suggests that the contribution of trade to wage inequality is relatively small. One estimate puts the contribution of trade with low-wage countries from 1980 to 2006 at something shy of 10 percent of the overall rise in the college wage premium.[35] Another study concludes that "without the impact on wage inequality between 1981 and 2006, the wages of blue-collar workers would have been 1.4 percent

---

[33] See the papers in Collins 1998, Feenstra 2000, and Feenstra and Hanson 2003 for an overview of this literature.

[34] Borjas, Freeman, and Katz 1997. However, they found that these factors are somewhat more important in explaining the wage gap between high school graduates and high school drop outs.

[35] See Lawrence Katz's comments in Krugman 2008.

higher than they were in 2006 and that almost all of this took place before 2000."[36] Indeed, "the timing of wage inequality is not what might have been expected if increased trade penetration in the U.S. economy always gives rise to increased wage inequality" because inequality grew rapidly in the 1980s when trade with developing countries was growing slowly, whereas inequality has leveled off when imports from low-wage countries were accelerating.[37]

Trade, then, does not appear to be primarily responsible for increased wage inequality in recent decades. Evidence instead points to technological change as having raised the demand for more highly educated workers. For example, the advent of ATM machines and personal computers reduced the demand for bank tellers and office assistants and increased the demand for skilled technicians and highly trained or educated personnel. Whereas international trade would shift the demand for skills between sectors of the economy, skill-biased technical change would increase the demand for skilled workers in all sectors.[38] Some labor economists cite the slowdown in the growth of the supply of skilled labor since 1980 as another factor behind the rising relative wages of educated workers.[39] Furthermore, the relative wage of educated workers in many developing countries has been increasing as well, a pattern that can be explained by skill-biased technical change but is more difficult to explain as a result of international trade.[40]

But if trade has contributed even modestly to increased wage inequality, we can understand why adversely affected workers would oppose free trade. Survey evidence indicates that workers with less

[36] Lawrence 2008, 37.

[37] "After 2000, the share of imports from non-OPEC developing countries continued to grow rapidly, while the share of imports from developing countries actually declined . . . Yet this was a period of slow wage growth for almost all workers, with very little additional inequality." Lawrence 2008, 31, 34. One hypothesis for trade's lack of impact on wage inequality more recently is that the factor content of imports appears to be roughly similar to that of the U.S. economy overall, so it does not have a disproportionate impact on unskilled workers in particular.

[38] Berman, Bound, and Griliches (1994) found that nearly three-quarters of the overall shift in labor demand (for nonproduction workers) was a change in demand within industries rather than between industries.

[39] Goldin and Katz 2007.

[40] Goldberg and Pavcnik 2007.

educational attainment, those whose wages have lagged the most in recent decades, are also the most skeptical of the benefits of free trade.[41] Although these workers may have a legitimate economic interest in preventing trade, it does not make sense to deal with their concerns by harming the overall economy. It is no more reasonable to help them by imposing barriers to trade than it would be to ban ATM machines or word processing so as to increase the demand for bank tellers and office assistants. This might help them in the short run, but it would also reduce economic opportunities for others now and for their children in the future. A more constructive response is to encourage workers to make investments in education and, where possible, cushion the blow for those who are adversely affected by trade. One reason the debate over trade policy is never-ending, however, is that policies to cushion the blow are often viewed as inadequate.

The general finding that industries that compete against imports tend to be low-wage has two important exceptions: steel and automobiles. Wages are high in these two industries, and yet they confront competition from imports and are relatively unsuccessful in exporting. Not coincidentally, they also have strong labor unions. Could protecting these unionized manufacturing industries be justified on the basis of preserving high-wages jobs? Some researchers suggest yes, arguing that the existence of wage premiums in such industries justifies government support.[42]

But the case for protecting these industries to preserve the wage premium is extremely dubious. First, it is not clear that these unexplained variations in the inter-industry wage structure should be attributed to labor market rents that might justify government intervention. If the variation is unexplained, it is a questionable target for intervention because we cannot be certain of what it represents. Second, even if workers in

---

[41] Scheve and Slaughter 2001a.

[42] Katz and Summers (1989, 264) argue that this generally would imply export promotion schemes, since "as a rule export-intensive industries are the ones that have substantial wage premiums," but the automobile and steel industries are the atypical import-competing sectors in which wages are above average. They argue that the abnormally high wages reflect the high marginal product of workers, which they take to be indicative of an economic distortion that results in too few workers being employed in such industries. In principle, therefore, policies to increase employment in these industries would capture these rents for the economy, offset the underlying distortion, and thereby improve national welfare.

certain industries earn a wage premium, the case for promoting those industries depends on those premiums being taken as given. If instead the wage premium is determined by the behavior of labor unions, then using protection to promote the industry might enhance the union's ability to raise wages above the competitive level and raise the wage premium without significantly increasing employment.[43] In this case, protectionist policies exacerbate rather than ameliorate the underlying distortion, namely, the union's ability to raise wages above the competitive level. In this way, the policy negates the benefits that it aimed to capture and imposes costs on other industries.[44]

Finally, the structure of the automobile and steel industries has changed significantly over the past twenty years. A large share of output in both industries is now produced in the United States by nonunionized workers. Japanese and European automakers in the United States and the domestic minimills of the steel industry hire workers who are not part of the United Auto Workers or the United Steelworkers of America. Thus, the large wage premiums earned by unionized workers in these industries have been compressed because of greater domestic competition coming from firms using nonunion workers.

Displaced Workers and Trade Adjustment Assistance

Although free trade may be good for the economy as a whole, some workers in import-competing industries will be displaced from their jobs as a result of foreign competition. Without some policy to help these workers, opposition to free trade will always be politically potent.

---

[43] Unions strive to attain a combination of higher wages and greater employment for their members. If imports are restricted and the demand for steelworkers increases as domestic firms expand their production, the union can focus more on obtaining higher wages and less on increasing employment. Several studies show that this response, in which unions increase their pressure to raise wages, can ultimately undermine the policy's aim of increasing employment and capturing wage premiums. See de Melo and Tarr 1992 and Swagel 2000.

[44] Dickens (1995) also points out that workers who will fill the high-wage vacancies are themselves likely to come from fairly high-wage jobs. This undercuts the ability of activist policies to capture labor rents. There is also the issue of equity. By restricting imports, the government is implicitly forcing workers in other industries earning average wages or below to pay more for automobiles and steel products so that already highly paid workers in those industries can earn even more.

What government programs exist to help workers displaced from their jobs as a result of imports? Do these programs work well, and should trade-displaced workers get better treatment than workers displaced for other reasons?

As discussed earlier in this chapter, import competition accounts for only a small fraction of workers who lose their job every year. Even so, who are the displaced workers in import-competing industries and what is being done to help them? Workers in import-sensitive industries "are similar to other displaced manufacturing workers—slightly older, with virtually no difference in educational attainment or job tenure"—but are more likely to be women.[45] And even among import-sensitive industries, workers in very high import-share industries tend to have less education, have shorter job tenure, and are more likely to be female than workers in medium and low import-share industries.[46] The two most salient of these characteristics are gender and relatively low levels of education. These underlying characteristics tend to determine the labor market experiences of these workers, not the fact that they are employed in industries that compete against imports.

For example, workers displaced from high import-share industries are less likely to find new employment within a certain time period. This fact could be interpreted as indicating that the reemployment prospects of workers who have been laid off from industries that compete against imports are worse than average. But this correlation disappears once one controls for the higher proportion of female workers in those industries. In other words, women in general tend to have lower reemployment rates after being laid off any job. They may opt to leave the labor force, for example, or take more time off between jobs than men do. It is this characteristic, rather than anything special about import-competing industries per se, that accounts for the lower reemployment rate of workers displaced from high import-share industries. As one

---

[45] "The most striking difference between import-competing displaced workers and other displaced manufacturing workers is the degree to which import-competing industries employ and displace women. Women account for 45 percent of import-sensitive displaced workers, relative to 37 percent of the overall manufacturing displaced. Some industries stand out: Women account for 80 percent of those displaced from apparel, 66 percent from footwear, and 76 percent from knitting mills (part of the textile industry)." Kletzer 2001, 3.

[46] Kletzer 1998b, 450.

researcher concludes, "Trade-displaced workers may have more difficult labor market adjustments, but the source of the difficulty is their otherwise disadvantaged characteristics, not the characteristics of their displacement industry."[47]

What about the wage losses suffered by workers thrown out of work as a result of imports? As it turns out, workers displaced from industries in which import penetration was increasing rapidly had lower earnings losses than other displaced workers.[48] In general, the size of the earnings losses depends largely on how long the workers had been employed in the jobs from which they were displaced (the longer they were employed, the greater the earnings loss) and whether the workers found reemployment in the same industry or in a different industry (if reemployed in a different industry, then the earnings losses are greater). Because workers in import-sensitive sectors tend to be low-wage workers with shorter job tenures, workers displaced from industries that compete with imports generally have lower earnings losses than the average displaced worker. This is particularly true in one of the most trade-sensitive industries, the textile and apparel industry, which lost more than 800,000 jobs between 1990 and 2004, due to technological change as well as imports.[49]

Table 4.2 presents recent data on all displaced workers in the United States. About two-thirds of workers displaced for any reason (not just trade) were reemployed; a sizable fraction remained unemployed or left the labor force. Particularly in the apparel industry, displaced workers tend to be older women who never earned a high school diploma, and therefore are more likely to have difficulty finding new employment or to no longer seek employment. Of the manufacturing workers who found employment, about half make more and about half make less than they did in their previous job, although displaced textile and apparel

---

[47] Kletzer 2000, 375.

[48] Addison, Fox, and Ruhm 1995.

[49] According to Field and Graham (1997), in contrast to displaced workers in other manufacturing industries, who experienced an average 10 percent drop in wages after finding new employment, displaced apparel workers who found new jobs actually received higher wages, while textile workers experienced little change in their wages. The explanation is that apparel workers receive very low wages in the first place and that over 60 percent of laid-off apparel workers found reemployment in another manufacturing industry.

_____Table 4.2
**Status of Workers Displaced from Full-Time Jobs between January 2003 and December 2005
(as of January 2006)**

	Labor Market Outcome (percentage distribution)			Of Those Reemployed, Full-Time (percentage distribution)	
	Reemployed	Unemployed	Not in Labor Force	At Lower Wage	At Same or Higher Wage
Textiles and Apparel	63	19	18	45	55
Manufacturing	65	16	18	54	46

Source: Displaced Workers Survey, Bureau of Labor Statistics, August 17, 2006 press release available at http://stats.bls.gov/newsrelease.htm.

Note: For workers over age 20 with job tenure of at least three years.

**Status of Workers Displaced from Full-Time Jobs between January 2005 and December 2007
(as of January 2008)**

	Labor Market Outcome (percentage distribution)			Of Those Reemployed, Full-Time (percentage distribution)	
	Reemployed	Unemployed	Not in Labor Force	At Lower Wage	At Same or Higher Wage
Textiles and Apparel	n.a.	n.a.	n.a.	—	—
Manufacturing	64	18	17	49	51

Source: Displaced Workers Survey, Bureau of Labor Statistics, August 20, 2008 press release available at http://stats.bls.gov/newsrelease.htm.

Note: For workers over age 20 with job tenure of at least three years.

workers were slightly more likely to make as much or more than they had before.

While most workers displaced from industries that compete against imports eventually find employment in the same industry, in related manufacturing industries, or in the nontraded service sector, they almost never find employment in export-oriented industries. A worker laid off from the apparel industry, for example, is extremely unlikely to find employment in the aircraft industry, because a different skill mix is required. This pattern creates a problem for policymakers: workers harmed by imports will not reap the benefits of new employment opportunities in export-oriented industries. Telling these workers that rising employment in export industries will offset the decline in their current industry of employment is not likely to persuade them that free trade is a good thing.

The plight of displaced workers should not be trivialized; numerous studies have shown that their earnings losses are generally sizable and persistent.[50] There is no debate about whether unemployed workers should receive government assistance. The question is whether trade-displaced workers should benefit from a special government program beyond that given to the far more numerous workers who are displaced for other reasons. Special adjustment assistance for workers laid off as a result of imports has been justified on efficiency, equity, and political grounds, but unfortunately all three rationales are open to question.

The efficiency rationale is that government assistance can speed up the process of adjusting to trade and thereby make it more efficient. This is doubtful on both theoretical and empirical grounds. In theory, the government should intervene to accelerate adjustment only if some market failure is associated with that process. The simple fact that the adjustment process sometimes operates slowly and with friction is insufficient grounds for intervention.[51] In addition, the empirical studies of displaced workers alluded to earlier generally suggest that the labor market experiences of those displaced from trade-sensitive industries are not much different from workers with similar characteristics who have been displaced from industries not sensitive to trade. Therefore, efficiency considerations do not seem to justify singling out trade-affected workers for more generous treatment than that given to other displaced workers. Then there is the more general point related to the potential inefficiency of any government program that attempts to redistribute income to a targeted group. The costs of administering a compensation program might well be much higher than the losses incurred by displaced workers.[52]

The equity rationale—that fairness requires giving workers displaced by imports special treatment—is also questionable. Workers may lose their jobs for any number of reasons: increasing domestic competition, fluctuations in the weather, substitution of capital for labor, changes in technology, shifts in consumer tastes, and so on. Even if it were

[50] Kletzer 1998a.

[51] Mussa 1982.

[52] Jacobson (1998, 476) suggests that the "transactions costs associated with [compensation] are likely to be many times larger than the costs imposed on those adversely affected by change."

possible to single out workers who have been dislocated for trade-related reasons, there is no compelling case for treating them differently from those who have lost their job for other reasons. In fact, it seems grossly unfair to provide a more comfortable cushion for the workers displaced because of imports and not for those laid off because of, say, a painful recession brought on by the collapse of a bubble in housing prices. What is the reason for providing more generous compensation to the apparel worker in Georgia who loses a job to imports than to the typewriter assembler at Smith-Corona displaced because of computers or the Kellogg's worker laid off because General Mills begins producing tastier cereals?

The political argument for trade adjustment assistance is that the public does view these various causes of job loss as different. Trade displacement is much more politically sensitive than job loss due to domestic competition or technological change or an economic recession. Therefore, trade adjustment assistance can mitigate the opposition to trade legislation by reducing the concentrated losses from liberalization. Still, there is little direct evidence that trade adjustment assistance (TAA) has proven important in obtaining negotiating authority, in securing the passage of legislation, or in maintaining support for the system of open trade. The ability of TAA to buy the political support of labor groups has weakened due to the well-known shortcomings of the program.[53]

Yet ever since the Trade Expansion Act of 1962, Congress has ensured that trade adjustment assistance has been a component of trade legislation. The original purpose of TAA was to compensate workers for loss of income, but since then, the goal has shifted toward other assistance, such as training and reemployment services.

TAA was revamped in 2002 and currently works in the following way.[54] Unemployed workers can typically receive up to twenty-six weeks of unemployment insurance. If they exhaust this benefit and are declared eligible for TAA by the Department of Labor, they can then receive financial support under the trade readjustment allowance (TRA) for an additional fifty-two weeks, bringing total support to seventy-eight weeks

---

[53] TAA may have facilitated the passage of trade bills in 1962 and 1974, when Congress included it in exchange for labor's support for (or muted opposition to) the trade legislation. Destler 1998.

[54] Baicker and Rehavi 2004.

(about a year and a half).[55] Eligible workers are those where increased imports have "contributed importantly" to declining production and layoffs in their industry. In addition, workers in firms whose upstream suppliers or downstream customers have been adversely affected are also eligible for assistance, as are those whose firms shifted production to another country with a free trade agreement with the United States or that receives preferential access.

A special NAFTA assistance program was set up in 1994, relating only to those affected by trade with Canada and Mexico. Under this program, workers could receive benefits even as a result of trade diversion. In other words, if NAFTA diverts trade to Mexico in such a way that higher imports from Mexico substitute for lower imports from another country, workers may be eligible for assistance. As long as Mexican imports have increased, no causal link from NAFTA to the job loss is required. For example, when a sawmill in the state of Washington shut down because federal forest lands were declared off limits to save the spotted owl, the 135 workers affected were declared eligible for NAFTA-TAA because timber imports from Canada subsequently increased.[56] A unique feature of the NAFTA program is that assistance is available not just to workers who lose their jobs as a result of imports, but also to those who lose their jobs if their employer shifts production to Canada or Mexico. Once again, participation in a government-approved training program is required for those receiving benefits.

In fiscal year 2006, the Labor Department spent about $775 million in TRA assistance (extended unemployment insurance payments) and TAA benefits (mainly training). These expenditures are a fraction of total spending on unemployment insurance. The program is inexpensive because few workers are actually involved in it; workers declared eligible for TRA do not necessarily collect benefits. In fact, usually less than half of all workers who are declared eligible for some form of trade adjustment assistance actually take advantage of it. For example, in fiscal year 2006,

[55] In the past, when the financial benefits of unemployment insurance were more generous, workers receiving TRA were apparently quite happy to take the benefits and wait for their old jobs to reappear, rather than seek retraining in an effort to adjust to the import competition. In 1988, therefore, Congress shifted the program's focus away from financial compensation and toward adjustment assistance by making enrollment in a government-certified training course a requirement for receiving TRA allowances.

[56] Richards 1997.

nearly 120,000 workers were certified as eligible to receive TAA benefits, and about 60,000 workers began to receive such benefits.[57] This is because workers are either rehired or reemployed in the interim, receive union compensation, or do not wish to enroll in a training program.

While the budgetary outlays are relatively small, the TAA program is not perfect. Workers provided with benefits over a longer period of time do not have an incentive to find a new job quickly. And prolonging the period of unemployment—as the TAA does—does not usually result in better labor market matches for those workers. The mandatory training programs have not addressed this problem because they are not very successful. As one study found, although TAA was well targeted in serving workers who were permanently displaced from their jobs and who experienced significant earnings losses, there was no evidence that training had a substantial positive impact on the earnings of the trainees. Those who went through the training program did not find better-paying jobs than those who did not attend the program.[58] This bleak assessment is not unique to TAA: there is little evidence that any government training program works well. After studying many such training programs, the OECD reached the sober conclusion that "broad training programs aimed at large groups of the unemployed have seldom proved a good investment, whether for society or for the program participants."[59]

Thus, as currently designed, TAA is not ideal. To the extent that the program merely provides an incentive for trade-displaced workers to remain unemployed for a longer period of time than other displaced workers, it fails to help workers or improve economic efficiency. So how should the system be changed? Some argue that the training requirement should be dumped: workers do not like it anyway, and it provides no economic value. The benefits should not be tied to time out of work because doing so only prolongs the period of unemployment. Since it is not

[57] Congressional Budget Office 2007.

[58] Decker and Corson 1995.

[59] Organization for Economic Cooperation and Development 1994, 37. Heckman (1999, 106) is more blunt about government-sponsored job training programs: "the evidence strongly suggests that investing in low skilled, disadvantaged adult workers makes no economic sense." There is some evidence that programs targeted at specific groups, such as youths and women, may work better than others, but even here those who enter such programs seldom experience labor market outcomes that are much different from those who do not enter such programs.

the case that a longer search leads to a better job match for workers, assistance programs should encourage quick reemployment.

The 2002 trade adjustment assistance legislation contained an interesting pilot program—wage insurance—that deserves careful study. Because the current TAA discourages work and fails to compensate for income losses, since payments cease when a worker takes a lower-paying job, time-limited earnings insurance was introduced to provide compensation while preserving the incentive to find work. This Alternative Trade Adjustment Assistance (ATAA) gives selected workers over fifty years old cash benefits equal to 50 percent of the difference between their old pay and their new pay (capped at $10,000) if they are reemployed at a lower wage within twenty-six weeks of being laid off and earn less than $50,000 in their new job.[60] Under this scheme, workers would receive these special payments only when they became reemployed.

Any proposal that seeks to provide compensation while preserving the incentive of workers to find employment is worth exploring. It is too soon to say how well the wage insurance and other new provisions of the 2002 TAA will work.[61] Such a scheme, however, would force a reexamination of the entire concept of unemployment insurance. A potential problem with earnings insurance is that it could be costly, although it could replace existing programs rather than be added to them. Aside from the high costs of such a program, basing a compensation program on past earnings runs the risk of trying to create a riskless society. Should the government insure against all losses that individuals incur in the labor market, particularly when the individuals themselves do not seem interested in purchasing such insurance?[62]

The 2002 Trade Adjustment Assistance was due to expire in 2007, but has been extended until new TAA legislation can be formulated. In the 2009 economic stimulus bill, Congress extended TAA benefits to

---

[60] Baicker and Rehavi 2004.

[61] Kletzer (2004) reports that a wage insurance trial in Canada had modest effects in accelerating reemployment.

[62] As Jacobson (1998, 475) notes, "Neither society at large nor members of the risk pool potentially affected by costly job loss appear willing to pay for such (earnings) insurance . . . individuals adversely threatened by trade and other factors appear to lack the willingness to pay actuarially fair insurance," although this may be due in part to the existence of government compensation programs. However, see Kaivanto (2007) for an economic rationale for wage insurance.

service workers affected by trade, relaxed eligibility criteria, and raised benefit levels. The Congressional Budget Office has priced out these changes as costing more than $1 billion per year.[63] Although this would double expenditures on TAA, it is still relatively inexpensive in comparison to the gains from keeping markets open to trade. Other public policies geared toward helping workers manage their best in this period of rapid economic change include such things as ensuring the portability of health and pension benefits in order to reduce the adverse impact of changing jobs, which must inevitably happen in an ever-changing economy.

The lamentable conclusion is that there is no easy solution and no obvious government policy that can address all of the concerns of workers adversely affected by economic change, whether it be due to imports or new technology. Trade adjustment assistance has not worked as promised, and may even be an impediment to economic efficiency. A broader government program to help displaced workers should be examined and might be a small price to pay to reduce anxieties about international trade and maintain political support for open markets. But even if such a program is affordable and gets the incentives right, there is absolutely no guarantee that demands for import barriers by labor groups in import-competing sectors (such as the steelworkers union) will diminish. Even if fully compensated for losing their job, these workers simply may not want to move to a different job in a different location when there is a chance they can stay employed where they are by stopping imports.

_____*What About the Trade Deficit?*

In every year since 1976, the value of goods and services imported into the United States has exceeded the value of goods and services exported. Does the trade deficit injure domestic industries and have adverse effects on employment? Should the trade deficit be a matter of concern and reversing it an objective for trade policy?

The connection between the trade deficit and employment is much more complex than the simple view that jobs are lost because

[63] Congressional Budget Office 2007.

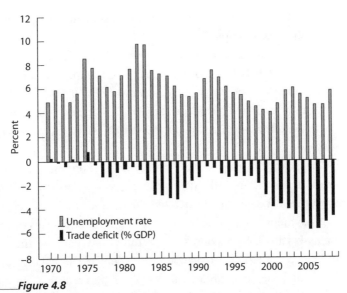

_____*Figure 4.8*
Unemployment and the Trade Deficit, 1970–2008.
Source: Council of Economic Advisers 2009, tables B-1, B-35, and B-103.

imports exceed exports. As figure 4.8 shows, the correlation between the merchandise trade deficit and the unemployment rate is actually negative: most of the time, the trade deficit has risen during periods of falling unemployment and has fallen during periods of rising unemployment. As noted earlier, the business cycle may be driving this relationship: a booming economy in which many people are finding employment is also an economy that sucks in many imports, whereas a sluggish economy is one in which spending on imports slacken.

Yet these imports are not free: in order to acquire them, a country must sell something in return. Imports are usually paid for in one of two ways: the sale of goods and services or the sale of assets to foreign countries. In other words, all of the dollars that U.S. consumers hand over to other countries in purchasing imports do not accumulate there, but eventually return to purchase either U.S. goods (exports) or U.S. assets (foreign investment). Both exports and foreign investment create new jobs: employment in export-oriented sectors such as farming and aircraft production is higher because of those foreign sales, and foreign investment either contributes directly to the national capital stock with new plants and equipment or facilitates domestic capital accumulation by reducing the cost of capital.

A deeper understanding of the trade deficit, however, requires some familiarity with balance-of-payments accounting. Balance-of-payments accounting may be a dry subject, but it helps lift the fog that surrounds the trade deficit. This accounting also suggests which remedies are likely to be effective in reducing the deficit, should that be considered desirable.

The balance of payments is simply an accounting of a country's international transactions. All sales of U.S. goods or assets to nonresidents constitute a receipt to the United States and are recorded in the balance of payments as a positive entry (credit); all purchases of foreign goods or assets by U.S. residents constitute a payment by the United States and are recorded as a negative entry (debit). The balance of payments is divided into two broad categories of transactions: the current account, which includes all trade in goods and services, plus a few smaller categories; and the financial account, which includes all trade in assets, mainly portfolio and direct investments.

The first accounting lesson is that the balance of payments always balances. By accounting identity, which is to say by definition, the balance of payments sums to zero. This implies that

current account + financial account = 0.

Because the overall balance of payments always balances, a country with a current account deficit must have an offsetting financial account surplus. In other words, if a country is buying more goods and services from the rest of the world than it is selling, then the country must also be selling more assets to the rest of the world than it is purchasing.[64]

To make the link clearer, consider the case of an individual. Each of us as individuals exports our labor services to others in the economy. For this work, we receive an income that can be used to import goods and services produced by others. If an individual's expenditures exactly match his or her income in a given year, that person has "balanced

[64] A country therefore cannot experience a "balance of payments deficit" unless one is using the old nomenclature that considers official reserve transactions (an important component of the balance of payments under fixed exchange rate regimes) as a separate part of the international accounts.

trade" with the rest of the economy: the value of exports (income) equals the value of imports (expenditures). Can individuals spend more in a given year than they earn in income, in other words, can a person import more than he or she exports? Of course, by one of two ways: either by receiving a loan (borrowing) or by selling existing financial assets to make up the difference. Either method generates a financial inflow—a financial account surplus—that can be used to finance the trade deficit while also reducing the individual's net assets. Can an individual spend less in a given year than that person earns in income? Of course, and that individual exports more than he or she imports, thereby running a trade surplus with the rest of the economy. The surplus earnings are saved, generating a financial outflow—a capital account deficit—due to the purchase of financial investments.

What does this mean in the context of the United States? In 2008, the United States had a merchandise trade deficit of about $820 billion and a services trade surplus of $140 billion. The balance on goods and services was therefore a deficit of about $680 billion, but owing to other factors (net income payments and net unilateral transfers) the current account deficit was nearly $673 billion, or 4.7 percent of that year's GDP. This implies that there must have been a capital account surplus of roughly the same magnitude. Sure enough, in that year U.S. residents (corporations and households) increased their ownership of foreign assets by just under $52 billion, while foreigners increased their ownership of U.S. assets by over $599 billion. Therefore, the capital account surplus was approximately $550 billion. In other words, foreigners increased their ownership stake in U.S. assets more than U.S. residents increased their holdings of foreign assets, thus forming the mirror image of the current account deficit.[65]

The balance of payments "balances" in the sense that every dollar we spend on imported goods must end up somewhere. Here's another way of thinking about it: in 2008, the United States imported almost $2,517 billion in goods and services from the rest of the world, but the rest of the world only purchased $1,836 billion of U.S. goods and services. What did the other countries do with the rest of our money? They invested most of it in the United States. In essence, for every dollar

[65] Council of Economic Advisers 2009, table B-103.

Americans handed over to foreigners in buying their goods (our imports), foreigners used seventy-three cents to purchase U.S. goods (our exports) and the remaining twenty-seven cents to purchase U.S. assets. What assets are foreign residents purchasing? Some are short-term financial assets (such as stocks and bonds) for portfolio reasons; some are direct investments (such as mergers and acquisitions) to acquire ownership rights; and some are real assets (such as buildings and land) for the same reasons.

Is the current account deficit sustainable? As long as foreign investors are willing to continue purchasing U.S. assets, the deficit can be sustained. Once foreign investors decide to stop buying U.S. assets or to sell them, then the dollar will tend to depreciate on foreign exchange markets, increasing exports and decreasing imports and thus tending to reduce the trade deficit. This process can be slow and orderly and does not require a "hard landing" or sudden collapse in the dollar.[66]

In running a current account deficit, the United States is selling assets to the rest of the world.[67] These foreign purchases of domestic assets allow the United States to finance more investment than it could through domestic savings alone. In essence, the United States is supplementing its domestic savings with foreign investment and thus is able to undertake more investment than if it had relied solely on domestic savings. The equation that expresses this relationship is

current account = savings − investment.

[66] In the mid-1980s, many commentators feared that the current account deficit was unsustainable and that the economy would face a "hard landing" once foreign capital stopped flowing into the United States. These fears proved to be misplaced: the economy did not suffer a hard landing when capital inflows slowed in the late 1980s, the dollar depreciated in an orderly way, and the current account deficits fell as a share of GDP.

[67] Sometimes the United States is likened to a developing country that has become a debtor nation. The United States is a "debtor" country in the sense that the stock of foreigners own more U.S. assets than U.S. residents own foreign assets. But the U.S. situation is not really comparable to those of developing countries. In developing countries, foreign investment sometimes includes large amounts of short-term government debt, denominated in a foreign currency. It is misleading to compare these debts to the foreign purchase of U.S. assets by saying that the United States is borrowing from other countries. Borrowing implies a specific payback schedule, hence the repayment problems that developing countries sometimes encounter. In the U.S. case, foreign investors are simply choosing to purchase dollar-denominated assets from the owners of those assets. The investors often wish to take a direct, long-term ownership stake in the United States that they do not intend to reverse.

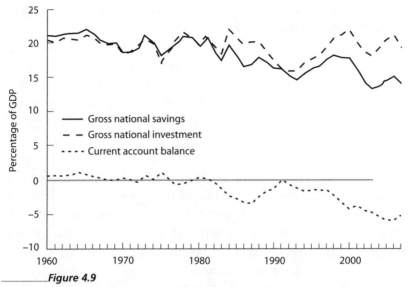

_____***Figure 4.9***

Savings and Investment as a Percentage of GDP, 1960–2007.
Source: Council of Economic Advisers 2009, tables B-32, B-24, and B-1.

Once again, this equation is an identity, meaning that it holds by definition. A current account deficit (the financial account surplus) implies that domestic investment exceeds domestic savings. Conversely, countries with current account surpluses have domestic savings in excess of domestic investment, the excess being used to purchase foreign assets via foreign investment (financial account deficit).

Figure 4.9 illustrates this point by presenting the U.S. current account as a percentage of GDP from 1960 to 2007, along with the evolution of savings and investment. The current account registered a slight surplus during the 1960s, indicating that the United States was making net foreign investments in the rest of the world. Since the early 1980s, however, domestic investment has been greater than domestic savings, meaning that the United States has been a net recipient of foreign investment.

That the U.S. current account was roughly balanced in the 1960s and 1970s is no coincidence. The ability of a country to run a current account surplus or deficit depends upon the degree to which capital is allowed to move between countries, which in turn is a function of the international monetary system and the exchange rate regime. In the absence of international capital mobility, domestic savings must equal domestic investment, and therefore the current account will be balanced. Under the Bretton Woods system of fixed exchange rates, which lasted from just after World War II until 1971, governments maintained fixed exchange rates by imposing controls on capital movements. As a result, capital flows were minimal by present-day standards. When the international monetary system suppresses capital account transactions, the financial account balance must be close to zero, and therefore the current account balance must also be close to zero.

The Bretton Woods system collapsed in 1971, and since then international capital movements have been deregulated. With the return of international capital mobility, relatively large current account imbalances also began to emerge. The United States became a magnet for capital from the rest of the world, particularly after the early 1980s. For example, after Japan eased restrictions on the holding of foreign assets in 1980, Japanese investors took part of their large pool of capital (invested in its domestic market as a result of its high savings rate) and sought higher rates of return in foreign capital markets, particularly in the United States. Now that they were free to buy U.S. assets as well as U.S. goods, Japanese residents chose to allocate some of the dollars they earned in selling products in the United States to buying U.S. assets rather than U.S. goods.

Why has the U.S. current account deficit grown so much since the late 1990s? Federal Reserve Chairman Ben Bernanke has put forward the hypothesis of a "global savings glut." In Bernanke's view, the principal causes of the current account deficit lie with factors outside the United States, in particular, the shift of rapidly growing East Asian economies and oil-producing countries from net borrowers to large net lenders on international capital markets. The windfall to oil exporters from higher petroleum prices and the buildup of foreign exchange reserves and foreign investment by East Asian countries have increased the savings in those countries and expanded their current account surpluses. They have chosen to invest their savings in the United States, resulting in the large U.S. current account deficit. Until the excess foreign savings gets dissipated in other ways, the current account deficit will continue.

The U.S. bilateral trade deficit with China is the most controversial part of the U.S. current account deficit. In 2008, the U.S. trade deficit with China was $266 billion, or 1.9 percent of GDP. An important factor behind China's trade surplus is that most of the dollars that it receives from exporting goods to the United States are used to buy U.S. debt rather than U.S. goods. In 2007, China purchased approximately $460 billion in U.S. Treasury bills and other securities. Such purchases have enabled China's foreign exchange reserves to swell from $166 billion in 2000 to an astounding $2 trillion by the end of 2008. (Similarly, China's current account surplus has ballooned from 1 percent of GDP in 2001 to 11 percent of GDP in 2007.)

For many years, China accomplished this by intervening in foreign exchange markets to peg the value of its currency, the renminbi, against the dollar at a relatively low rate. In 2005, as a result of U.S. pressure, China began to allow the renminbi to appreciate slowly against the dollar, but many economists still believe that the renminbi is undervalued by a substantial margin, perhaps as much as 40 percent.[68] This has led to charges that China is manipulating its currency to achieve unbalanced, export-led growth, and has suppressed domestic consumption. The undervaluation of the renminbi is an implicit subsidy to Chinese exports, and also an implicit subsidy to the U.S. Treasury since it enables the government to borrow at a lower interest rate than it otherwise could.

Just like the U.S. trade deficit with Japan in the 1980s, the trade deficit with China is highly controversial. According to the Economic Policy Institute, the trade deficit with China was responsible for the loss of 2.3 million U.S. jobs from 2001 to 2007.[69] This is unlikely for several reasons. First, China's leading exports to the United States are consumer electronics, machinery, sporting goods and toys, apparel and footwear, and furniture. As chapter 1 pointed out, the Chinese content in the consumer electronics exports tends to be relatively small (it imports the components and exports the assembled goods), so using the dollar value of imports from China to calculate the effect on employment grossly overstates its impact on the U.S. economy. The EPI study also assumes that if the United States did not import consumer electronics from China, the goods would be produced in the United States, creating jobs. But if the electronics were not imported from China, the United States would probably have imported them from another Asian country, as was done before China's economic rise.

[68] Goldstein and Lardy 2008.
[69] Scott 2008.

In fact, the Congressional Budget Office found "roughly one-third of the increase in the share of imports from China in U.S. markets from 1998 through 2005 was offset by reduced growth and, in some cases, declines in the shares of imports from other countries," an offset that was even higher prior to 1998.[70] To some degree, China has simply displaced other East Asian countries—Hong Kong, Taiwan, and Korea—as a source of U.S. imports. U.S. employment was already severely diminished in industries such as sporting goods, toys, apparel, and footwear as a result of foreign competition from Asia since the 1960s. China merely took over those markets from other foreign suppliers. Even in product categories that overlap with existing U.S. industries, U.S. and Chinese producers tend to sell in different markets: China has tended to specialize in selling cheaper, lower quality goods whereas U.S. manufacturers have specialized in selling more expensive, higher quality goods.[71]

Finally, it is difficult to say much about the impact of the trade deficit on the number of jobs in the economy because looking at the trade flows alone ignores the role of financial flows in keeping interest rates low. If the United States took action to reduce the trade deficit in an effort to reduce the number of jobs lost to trade, then net capital inflows from abroad would necessarily have to fall (i.e., China would no longer buy Treasury bills and the renminbi would appreciate and the dollar would depreciate). Then domestic investment would have to be financed by domestic savings, implying higher interest rates, which would reduce the number of jobs created by business investment. In the end, a lower trade deficit's positive impact on employment might be offset by the negative impact of lower domestic investment and higher interest rates.

So what are the implications for trade policy? The current account is fundamentally determined by international capital mobility and the gap between domestic savings and investment. The main determinants of savings and investment are macroeconomic in nature. Current account imbalances have nothing to do with whether a country is open or closed to foreign goods, engages in unfair trade practices or not, or is more "competitive" than other countries. If net capital flows are zero, the current account will be balanced. Japan's $11 billion current account

---

[70] Congressional Budget Office 2008, 9.
[71] Schott 2008.

deficit in 1980 became an $87 billion current account surplus in 1987 not because it closed its market, or because the United States opened its market, or because Japanese manufacturers suddenly became more competitive. The surplus emerged because of financial and macroeconomic policy changes in Japan and the United States. The current trade imbalance with China is more controversial because it involves efforts by the Chinese government to control the flow of capital between the two countries rather than allow it to be determined by private financial market participants.

Trade policy cannot directly affect the current account deficit because trade policy has little influence on domestic savings and investment, the ultimate determinants of the current account. If a country wishes to reduce its trade deficit, then it must undertake macroeconomic measures to reduce the gap between domestic savings and investment. Reducing the federal government's fiscal deficit, which acts to absorb domestic savings, could contribute to this result. Long ago it was believed that restrictions on imports would reduce the trade deficit. But that result would follow only if exports remained unaffected, an assumption that the Lerner symmetry theorem suggests, and experience demonstrates, is false. Adam Smith saw through such policies of restriction: "Nothing, however, can be more absurd than this whole doctrine of the balance of trade, upon which, not only these restraints, but almost all the other regulations of commerce are founded."[72]

To conclude, we have seen in the past two chapters that trade is a small part of the everyday shift of workers between various sectors of the economy, creating jobs in some industries but destroying jobs in others. While some workers are adversely affected by imports, government programs are in place to help them. Blocking imports may protect some jobs in industries that compete against imports, but harms employment in export-oriented and import-using industries, as chapter 3 explained. To fully understand trade policy, we must appreciate these oft-ignored indirect effects.

[72] Smith 1976, 488.

5

Relief from Foreign Competition: Antidumping and the Escape Clause

We have seen how trade policies aimed at reducing imports also reduce exports and employment elsewhere in the economy. Yet import restrictions are often justified as a way of providing relief to industries suffering from "unfair" foreign competition. Antidumping laws, which provide a means for tariffs on unfairly low-priced imports, have become the primary instrument for addressing such concerns. This chapter examines the U.S. antidumping laws and asks whether they provide a remedy for unfair trade, or are merely a convenient mechanism for protecting an industry from imports. We will also look at the escape clause procedure, which can provide industries with temporary relief from imports without the claim of unfair trade. Finally, we will examine whether trade protection really helps industries such as textiles and steel adjust to foreign competition and become more competitive.

Unfair Trade: Subsidies and Dumping

We are all familiar with the claim that imports cost jobs. But many people are also afraid that American industries are being harmed by unfair foreign trade practices. These include export subsidies and the dumping of goods at low prices that undermine the sales of U.S. firms. To counter such practices, the United States enforces several "fair trade" laws that allow import tariffs to be imposed. For example, when a foreign government subsidizes its exports to the United States, the subsidy is considered to be an actionable unfair trade practice if it injures domestic producers.

Of course, from a strictly economic point of view, an importing country might well benefit from receiving subsidized goods. Even if the subsidy harms domestic producers, the subsidy allows the importing country to purchase imports at a lower price, thanks to the generosity of foreign taxpayers. By improving the terms of trade, the foreign subsidy adds to the domestic gains from trade. For example, domestic oil producers would be understandably upset if the Organization of Petroleum Exporting Countries (OPEC) decided to subsidize oil exports to the United States, but the country as a whole would probably welcome the lower gas prices that would follow.

But such subsidies are not desirable from the standpoint of the world economy. For one thing, such subsidies cut into the exports of countries that have a natural comparative advantage in those products, and so distort the world's allocation of resources. Subsidies also generate political friction among trading partners, each viewing the other's government as putting its finger on the scales of international competition to tip the outcome toward its own favored producers.[1]

For these reasons, the United States led the effort to draw up an Agreement on Subsidies and Countervailing Measures in the Uruguay Round of multilateral trade negotiations in 1994. The subsidies agreement establishes rules on permissible types of subsidies and tries to ensure that such subsidies will not distort trade. Under the agreement, export subsidies and subsidies to industries that compete against imports are prohibited in principle, but subsidies related to research and development, regional development, and environmental compliance purposes are permissible.

In the United States, domestic firms have legal recourse against subsidized imports. The remedy takes the form of tariffs known as countervailing duties (CVDs). Domestic firms initiate the legal process by filing a petition with the Department of Commerce and the U.S. International Trade Commission (ITC) alleging that imports have been subsidized by a foreign government. If Commerce determines that the imports have been subsidized and if the ITC decides that the domestic industry has

[1] The United States, it should be noted, provides such export subsidies through the Export-Import Bank. In fiscal year 2006, the Export-Import Bank authorized $12.1 billion in support to U.S. exporters through loans, guarantees, and export credit insurance. Nearly half of that amount helped finance the sale of large commercial aircraft. Indeed, Boeing and General Electric receive the bulk of the funding support. World Trade Organization 2008, 59.

been injured as a result of the imports, tariffs of the magnitude of the subsidy margin (as determined by Commerce) will be imposed.

In recent years the CVD process has been rarely invoked by domestic firms. Are foreign countries subsidizing fewer of their exports to the United States? As a result of the multilateral subsidy agreement, perhaps so. But the more likely explanation is that domestic firms have found other ways to prevent such exports from entering the U.S. market. And in fact domestic firms find it much easier to obtain protection by accusing foreign firms of "dumping" in the U.S. market than by proving the existence of foreign subsidies.

From the standpoint of domestic firms seeking protection from imports, antidumping is where the action is. The number of dumping cases swamps those of other trade remedies: during the 1990s, five antidumping cases were initiated for every CVD case. At the end of 2007, the United States did not have any countervailing duties in place, while it maintained antidumping duties on nearly three hundred products. This emphasis on antidumping instead of countervailing duties exists around the world as well. In the year ending June 2006, WTO members initiated four countervailing duty investigations and 185 antidumping investigations.[2] What exactly is going on here?

Dumping has been deemed an unfair trade practice by country authorities and world trade agreements, and the antidumping law is intended to combat it. Yet the gap between the rhetoric and the reality of antidumping trade policy is simply enormous. Dumping sounds awful, as though foreign goods were being unloaded on America's docks and priced below cost to force domestic firms out of business. But under the law, dumping simply means that a foreign exporter charges a lower price in the U.S. market than it does in its home market. This is nothing more than price discrimination. If the foreign exporter is found guilty, the United States can impose import duties to offset the difference.

Figure 5.1 shows the annual number of U.S. antidumping investigations since 1970. As is evident, the number of investigations is quite cyclical. Fluctuations in antidumping activity are related to such factors as the exchange rate and the unemployment rate (an appreciation of the dollar and a higher unemployment rate increase the number of cases) as

[2] World Trade Organization 2007, 31–32.

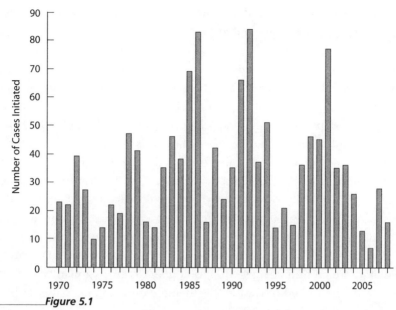

_____*Figure 5.1*

Annual Number of Antidumping Investigations, 1970–2008.
Source: Import Administration, U.S. Department of Commerce. www.ia.ita.doc
.gov.

well as the rise in the import-to-GDP ratio. Although the number of petitions filed has dropped off in recent years, it is likely to increase again
due to the recent economic downturn.[3]

    While the details of antidumping (AD) are quite complex, it is
important to understand why these laws have become problematic.[4] The
AD process is activated when a domestic industry, represented by an industry association or in some cases just a single firm, files a petition with
the Commerce Department and the ITC. The petitioners must have legal
standing to file a petition. (In 1999, for example, Commerce rejected an
antidumping case filed by a group of Texas oil producers against Saudi
Arabia, Mexico, Venezuela, and Iraq on the grounds that the petitioners
did not represent the entire industry.) The legal fees associated with filing

[3] Irwin 2005a.
[4] There is now a voluminous literature that finds fault with the antidumping laws.
For recent analyses, see Barfield 2003 and Lindsey and Ikenson 2003. Blonigen and Prusa
(2003) and Nelson (2006) survey the recent research on antidumping policy.

an AD case typically amount to about $1 million, although more complex cases can cost several million dollars.[5]

The Commerce Department determines whether dumping has occurred and, if so, calculates the dumping margin. Specifically, Commerce ascertains whether a foreign exporter made sales in the United States at prices that are at "less than fair value." Sales are less than fair value if the export price, the price charged in the U.S. market, is less than the so-called normal value. The normal value is determined one of three ways: by the price charged by the foreign exporter in home market sales, by the price it charged in third-country sales, or by constructed value, which is an estimate of what the price should have been based on the costs of production plus administrative expenses and a profit margin. The dumping margin is simply the difference between the export price and this determined normal value divided by the export price. For example, if a foreign firm charges $100 for a good in its own market and exports it to the United States for $80, then the dumping margin is 25 percent, or $(100 - 80)/80$.

After receiving a petition, Commerce almost always rules that dumping has occurred. From 1995 to 1998, Commerce ruled that dumping had occurred in 98 percent of all cases.[6] And the dumping margins were large: the average AD duty imposed during the same period was a whopping 58.8 percent.[7] However, the average dumping margin varies widely depending upon the method used to calculate the normal value. As table 5.1 shows, during the 1995 to 1998 period, the average margin on (affirmative) cases that compared the U.S. price to the exporter's home market price was just 7.36 percent. When Commerce compared the U.S. price to its constructed value, the average margin was 35.70 percent. In cases involving nonmarket economies, such as China and the former Soviet Union, the average margin was about 67 percent. In cases

[5]In the early 1990s, the U.S. International Trade Commission (1995, 4–3) surveyed petitioners and found a simple petition would cost about $250,000. The price is much higher today, particularly if the petitioner wants the law firm to provide additional support for the petition.

[6]Lindsey and Ikenson 2003, 24–25. From 1980 to 1992, Commerce ruled that dumping had occurred in 93 percent of all cases. Congressional Budget Office 1994, 50.

[7]Lindsey and Ikenson 2003, 26. The average antidumping duty imposed has risen over time. The average duty was 22 percent in the period from 1981 to 1983 and 56.8 percent in the period from 1991 to 1995. Congressional Budget Office 1998, 25.

_____Table 5.1
Antidumping Margins and Calculation Method, 1995–1998

Calculation Method	Determinations (Affirmative Only)	Average Dumping Margin (Affirmative Only)
U.S. Prices to Home Market Prices	4 (2)	4.00% (7.36%)
Constructed Value	20 (14)	25.07% (35.70%)
Non-Market Economy	47 (28)	40.03% (67.05%)
"Facts Available"	36 (36)	95.58% (95.58%)
Total	141 (107)	44.68% (58.79%)

Source: Lindsey and Ikenson 2003, 26.
Note: Not all methods shown.

using "facts available," in which Commerce essentially accepted the data presented by the petitioner, the average margin was nearly 96 percent. Because of a greater reliance on the constructed value method over the price comparison method, the average dumping margin has steadily increased over time.[8]

When U.S. prices are compared to actual foreign market prices, rather than to some constructed value, the dumping margins appear to be quite low. Yet even when a foreign firm charges exactly the same price in the U.S. market as in its home market, dumping can be found to exist. This is because Commerce compares the average of the foreign firm's home price to the prices charged on individual sales in the United States. If any *individual* U.S. price is below the *average* home market price, which must be the case if there is any movement in the prices over time, then dumping is found to occur. Instances in which the U.S. price exceeds the foreign price are ignored. This not only guarantees a finding of dumping, but artificially inflates the dumping margin.[9]

In contrast, something is clearly amiss when a method other than the price comparison approach is employed. When Commerce is

[8] See Blonigen 2006.
[9] Ikenson 2004. In 2006, the WTO Appellate Body upheld a ruling that the zeroing method is inconsistent with the fair comparison required by Article 2.4.2 of the WTO Agreement on Antidumping. The case was brought by the EU, and U.S. adherence has been mixed.

unable to collect enough data on the exporter's home market prices, it may resort to the constructed value method. When Commerce undertakes a constructed value calculation, it attempts to estimate the foreign exporter's costs of production plus an allowance for administrative, selling, and general expenses and profits. Prior to 1995, U.S. antidumping practice was to augment the estimated costs of production by at least 10 percent for administrative expenses and at least 8 percent for profits.[10] Multilateral agreements reached under the Uruguay Round mandate that Commerce cannot tack on these arbitrary amounts to the estimated costs, but must use the actual administrative expenses and the actual profit, when available. However, there is still room for Commerce to use questionable numbers and thereby raise the dumping margin.

When dealing with nonmarket economies, such as China and the states of the former Soviet Union, where prices may not be market-determined, Commerce estimates production costs using wage rates and other factor costs from a surrogate country of similar level of economic development. For example, in estimating China's costs of farming crawfish in 1997, Commerce used the cost of fish caught at sea in "comparable" economies with freer markets, such as India, Pakistan, Sri Lanka, and Indonesia, and took transport costs within China from a 1994 newspaper report on trucking costs in India. Not surprisingly, this method leads to unusually large dumping margins. In this case, Commerce announced dumping margins ranging from 85 to 201 percent, implying that Chinese crawfish farmers generously decided to sell their product for just one-third to two-thirds of production costs.

In another case using the constructed value method, Commerce once determined (with apparent precision) that natural bristle paintbrushes from China were sold at less than their fair value with a dumping margin of 351.9 percent, and imposed tariffs of the same amount. Such high dumping margins are typical in cases involving China. In June 2008, Commerce made its final determination in the case of laminated woven sacks from China and issued the following company-specific margins: Shandong Shouguang Jianyuan Chun at 352.82 percent, Shandong Qilu Plastic Fabric Group at 304.40 percent, Han Shing Chemical at 223.74 percent, and so forth. In July 2008, Commerce ruled that the dumping

[10] Congressional Budget Office 1994, 31.

margin on sodium nitrite from China was 190.74 percent. The finding of such high dumping margins is not limited to nonmarket economies. In June 2003, in a case involving polyethylene retail carrier bags (PRCBs, otherwise known as the thin plastic shopping bags one finds at grocery stores), the Commerce Department found margins as high as 123 percent for Thailand, 102 percent for Malaysia, and 77 percent for China.

The International Trade Commission's role in an antidumping case is to determine if the domestic industry has suffered or is threatened with "material injury" as a result of the less-than-fair-value imports. The definition of material injury, according to the law, is "harm which is not inconsequential, immaterial, or unimportant."[11] Only the harm to the competing industry is considered, not the harm or injury to consumers or other domestic industries that result from the imposition of import duties.

While Commerce almost always finds dumping, the injury determination is a more difficult hurdle for the domestic petitioner to clear. This is because of the injury standard itself and because the ITC is a quasi-independent agency (as opposed to Commerce, which is typically an advocate of the domestic industry in the process). Still, the ITC ruled affirmatively in about 83 percent of final determinations during the period 1999 to 2002.[12] Economic factors, such as changes in the industry's output, employment, and capacity utilization, are the main determinants of a favorable injury finding. But political factors, such as whether the industry is a constituent of the chairman of the ITC's congressional oversight committee, also appear to matter.[13]

If dumping is found to exist and the domestic industry is deemed to have suffered material injury, then antidumping duties are imposed. At the end of 2007, the United States had 232 AD duty orders in effect on goods coming from thirty-nine countries. The main targets of AD duties are China (62), the European Union (36), Japan (21), and Taiwan (15). Almost half of the duties are on iron and steel products, with chemicals a distant second.[14] AD orders existed on such narrowly defined goods as

[11] U.S. House of Representatives 2003b, 553.
[12] Lindsey and Ikenson 2003, 3. The ITC ruled affirmatively in 66 percent of final determinations during the period 1980 to 1992. Congressional Budget Office 1994, 50.
[13] See the survey by Blonigen and Prusa 2003.
[14] World Trade Organization 2008, 23.

_____Table 5.2
Trade Effects of Antidumping Duties (Comparing year prior and following initiation of AD investigation)

AD Duties	Import Volume	Import Price (Unit Value)
Over 50 percent	−73%	33%
Between 20 percent and 50 percent	−22%	2%
Under 20 percent	−16%	−10%
Nonaffirmative Decision	−3%	3%

Source: U.S. International Trade Commission 1995, 3–9.
Note: Import price effect does not include the AD duties.

frozen concentrated orange juice from Brazil, cotton shop towels from Bangladesh and China, oil country tubular goods from Canada, fresh salmon from Chile and Norway, paper clips from China, large newspaper printing presses from Germany, stainless steel wire rod from France and elsewhere, fresh kiwifruit from New Zealand, pasta from Italy and Turkey, aspirin from Turkey, and a host of other products.[15]

Of course, the United States is hardly alone in imposing antidumping duties. As of June 2007, India had 162 antidumping duties in place, followed by the EU (149), China (103), Turkey (99), Mexico (69), Argentina (62), South Africa (61), and Brazil (50).[16]

What happens when AD duties are imposed? Not surprisingly, imports fall sharply. Looking at table 5.2, we can see that imports subject to AD duties of over 50 percent fell 73 percent in volume and rose 33 percent in price, on average, from the year before the petition to the year after the petition. Imports subject to AD duties in the 20 to 50 percent range fell 22 percent in volume and rose 2 percent in price. The ITC study on which the table is based also found that developing countries were disproportionately harmed by AD duties: the quantity of their imports tended to fall over twice as much as imports from developed countries.

To a large extent, however, imports from countries not subject to the AD duties fill the void left by those smacked with the AD duties. This is because AD duties are only imposed on imports from countries named in the petition, leaving the market open to others who can produce similar

[15] For updated statistics and information on the administration of U.S. antidumping laws, see http://www.ita.doc.gov.
[16] World Trade Organization 2008a, 29.

_____**Table 5.3**
Evidence of Trade Diversion in Antidumping Actions

	Import Volume	Import Price (Unit Value)
Affirmative, subject country	−32%	5%
Affirmative, nonsubject country	24%	−5%
Nonaffirmative, subject country	−24%	4%
Nonaffirmative, nonsubject country	19%	−3%

Source: U.S. International Trade Commission 1995, 3–15.

Note: Affirmative denotes cases in which AD duties were imposed; subject are imports subject to the duties and nonsubject indicates imports from other countries or firms not subject to the duties.

products. Table 5.3 indicates that while imports from countries affected by the AD duties fell by 32 percent, imports of the same product from countries not subject to the duties rose 24 percent. Because of this effect, antidumping petitions are often filed sequentially to squash the imports that arise from other sources as a result of the initial antidumping action.

For example, Micron Technology, a producer of dynamic random access memory (DRAM) computer chips in Boise, Idaho, filed an AD petition against DRAM imports from Japan in 1985. After the imposition of restrictions on Japanese exports, foreign DRAM production shifted to South Korea, so Micron filed an AD petition against Korean producers in 1991. After Korean exports were similarly restricted, Taiwanese producers entered the market, so Micron filed an AD petition against DRAM exports from that country in 1998. The story is similar in the case of salmon. Antidumping duties were imposed against imports of fresh salmon from Norway in 1991. After Chile began to develop its fishing industry and filled the void left by the Norwegians, they too were hit with AD duties in 1998.

The simplest way for domestic petitioners to avoid this problem is to file multiple petitions against several sources. When the Coalition for Fair Preserved Mushroom Trade filed an AD petition concerning imports of preserved mushrooms in 1998, for example, it targeted imports from Chile, China, India, and Indonesia all at the same time. During 1999 to 2001, when the steel industry filed numerous antidumping cases, they named twelve countries in cold-rolled steel products, twelve countries in steel concrete reinforcing bars, and twenty countries in cold-rolled carbon steel flat products. The countries ranged from the usual suspects of Japan and Korea to more obscure producers such as Latvia and Moldova.

In 2004, the Shrimp Trade Action Committee filed a case on fresh and canned warm-water shrimp against Brazil, Ecuador, India, Thailand, China, and Vietnam.

Congress facilitated the move toward multiple filings by changing the law in 1984. Prior to that time, the injury determination was conducted on a country-by-country basis, even if multiple petitions were filed. After the 1984 change, the ITC had to consider the combined impact of imports from all named countries on the domestic industry. The cumulation provision is estimated to have raised the probability of an affirmative decision by 20 to 30 percent, thereby changing the ITC's determination from negative to positive in one-third of such cases.[17] This, in turn, has given petitioners an additional incentive to file petitions against multiple countries.

Sometimes petitioners exclude certain countries from petitions as a matter of corporate strategy. For example, in 1994, the Maui Pineapple Company in Hawaii filed an AD petition against imports of canned pineapples from Thailand, resulting in the imposition of AD duties up to 51 percent, depending on the company. Thailand's canned pineapple exports to the United States fell from $101 million in 1993 to $51 million in 1997. Over the same period, imports of canned pineapple from Indonesia jumped from $9 million to $51 million because that country's exports were not subject to AD duties. But Maui did not file an AD petition against Indonesian imports because at that time it was forming a joint venture with one of the country's largest pineapple producers. Similarly, in 1994 Bic filed a petition alleging that disposable lighters from China and Thailand were being dumped in the U.S. market, but did not include Mexico in the petition because Bic had a factory there.[18]

It is important to note that trade diversion occurs even in cases where the final ITC injury decision is negative and no duties are imposed. Even when the domestic industry was found not to have suffered injury, imports from countries that had been the target of the case fell 24 percent on average, while imports from countries not targeted rose 19 percent. Thus, simply filing an antidumping petition can reduce imports from targeted sources even if duties are not imposed. According to one

[17] Hansen and Prusa 1996.
[18] *Rushford Report*, September 1999, 3.

study, when a petition is ultimately rejected, imports from the sources named in the petition fall by about 15 to 20 percent, whereas if the petition is accepted, imports fall about 50 to 70 percent.[19]

A reason for this "chilling effect" on imports is the uncertainty surrounding the AD process: if dumping is found, domestic importers will be liable for the payment of dumping duties after Commerce issues its preliminary determination. To minimize their potential financial exposure, importers quickly stop purchasing from the foreign suppliers named in the petition. There is also an "investigation effect" on imports when an antidumping petition is filed: before Commerce has even made a preliminary determination about dumping, import volumes fall and prices rise by about one-half of the full effect of imposing duties.[20]

As if there was not already sufficient incentive for firms to file antidumping petitions, Senator Robert Byrd (D-W.Va.) opened the door to more mischief in the fall of 2000. Senator Byrd slipped into an agricultural appropriations bill a provision that hands over all the revenue from antidumping duties to the petitioning industry. Although the Clinton administration opposed the measure, the president signed the bill for its other provisions. During the period that the Byrd amendment was in effect, petitioning firms were not only able to charge domestic consumers higher prices for their products, but received a check from the government for a share of the tariff revenues. Studies have shown that this increased the incentive to file petitions by a significant margin.[21]

The Byrd amendment also led to a scramble for government cash, particularly because the legislation is retroactive. In 2001, companies put in requests for $1.2 trillion in back antidumping tariff revenue. The chief beneficiaries have been two ball bearing companies whose lawyers helped write the Byrd legislation. Torrington Company received $63 million in Byrd money in 2001 but has sought reimbursements of $23.4 billion (its sales in 2001 amounted to $1.1 billion).[22] The Byrd provision encourages domestic firms to become bounty hunters and start filing AD petitions to receive tariff revenue payments from the government.

---

[19] Prusa 2001.

[20] See Blonigen and Prusa 2003.

[21] Reynolds 2006. For some of the issues raised by the Byrd amendment, see U.S. GAO 2005.

[22] King 2002.

However, in a dispute initiated by the EU and seven other countries, a WTO panel ruled in 2002 that the subsidy was inconsistent with the multilateral rules, a finding affirmed by the WTO's Appellate Body in 2003. In 2005, Congress repealed the Byrd amendment, but still allowed the distribution of antidumping tariff revenue to members of the affected U.S. industry who supported the petition for investigation on goods that entered before October 2007. The government disbursed about $380 million in FY2006 and, since the amendment came into force, the government has disbursed some $1.9 billion in revenue to petitioners.

However, the issue is still alive: the original complainants have charged that the United States has not fully complied with the WTO ruling and some members of Congress want to re-enact the Byrd amendment.

_____The Costs of Antidumping

Despite the apparent ease with which domestic firms can obtain some form of protection under the antidumping laws, only a tiny fraction of total U.S. imports are covered by AD duties. AD orders covered just 0.1 percent of all imports in 2007.[23] In any given year, the value of imports targeted by antidumping petitions is usually much less than this amount. Given these small figures, does the antidumping process really matter?

There are several reasons why antidumping continues to merit close scrutiny. First, these tariffs quickly add up. The net welfare cost of AD and CVD actions in the United States was a whopping $4 billion in 1993.[24] With the demise of the Multi-Fiber Arrangement in 2005, it is likely that they are collectively the most costly of all U.S. import restrictions.

These costs are only going to mount over time as more cases are filed. This is because AD duties are hard to remove once they are imposed. The average duration of AD measures in place is eleven years.[25] The oldest antidumping duty in place dates from 1973, and more than thirty have been imposed for more than twenty years. One of the few reforms of AD actions in the Uruguay Round was to introduce a sunset rule starting in 1995. This required that all AD duties be terminated after five

[23] World Trade Organization 2008, 23. In 1991, the figure was 1.8 percent; U.S. International Trade Commission 1995, 4–1.
[24] Gallaway, Blonigen, and Flynn 1999.
[25] World Trade Organization 2008, 23.

years unless a review finds that this would lead to a recurrence of dumping and injury. Yet Commerce is unlikely to revoke an antidumping order over the objections of the domestic industry. In 210 reviews conducted from 2000 to 2007, only fifty-eight duties were revoked.[26]

Second, the coverage figures understate the harm in antidumping actions. The very existence of the antidumping law allows it to be used as a tool to enforce collusive agreements. For example, in 1989 U.S. producers of ferrosilicon formed a cartel and reduced output. The lower output was used to prove injury and justify the imposition of antidumping duties against five foreign competitors. When Brazil started exporting ferrosilicon in place of the others, their producers were invited to join the U.S. cartel. When they refused, they too were hit with an antidumping case.[27]

When an exporter is confronted with the prospect of potentially severe duties that exporters from other countries will not have to endure, the target has a powerful incentive to negotiate some sort of export restraint agreement that will allow the exporter to avoid the imposition of duties. In some cases, the foreign exporter tries to reach a suspension agreement with Commerce (and approved by the petitioner) that terminates the petition. The quantity of imports falls by the same margin in cases that are settled as those in which duties are imposed, although the import price does not rise as much in settled cases.[28] The Uruguay Round also allows "price undertakings," in which exporters can agree to minimum export prices in order to avoid the imposition of duties. Thus, even when no duties are imposed, antidumping can result in trade restrictions and even collusive outcomes.[29]

Third, the antidumping process is so heavily biased against foreign firms that it is prone to abuse and manipulation by domestic firms.

[26] World Trade Organization 2008b, 40. In 180 sunset cases considered between July 1998 and December 1999, the ITC revoked AD or CVD duties only 31 percent of the time. Moore 1999.

[27] Eventually, criminal and civil legal actions were taken against the cartel members. Pierce 2000.

[28] Only about 10 percent of all petitions in the United States were withdrawn in the 1990s. Withdrawn petitions used to be considered a signal of a collusive settlement, but Taylor (2004) shows this not to be the case. However, Rutkowski (2006) questions this and shows that withdrawals may be related to collusion in the EU.

[29] See Moore 2005.

The problem is not that the process is overtly political and subject to political influence, although that problem can arise in some high-profile cases. Rather, AD rules are intentionally stacked in favor of the domestic petitioner, both in reaching a conclusion that dumping has occurred and in the size of the dumping margin. Even the Congressional Budget Office notes that the Commerce Department "effectively serves as investigator, prosecutor, judge, and jury in dumping and subsidy determinations." And although it should be neutral in these roles, Commerce is "actually an advocate of one of the parties to the case."[30]

The antidumping process is riddled with subtle tricks and arbitrary biases that invariably favor the domestic petitioner, making it ironic that AD rules are a part of the "fair trade" laws. The application of AD measures often hinges on a narrow technicality, such as the definition of the relevant industry. In the case of cut flowers from Colombia, the ITC initially ruled that the domestic industry was not materially injured. After Commerce later accepted petitions maintaining that each individual flower species was a different "industry" (the rose "industry," the chrysanthemum "industry," etc.), the ITC then made an affirmative injury ruling. In the case of frozen concentrated orange juice, Commerce ruled that fresh oranges and industrial concentrate orange juice are "like products" even though the markets and pricing for the two products are quite different.

Even the Commerce Department's Office of Inspector General was critical of the way that the Department's Office of Import Administration handled the eighty-four antidumping and countervailing duty petitions filed by the steel industry in June 1992. The office said that the agency "adopted several controversial and confusing policies that undermined the principles of transparency and consistency . . . [and were] not only inconsistent with past practice, but were also applied inconsistently from one case to the next." The report added that Import Administration "applied policies that made reporting more onerous for respondents, caused confusion among analysts, and made IA's decisions appear arbitrary, even to its own staff."[31]

Finally, perhaps the biggest concern about antidumping is that the antidumping genie is out of the bottle and has spread around the

[30] Congressional Budget Office 1994, 41.
[31] U.S. Department of Commerce 1993, 20.

world. Whereas antidumping actions were once instituted mainly by the United States, European Union, Australia, and Canada, now developing countries (such as Mexico, India, China, Argentina, South Africa, and others) have copied them and have become aggressive users of these measures.[32] The more this "legal" form of protectionism has been adopted around the world, the harder it will be to contain its adverse effects on trade.

Furthermore, the motivation for this spread appears to be retaliation for developed countries' use of antidumping, rather than an increase in unfair trade.[33] This means that U.S. exporters may face more accusations that they are dumping in foreign markets.[34] For example, Micron Technology, previously mentioned as the DRAM producer who filed a series of petitions, was itself accused of dumping memory chips in Taiwan shortly after it succeeded in getting AD duties imposed on Taiwanese exports. And even though the ITC rejected a petition accusing Mexico of dumping emulsion styrenebutadiene rubber, the U.S. petitioner soon faced charges by its Mexican competitor of dumping the same product in that country. If antidumping actions remain unchecked, such retaliatory cases can only be expected to multiply in coming years. Yet the United States refused to put antidumping reform on the agenda for future trade negotiations until the WTO ministerial conference in Doha, Qatar, in November 2001. It is difficult to be optimistic that antidumping policies will change anytime soon.[35]

Is Antidumping Defensible?

The antidumping process involves many arbitrary judgments and is subject to abuse. Can any economic rationale be mustered in favor of the AD laws? The problem is that price discrimination, charging different prices in different markets, is a normal business practice and an accepted feature

[32] See Prusa 2001 and Zanardi 2006.

[33] Vandenbussche and Zanardi 2008. While the Congressional Budget Office did not find systematic evidence prior to 1995 that other countries were singling out American firms for antidumping enforcement in retaliation for AD actions, evidence did "lend some credence to fears that U.S. policy may be starting to come back to haunt U.S. exporters as other countries follow its lead." Congressional Budget Office 1998, xiv.

[34] Feinberg and Reynolds 2008.

[35] Moore 2007.

of domestic competition. Exporters often find that competition is more intense in the international market than in their home market, where they have a more secure position with domestic consumers. Therefore, exporters have to offer price discounts in foreign markets.

On economic grounds, the fact that a firm charges different prices in different markets is neither unfair nor a problem unless it harms competition (such as through anticompetitive actions or predatory practices) or reflects a market-distorting policy. If geared toward preventing these actions, antidumping policy could have some merit as a means of preserving competition or correcting alleged market distortions. Unfortunately, the antidumping laws are not written to identify and respond to such situations. This leaves the impression that the laws exist only to protect domestic firms if they can jump through a few bureaucratic hoops.

For example, the antidumping laws might be worthwhile if they prevented predatory pricing by foreign exporters. Predatory pricing would occur when an exporter prices its goods below cost in an effort to eliminate American producers and achieve a monopoly position. Firms engaging in predatory pricing must be prepared to incur substantial losses initially and then recoup those losses through the future exercise of monopoly position. But this makes sense only if the firm can effectively knock out most of its competitors in the United States and in other countries. Were the Bangladesh shop towel producers trying to eliminate their foreign rivals and achieve a monopoly position? Were the flower growers from Colombia trying to do the same? Most foreign exporters want to receive as high a price as possible from their sales. Few companies entertain the delusion of driving all of their competitors out of business in the world market.

In fact, in the overwhelming majority of AD cases, such predatory motives can be ruled out as utterly implausible. One researcher examined the structural characteristics of every one of the 282 industries involved in every dumping case in the 1980s in which duties were imposed or in which the case was suspended or terminated.[36] To isolate the cases in which predatory pricing might be considered plausible, she first eliminated all cases in which the industry in the United States and in the challenged country was relatively unconcentrated. These were excluded

[36] Shin 1998.

on the grounds that barriers to entry in such industries are probably not substantial. And without barriers to entry, anticompetitive practices are unlikely to exist because even if the firm drives rivals out of business, it cannot raise prices to finance the losses sustained in the price war if other firms can simply reenter the market once prices go up.

The researcher also eliminated cases in which there were multiple exporters from a single country or from several countries, reasoning that successful collusion by such firms would be unlikely and that there are enough firms to preserve competition. Finally, she eliminated all cases in which the import penetration level was not significant, or in which import growth was not rapid, since the imports would be unlikely to create market power if they did not comprise a large share of the U.S. market. In the end, only thirty-nine cases were left, just 14 percent of all those considered, in which the industries were characterized by substantial domestic or foreign concentration. Of these remaining cases in which the preconditions for predation did exist, we cannot say for sure that predation was in fact a motive, only that it could not be ruled out.

The antidumping statute is not employed to prevent predatory conduct or preserve competition, but simply to protect the domestic industry from foreign competition—at the expense of domestic consumers, of course. One legal scholar concludes that while the antidumping laws were "originally marketed as anti-predation measures, they are now written in a way that compels the administering authorities to impose antidumping measures in a vastly broader class of cases—all instances in which dumping causes material harm to competing domestic firms."[37] A ITC commissioner once tried to shift the interpretation toward an anti-predation remedy. But petitioners appealed to the U.S. Court of International Trade, which ruled that focusing on competition effects "seems to assume that the purpose of the antidumping statute is merely to prevent a particular type of 'injury to competition' rather than merely 'material injury' to industry."[38]

Some antidumping advocates claim that foreign firms have a protected home market in which they can earn high profits, and from which they can subsidize export sales. In this view, any price discrimination

[37] Sykes 1998, 29–30.
[38] Sykes 1998, 29–30.

due to a sanctuary home market counts as a market-distorting practice that antidumping should attempt to remedy. But as one antidumping critic aptly notes, "the [antidumping] law lacks any mechanism for determining whether the price practices it condemns as unfair have any connection to market-distorting policies abroad."[39] The law does not distinguish cases in which there may be a sanctuary market effect, or ask if dumping is at all related to market distortions. If antidumping advocates are sincere in their desire for an antipredation remedy that is not simply protectionism, they should be willing to amend the current law and include an explicit test for the protected sanctuary home market that is often alleged to exist.

The problem with antidumping is not just the way the law is administered. The fundamental problem is that antidumping laws are written with the presumption that price discrimination is a problem. But there is nothing inherently harmful or anticompetitive about price discrimination. Price discrimination is an accepted feature of domestic competition. It would be surprising if domestic prices were *exactly* the same as an exporter's home price.[40] As already noted, the government rarely undertakes direct price comparisons when making a dumping determination, but more frequently makes arbitrary calculations about production costs. The result is that "dumping is whatever you can get the government to act against under the dumping law."[41] It is hard to avoid the conclusion that the antidumping laws are simply a popular means by which domestic firms can stifle foreign competition under the pretense of "fair trade."

Except in cases of gross abuse, antidumping is most frequently used by firms to insulate themselves from falling import prices. Some industries will always be faced with import surges, such as the domestic steel industry in the aftermath of the Asian financial crisis of 1997–98,

---

[39] Lindsey 2001, 1.

[40] "In the typical antidumping investigation, the DOC compares home-market and U.S. prices of physically different goods, in different kinds of packaging, sold at different times, in different and fluctuating currencies, to different customers at different levels of trade, in different quantities, with different freight and other movement costs, different credit terms, and other differences directly associated selling expenses (e.g., commissions, warranties, royalties, and advertising). Is it any wonder that the prices aren't identical?" Lindsey and Ikenson 2003, 21.

[41] Finger 1993, viii.

when a collapse in foreign demand sent world steel prices tumbling. After the domestic computer production outstripped demand in 1985, world prices of semiconductors fell through the floor, triggering a round of dumping complaints.

In such cases, the problem facing the petitioning industry is not any price differential between markets, that is, foreign firms charging a higher price in their domestic market than in the United States. The afflicted industry would find no consolation if the U.S. price were higher than the foreign price even as both were falling sharply. Rather, the basic problem for the industry is that prices everywhere are falling due to unforeseen circumstances. It may be reasonable to provide an industry facing such difficulties with temporary protection without any claim that trade is "unfair." And that is precisely what the escape clause is designed to do.

The Escape Clause

If a domestic industry is suffering as a result of import competition and yet does not allege that the imports are unfairly dumped or subsidized, the industry can still receive temporary protection. Ever since the passage of the Reciprocal Trade Agreements Act in 1934, when the United States embarked on its policy of negotiating tariff reductions with other countries, Congress recognized that trade liberalization might force difficult economic adjustments on particular sectors of the economy. Because of this, Congress insisted that if lower tariffs brought about serious injury to certain domestic industries, they should be provided with temporary relief to help them adjust to the new conditions of trade. To this end, the "escape clause" provides a mechanism for domestic industries to get a temporary exception to any negotiated tariff reduction.

Section 201 of the Trade Act of 1974 provides the current statutory basis for the escape clause.[42] It allows representatives of an industry (a trade association, firm, union, or group of workers) to file a petition with the International Trade Commission for temporary relief from import competition. The petition must include a specific plan that details

---

[42] The escape clause is also contained in Article 19 of the GATT and in the Agreement on Safeguards as part of the Uruguay Round negotiations.

how protection will be used to help the industry adjust. The ITC must then determine if the imports are, or threaten to be, "a substantial cause of serious injury," where "substantial cause" is defined as "a cause which is important and not less than any other cause."[43] Cutting through the legal verbiage, this simply means that imports must be the most important cause of injury. This legalistic language is nontrivial: The ITC rejected a Section 201 petition from the automobile industry in 1980 on the grounds that the most important source of the industry's difficulty was not imports, but the recession of that year.

If the ITC reaches an affirmative finding of injury, it must then recommend an appropriate remedy to the president. This remedy can include action on trade, such as higher tariffs, or other policies that would help facilitate the adjustment efforts of the domestic industry. The president then has wide discretion as to what action is taken. The import relief can take place over a period of four to eight years and must apply to imports from all sources (unlike antidumping, which, as we have seen, is selective).

Section 201 has been criticized as being merely a protectionist loophole that allows firms to obtain protection, with no allegation of unfair trade, and therefore permits a country to backslide away from open markets.[44] But such provisions function as essential safeguards that make trade liberalizing agreements possible. As other economists have noted, "Safeguard provisions are often critical to the existence and operation of trade-liberalizing agreements, as they function as both insurance mechanisms and safety-valves. They provide governments with the means to renege on specific liberalization commitments—subject to certain conditions—should the need for this arise (safety valve). Without them governments may refrain from signing an agreement that reduces protection substantially (insurance motive)."[45] The presence of the escape clause, it

[43] U.S. House of Representatives 2003a, 666.

[44] Expressing skepticism about the "safety valve" explanation for the escape clause, Sykes (2003) argues that the likelihood of direct protectionist legislation decreases if such legislation violates international obligations and results in international sanction. Therefore, "the ability of Congress to resist special interest pressures for protection . . . would likely be greater in the absence of Article XIX." Finger (1996) is equally skeptical about safeguards, dubbing them "legalized backsliding."

[45] Hoekman and Kostecki 2009, 303.

can be argued, has encouraged cautious governments to liberalize trade more than might otherwise be the case.

Section 201 was invoked frequently in the 1970s, but has been used only sporadically in recent decades. Just nineteen cases were filed in the 1980s and only ten cases in the 1990s. At the end of 2008, no safeguard tariffs were in place. This is partly because it has proven too difficult a way of getting protection: of the nineteen cases considered in the 1980s, for example, the ITC ruled affirmatively in only seven. Even then, there is no guarantee that the president will provide relief to the industry, and in practice presidents are often reluctant to grant it. This record is why Senator Ernest Hollings (D-S.C.) once made the dismissive quip that "Section 201 is for suckers."[46] The escape clause has been completely overshadowed by antidumping, where the injury standard is not as strict and presidential action is not required. In view of the ease with which antidumping actions can be initiated and affect trade, it comes as no surprise that firms have avoided Section 201.

The steel industry recently discovered two more reasons why escape clause actions are of limited value—administrative exemptions and WTO review. As a result of a campaign promise, President Bush initiated a large steel Section 201 case in 2001 and later imposed duties of up to 30 percent for three years on several types of steel products. But imports from countries having free trade agreements with the United States—Canada, Mexico, Israel, and Jordan—were exempt from the duties, and the Bush administration granted many additional product exclusions that allowed the import of specialized steel products. The European Union and seven additional countries also challenged the steel tariffs at the WTO, claiming they violated international agreements. A WTO panel ruled that the safeguard decision was inconsistent with the Agreement on Safeguards, which allows tariffs to be imposed only when foreign products are being imported in a quantity sufficiently increased so as to cause serious injury. But the 2002 safeguard action was taken well after the Asian financial crisis of 1997–98 caused U.S. steel imports to swell, and imports generally declined from 1999 to 2001. In addition, the panel indicated that the U.S. recession rather than imports may have been the major cause of injury.

[46] Quoted in Low 1993, 57.

The Bush administration faced the decision of whether to maintain the safeguard duties and face possible foreign retaliation for violating the WTO agreement, or to rescind the duties and comply with the WTO finding. When the EU threatened to impose tariffs on $2.2 billion of U.S. exports, the government decided to lift the duties in December 2003, after just twenty-one months. The safeguard action proved to be much less valuable to the steel industry than it had hoped.[47]

With the increasing abuse of antidumping measures, escape clause actions have come to be viewed in a more benign light. Section 201 is now seen as a potential solution to the problem of antidumping. Escape clause actions have several advantages over antidumping measures: there are no bogus claims of unfair trade, they provide greater flexibility in the scope and duration of nondiscriminatory protection, and the president is allowed to take into account the overall economic, security, and political interests of the United States in tailoring a relief package. Relaxing the high standards of the escape clause would make it a more attractive method of obtaining import relief and provide an opportunity to rein in the use of antidumping. The danger, of course, is that Congress might simply expand the use of the escape clause without constraining the use of antidumping.

Clearly, the challenge for policymakers operating in an era of greater economic integration is one of balance—making the escape clause available without compromising open markets: "If the standards for obtaining import-related remedies are too restrictive, the escape clause mechanism cannot serve as an effective shock absorber for protectionist pressures. On the other hand, if the eligibility criteria are too weak, any domestic industry that faces import competition may become eligible for temporary protection."[48] This trade-off is one of the most difficult challenges in trade policy.

Does Temporary Relief from Imports Work?

Some form of safeguards seems to be a political necessity. And we have seen that the escape clause can be a desirable alternative to antidumping actions. But does temporary relief from imports actually provide a rem-

[47] For an overview of this case, see Read 2005.
[48] Lawrence and Litan 1986, 79.

edy for the ills afflicting the domestic industry? Although protection has been justified as a way of revitalizing certain industries, it may not be able to accomplish this objective.[49]

Ideally, such relief would offer temporary protection to industries that compete against imports, in exchange for assurances that the industry will undertake measures to adjust to the new competition. But in providing temporary relief, the government encounters a problem with time consistency. The industry would like to reap the benefits of protection without undertaking the costs of adjustment. When the government cannot credibly commit to eliminating protection in the future, an industry may find itself able to perpetuate the protection by not investing sufficiently in cost reductions. If the government bases its decision to renew protection on whether the industry has adjusted to the foreign competition, then the industry may have an incentive not to adjust in order to trigger a renewal of protection. Even making trade relief contingent on such investment does not eliminate the time consistency problem. Temporary, contingent protection may still become permanent protection.[50]

This pattern of repeated renewals of protection is sometimes seen in practice. Some industries have used temporary protection to adjust to competition from imports. The automobile, consumer electronics, and semiconductor industries have received temporary protection at one time or another, but adjusted to the new conditions of competition. This does not mean that protection helped promote the adjustment, just that protection was temporary. Indeed, blocking imports failed to solve the fundamental problem these industries faced, either because foreign competition was located in the United States through direct investments or because the industry depended heavily upon foreign export sales and the importation of components. Given the inability of trade policy to solve the underlying problems confronting these industries, domestic firms adjusted by adopting new technology, moving to new market niches, and forming global alliances.[51]

[49] In addition to the discussion of certain industries below, Krueger (1996) presents a series of case studies on protection that examine whether import limits actually helped the domestic industry. Baldwin (1988) also discusses the inefficacy of protectionist measures in helping domestic industries.

[50] Tornell 1991.

[51] Another way to adjust to import competition is simply to fade away, as has been the fate of the domestic footwear industry. Import penetration in the domestic footwear

Other industries have essentially received permanent protection over the past few decades by seeking and repeatedly receiving "temporary" protection. Two that stand out are the steel industry and the textile and apparel industry. Both face long-term structural adjustments to domestic and foreign competition and have stubbornly resisted pressures to adapt. The steel industry suffers from excess capacity worldwide, a strong union that has helped price domestic producers out of the world market, and growing domestic competition from smaller mills. The textiles and apparel industry, on the other hand, is struggling against the loss of comparative advantage in labor-intensive manufactures by becoming more capital-intensive, upgrading technology, and outsourcing.

The steel industry has received nearly continuous protection for over thirty years and is still seeking limits on imports. From 1969 to 1974, the large, integrated producers were protected from imports by a series of voluntary restraint agreements (VRAs). From 1978 to 1982, a Trigger Price Mechanism, consisting of minimum import prices, was in effect. From 1982 to 1992, a new round of VRAs was in place. When the industry failed to persuade the government to renew the VRAs, the industry filed a massive number of AD and CVD complaints in 1992–93. When the Asian financial crisis struck in 1997–98, sharply depressing world steel prices, the industry again filed many AD cases. As a result of the Section 201 escape clause case initiated by President Bush in 2001, the industry benefited from 30 percent tariffs on imports during 2002 and 2003.

Yet all this trade protection has never been enough for the steel industry. In fact, there are two steel industries in the United States—large integrated firms and smaller minimills. The big integrated firms—U.S. Steel, the former Bethlehem Steel, and others—use blast furnaces to create steel from raw inputs and then shape it into various products. Production is concentrated in Pennsylvania, Ohio, and West Virginia, and labor is represented by the United Steelworkers of America. The management and unions of Big Steel perpetually blame their problems on imports and are continually calling for import restraints to allow the industry to revitalize itself.

---

market rose from 13 percent in 1966 to 90 percent in 1996, while employment fell from 233,400 in 1966 to 46,100 in 1996. See Freeman and Kleiner (2005) on how the remaining firms in the domestic industry have adjusted their labor practices in order to survive.

The smaller minimills take scrap steel and use electric-arc furnaces to produce various final products. Because they do not require iron ore and coal supplies, these firms are not geographically concentrated but spread around the country close to the markets they serve. Minimills have much lower costs than the big integrated steel firms, partly because their workers are not unionized. As a result, the minimills have grabbed U.S. market share away from the big integrated producers. The minimills accounted for about 10 percent of U.S. production in the late 1960s, but nearly 50 percent today. As the market share held by imports has remained steady at about 20 percent, almost all of the erosion in the market share held by the integrated producers is due to the minimills.

Thus, changes in market demand and competition from the minimills are mainly responsible for pushing several large steel producers into bankruptcy. Unlike imports, this domestic competition cannot be stopped at the border and is slowly forcing the integrated producers to adjust. But the process has been prolonged in part due to import restraints and the recalcitrant steelworkers union. The strength of the "steel triangle"—the Big Steel firms, the United Steelworkers union, and their powerful representatives in the Congressional Steel Caucus—have ensured that the large producers continue to receive corporate welfare at the expense of taxpayers and consumers. In 2002, for example, the Pension Benefit Guaranty Corporation, a U.S. government agency, took over the pension plans of several steel firms whose unfunded pension liabilities exceed $8 billion.[52]

The textiles and apparel industry has also used its political influence to maintain an array of barriers designed to stop foreign competition. The United States negotiated export restrictions on cotton textile products with Japan in the 1950s. Although these trade restrictions were designed as a temporary measure to give the industry some breathing space to become more efficient, the industry always complained that the protection was inadequate. Rather than being eliminated, the temporary restraints slowly spread to include other countries and products, gradually filling in the gaps from which imports were seeping in. The Short Term Arrangement on Cotton Textiles trade was signed in 1961, followed

---

[52] For an expose of steel's lobbying tactics and demands for corporate welfare, see Barringer and Pierce 2000.

by the Long-Term Arrangement on Cotton Textiles in 1962. Set to last for five years, the long-term arrangement was renewed for three years in 1967 and again in 1970. These trade restrictions were extended to wool and man-made textiles products in the first Multi-Fiber Arrangement in 1974. This was followed by the second MFA in 1978, the third MFA in 1982, and the fourth MFA in 1986, each of which continued to tighten the restrictions by expanding the country and product coverage. The MFA was finally abolished in 2005 (after a ten-year phaseout) over the strenuous objections of the industry, but its proponents have not given up the fight for more import restraints.

Unlike the large integrated steel producers, the textile and apparel industry has made some adjustments to compete against foreign imports. The textile industry has become less dependent upon unskilled labor-intensive production techniques by adopting advanced technology and more capital-intensive production methods (often using imported machinery). The consequent increase in productivity has sharply reduced industry employment. The apparel sector, which is less able to substitute capital for labor, has been harder hit and has turned instead to foreign outsourcing to remain competitive. Despite the plant closings and employment losses at the aggregate level, new firms have entered the industry, and within-plant productivity has increased in both textiles and apparel.[53]

Despite the inefficacy of import protection in solving an industry's problems, many industries still identify imports as the problem and protection as the cure. Some have even claimed that temporary protection "played a major role in revitalizing key American industries" in the 1980s. For example, the steel and auto industries faced many difficulties in the early 1980s, but received import relief and by the late 1980s had significantly improved their output, employment, and productivity.[54]

This view of protection completely misrepresents the experience of the 1980s. Revitalization was in fact the result of the economic recovery after the recession of 1981–82, which had been the worst economic downturn since the Great Depression. In addition, the appreciation of

[53] Levinsohn and Petropoulos 2001.

[54] Tonelson 1994. His article is entitled "Beating Back Predatory Trade," but it is absurd to think that the woes of the steel, automobile, and textile industries were due to foreign predatory practices.

the dollar in the early 1980s squeezed import-competing and export industries, with relief coming when the dollar began to depreciate after 1985. To conclude from the 1980s that temporary protection is a proven method of boosting industrial competitiveness not only overlooks the more important macroeconomic context of that period, but ignores the fact that foreign competition is precisely what motivated American manufacturers to cut costs and improve their productivity. Diminishing competition through import restraints takes the pressure off domestic industries and dulls their incentive to improve efficiency.

For example, let us consider the celebrated Harley-Davidson motorcycle case. Even today, this is frequently heralded as a great success of "breathing space" protection. The story, as conventionally told, is that in the early 1980s Harley-Davidson was pushed to the wall by Japanese competition. After receiving temporary import relief in 1983 under the Section 201 escape clause, the company got its act together and came back stronger than ever.[55] In fact, Harley recovered so swiftly that it even requested that the final year of tariff protection be canceled.

The real story is different: import relief had nothing to do with Harley-Davidson's turnaround. At the time, Harley-Davidson produced only "heavyweight" motorcycles with piston displacements of over 1000cc, while Japanese producers mainly exported medium-weight bikes (700cc to 850cc of piston displacement) to the United States. But in 1975, Kawasaki opened a production plant in Nebraska, and in 1979, Honda opened a plant in Ohio, both of which produced heavyweight motorcycles to compete directly with Harley-Davidson. They did not produce them in Japan because there was virtually no market for such large motorcycles in Asia.

The deep recession of 1981–82 particularly affected blue-collar workers, the main consumer base for Harley's products, and put the company under severe financial pressure. So they filed for import relief under Section 201 in September 1982, making no allegation of unfair dumping or subsidies. The ITC had problems determining that imports were the substantial cause of Harley's injury because imports were plummeting from the recession too. They finally decided that Harley had been

---

[55] The company's management fully conceded that Harley's production process was far behind the cutting-edge Japanese manufacturing practices at the time the Section 201 petition was filed; see Reid 1990.

injured because unsold inventories of imported medium-weight bikes (700–850cc) were accumulating.[56] The ITC also ruled that Honda's Ohio plant and Kawasaki's Nebraska plant were part of the domestic industry that deserved protection.

The Reagan administration accepted the ITC's recommendation and adopted a tariff-rate quota on imports of motorcycles over 700cc. A tariff-rate quota allows a certain quantity of imports to enter paying the usual tariff, but imports above that quantity have to pay the higher protective tariffs. These were initially set at 45 percent and then declined over five years. The protection had almost no impact on Harley-Davidson because Honda and Kawasaki were already producing heavyweight motorcycles in the United States, production that was not constrained. In fact, Honda and Kawasaki favored the Section 201 case because it could protect them from their Japan-based rivals Suzuki and Yamaha. But even Suzuki and Yamaha were able to evade the tariff-rate quota on imports of motorcycles over 700cc: they simply produced a 699cc version that was not subject to the quota.[57] Then Suzuki and Yamaha had room under the quota to export a greater quantity of larger (1000cc) bikes before they had to pay the extra 45 percent duty.

Harley was deeply disappointed with the import relief. Because the final year of tariffs would have been very low and had virtually no effect on the motorcycle market, the company gave up the Section 201 relief a year before it was set to expire. Doing so gained Harley favorable publicity and helped convince President Reagan to visit a Harley plant in Pennsylvania, where he declared, amid a sea of red, white, and blue, that his administration was glad to lend Harley a helping hand.

Harley saved itself from bankruptcy and turned itself around because a new management team, appalled at the lax inventory control system and antiquated production methods, dramatically improved the efficiency of the production process. Close attention to production detail, as well as the rebounding economy, helped rejuvenate Harley's economic

[56] The inventory of medium bikes accounted for 80 percent of all unsold motorcycles, and the inventory buildup was much less for models larger than 1000cc because of production cutbacks.

[57] Harley engineers purchased two imported motorcycles because they suspected that only the label on the engine had changed, but to their astonishment the engines were exactly 699cc! Reid 1990, 89.

prospects. Blocking imports contributed virtually nothing to Harley's recovery. A recent counterfactual study of the episode found that the safeguard measures increased Harley's sales by just 6 percent.[58]

Thus, one should not be overly optimistic about the ability of trade protection to help sectors with adjustment problems more severe than coping with a temporary surge of imports. Whether import restraints actually assist the domestic industry in its adjustment efforts is a debatable proposition. But even if protection contributes little to adjustment, the escape clause has been a political necessity and has helped maintain domestic support for the open world trading system.

[58] Kitano and Ohashi 2007. As the chief economist of the ITC during this period later recalled, "If the case of heavyweight motorcycles is to be considered the only successful escape-clause case, it is because it caused little harm and it helped Harley-Davidson get a bank loan so it could diversify." Suomela 1993, 135. In 1986, the company bought a mobile home producer, Holiday Rambler Corp.

6

Developing Countries and Open Markets

Previous chapters have described the benefits of free trade and the costs of import protection, but many observers are skeptical that open trade policies can improve conditions in poor countries where a majority of the world's population live. This chapter examines whether the case for free trade is qualified by the special circumstances of developing countries. Recent experience suggests that developing countries can reap substantial benefits from adopting more open trade policies, but that such policies alone do not guarantee development, particularly when corruption, civil conflict, excessive regulation, and other institutional failings prevent local entrepreneurs from taking advantage of world markets. This chapter also discusses developed country policies that are harmful to developing countries, such as agricultural protectionism, import barriers on labor-intensive manufactured goods, and requirements that labor standards be a condition for trade.

Trade Policy and Developing Countries

In past decades, developing countries were reluctant to participate in the world economy. Many people in poorer countries feared that rich countries would dominate and exploit them.[1] Powerful foreign multinationals, it was believed, would gain control of small economies unless governments restricted their activities. Furthermore, the prevailing view among

---

[1] "It is sometimes difficult for sophisticated economists and politicians to understand the deep historic and cultural problems some [developing] countries have with the idea of free trade. Some still equate it with oppression from colonial days." This comment comes from Mike Moore, the former director-general of the WTO. Moore 2003, 133.

economic experts in the 1950s and 1960s was that developing countries had limited opportunities to achieve growth through exports. International trade was expected to reinforce their comparative advantage in the production of simple primary commodities, thereby locking them into a pattern of specialization that would forever prevent their economic development.

Over the past two decades, these conclusions have been proven false. Countries that restricted foreign trade and investment may have avoided foreign exploitation, but remained desperately poor nonetheless. Meanwhile, international trade created opportunities that in fact promoted development and reduced poverty. Many countries that encouraged trade did not remain stuck producing just raw materials, but began exporting an increasing array of labor-intensive manufactured goods.[2]

However, as a legacy of the past, developing countries have had to overcome severe trade-related policy distortions, including quantitative restrictions on imports and exports, high tariffs, overvalued exchange rates, and administrative controls on foreign exchange allocation. Politically powerful interest groups, including state-owned enterprises that fear competition and government bureaucrats whose power is derived from their decision-making authority, have fiercely resisted trade liberalization and often have been able to block trade reforms. As a result, even after many developing countries have reduced tariffs and liberalized trade policies, they still have much higher tariffs than developed countries. As table 3.1 showed, import tariffs in developed countries are less than 5 percent, on average, while those in developing countries are substantially higher, in the range of 10 to 30 percent, on average. Although developing country tariffs are significantly lower than a decade ago, these tariffs are often just the tip of the iceberg, as many of these countries have in place significant nontariff barriers to trade. Thus, there is ample room for further reforms of trade policy in the developing world.

Of course, free trade is not the single most important factor behind economic development. For many countries, reforms in other areas may be of greater importance and hence a more urgent priority. These include ensuring the security of property rights, providing legal institutions

---

[2] Krueger (1997) provides an excellent analysis of how the old view of trade and development, based on erroneous assumptions and expectations, eventually gave way in the face of contrary evidence.

that support market transactions (enforcing contracts, etc.), and encouraging the development of financial markets. In many instances, these goals can be achieved not by proactive government policies, but by eliminating poor policies and counterproductive practices: the government should not arbitrarily confiscate or expropriate goods or property, should not protect monopolies and create obstacles to new business formation, should not suppress financial markets with heavy-handed regulations, and so forth. Other nontrade reforms may require proactive government policies, such as improving public health and access to schools.

Still, trade policy reforms can play an important contributing role in promoting development. Recent experience has demonstrated that a shift toward more liberal trade policies can bring about striking improvements in economic performance. This in turn leads to improved socioeconomic outcomes, including the reduction of poverty, malnutrition, and infant mortality.

Consider the following statement:

History makes a mockery of the claim that trade cannot work for the poor. Participation in world trade has figured prominently in many of the most successful cases of poverty reduction—and, compared with aid, it has far more potential to benefit the poor. . . . Apart from financial benefits, export growth can be a more efficient engine of poverty reduction than aid. Export production can concentrate income directly in the hands of the poor, creating new opportunities for employment and investment in the process. . . . Experience from East Asia illustrates what is possible when export growth is broad-based. Since the mid-1970s, rapid growth in exports has contributed to a wider process of economic growth which has lifted more than 400 million people out of poverty. In countries such as Vietnam and Uganda, production for export markets has helped to generate unprecedented declines in the levels of rural poverty. Where export growth is based on labour-intensive manufactured goods, as in Bangladesh, it can generate large income gains for women. . . . The benefits of trade are not automatic—and rapid export growth is no guarantee of accelerated poverty reduction. Yet when the potential of trade is harnessed to effective strategies for achieving equitable growth, it can provide a powerful impetus to the achievement of human development targets.

This statement did not come from a globalization cheerleader, but from Oxfam, the British charitable organization that is also very critical of the current system of world trade.[3] Oxfam is among the growing number of nongovernmental development organizations recognizing that open trade policies enable countries to benefit from the growth of world trade.

The conclusions expressed in Oxfam's statement are supported by empirical analyses of the relationship between trade and growth focusing specifically on developing countries. One recent study by David Dollar and Aart Kraay examined the top one-third of all developing countries in terms of the increase in their trade-to-GDP ratio since 1980. These countries—the "globalizers"—experienced a 5 percent annual increase in real per capita income, whereas the other developing countries—the "nonglobalizers"—saw only a 1.4 percent annual increase in real per capita income.[4] The globalizers also cut import tariffs by twice the margin of nonglobalizers.

Individual country case studies reinforce the conclusions of the cross-country studies. As Dollar and Kraay note: "There are many interesting pair-wise comparisons between the globalising group and the non-globalising group: Vietnam versus Burma, Bangladesh versus Pakistan, Costa Rica versus Honduras. In each of these cases, the economy that has opened up more has had better economic performance."[5] Indeed, greater trade openness—marked by rising trade and low or declining trade barriers—has been a feature of virtually all rapid-growth developing country experiences in the last fifty years.[6]

It is sometimes believed that globalization has been imposed on countries. Yet globalization is also a choice. Through their trade and foreign investment policies, countries can choose the degree to which they want to be a part of the world economy. Cambodia, Vietnam, and Uganda

[3] Oxfam 2002, 8–9.
[4] Dollar and Kraay 2004.
[5] Dollar and Kraay 2004, F24.
[6] Panagariya 2004.

have embraced the world market and have seen their trade-to-GDP ratios soar. Meanwhile, trade has shrunk as a part of the economies of Egypt, Nigeria, and the Dominican Republic. Some of these declines may be due to domestic disorder, macroeconomic mismanagement, or reduction in demand for country-specific goods (such as Zambia's copper), but some also represent government policies that deliberately hinder the ability of citizens to participate in the world economy. For example, Egypt, once one of the great trading nations of the world, currently has an export- (or import-) to-GDP ratio of only about 12 percent, a fraction of what it is for many export-oriented developing countries. Egypt's own policies have stifled trade and kept this ratio artificially low. Many parts of the world that chose not to participate in the world economy have succeeded in being marginalized.

The greatest example of a country turning its back on the world economy is China in the fourteenth century. The imperial court prohibited any foreign trade (without official permission) for about two centuries after 1371, even going so far as to forbid the construction of new seagoing ships in 1436. While these efforts did not completely eliminate trade, they severely curtailed it at a time when Chinese merchants were very active in the Indian Ocean and Africa. China's action did not stop globalization. But China lost its technological leadership and fell very far behind the rest of the world in military and commercial strength. Eventually it fell prey to political domination by the West in the nineteenth century.

That lesson still holds true today: countries that deliberately seek to isolate themselves from the world will only find their living standards falling behind those of other countries. The failed, autarkic state of Burma is a sad reminder of this fact. In the Middle East, too, many countries have resisted joining the world economy. At the time of the September 11, 2001, attack on the World Trade Center and Pentagon, Saudi Arabia, Iran, Iraq, Syria, Afghanistan, Algeria, and other countries in the region had one thing in common: they were not members of the World Trade Organization. With over 150 members, the WTO is not an exclusive club that has shunned them. Instead, these countries did not (until recently) feel compelled to become part of the club, a symptom of their disengagement with the rest of the world.[7] According to the UN's Arab Human Develop-

[7] Lindsey 2001.

ment Report, many societies in the Middle East are closed, their economies stifled, their peoples repressed. They do not encourage business formation or welcome foreign investment, the exchange of goods across borders, or even international trade in ideas. According to the report, the Arab world translates about 330 foreign books annually, one-fifth of the number that Greece alone translates. Perhaps not surprisingly, the report found that one in two Arab youths is dissatisfied with the prospect of living in a closed society and has expressed a desire to emigrate.[8]

_____Two Billion People—China and India

Perhaps the most compelling examples of how more open trade policies can facilitate economic growth and development come from the two most populous countries in the world—China and India. Over the past quarter century, both countries have shifted from economic isolation to economic integration with the rest of the world. Both countries are now growing rapidly and have made remarkable strides in reducing poverty and raising the standards of living of their citizens.

Before 1979, China was virtually closed to world trade. China's trade operated under a strict system of state trading in which about a dozen foreign trade corporations monopolized all international trade. China followed a Soviet-style system of central planning that suppressed foreign trade and made import-substitution industrialization its overriding objective. Imports were minimized and exports were authorized only to the extent required to pay for imports.[9] The policy succeeded in building up domestic manufacturing, but investments in heavy industry failed to improve the welfare of China's citizens.

In December 1978, China began to end its policy of economic isolation. Under the leadership of Deng Xiaoping, the government de-collectivized agriculture, freed foreign exchange transactions, allowed private entities to trade, and permitted foreign investment. Although reforms

[8] United Nations Development Program 2002, 30.

[9] "To achieve the goal of a self-reliant industrial economy, domestic industry was protected from foreign competition by direct controls on imports and investment and administrative allocation of foreign exchange combined with an overvalued currency. These policies, enforced by central planners and a central foreign trade monopoly, built an airtight wall between the domestic economy and the world economy." Shirk 1994, 8.

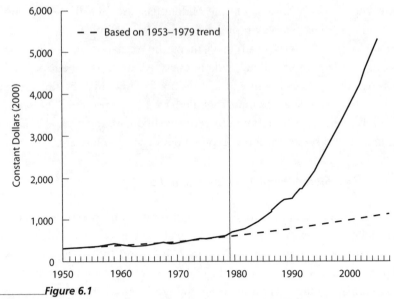

_____*Figure 6.1*

Real per Capita GDP in China, 1953–2004. Major reforms were initiated in 1979. Source: Data from Penn World Tables, 6.2. http://pwt.econ.upenn.edu.

were gradually introduced over the 1980s and 1990s and went well beyond trade policy alone, the opening of China's economy to the world was a critical component of these changes. In 1992, the weighted average tariff on manufactured goods was over 45 percent. Since China joined the WTO in 2001, the country's average tariff will eventually fall to less than 7 percent.[10]

The results have been stunning. China's exports and imports have soared, as figure 3.1 illustrated. China's share of world trade rose from about 1 percent in 1980 to more than 8 percent in 2006. Foreign investment in China has grown from virtually nothing in 1979 to more than $600 billion in 2006. As figure 6.1 shows, China's real per capita income has grown at near double-digit rates since the 1980s, making it one of the fastest-growing countries in the world. As a result, the official rate of poverty fell from 28 percent in 1978 to 9 percent in 1998.[11]

Of course, China did not just open up to trade, it fundamentally changed the way its economy was organized. Yet the decision to open to

[10] Ianchovichina and Martin 2004, 9.
[11] Bhagwati and Srinivasan 2002.

the world was not inevitable; it had a large internal market and could have pursued import substitution or industrial policies. But its trade policy reforms were a vital component of its broader reforms and have played a critical role in its economic success.

India is another example of a country that dramatically improved its economic performance after moving to freer trade policies. For about four decades after becoming independent in 1947, India pursued a policy of self-sufficiency and industrial planning that required elaborate and complex import restrictions. Importing anything that was not explicitly on a government list of approved items was forbidden. Imports of "nonessential" consumer goods were banned, and those deemed "essential" (food, pharmaceuticals, etc.) were imported and sold only by state agencies. A labyrinth of government requirements—permissions, licenses, and certifications—had to be met before intermediate and capital goods could be imported.

Bureaucrats and politicians justified these draconian policies on several grounds. Government control over industry and trade was deemed essential to conserve resources and eliminate wasteful competition. The scarcity of capital was held to justify government approval for investment projects. The shortage of foreign exchange, it was believed, meant that hard currency should be allocated by government officials rather than by the market to ensure its use for projects in the "national interest." The fear of foreign domination lurked behind many of these policies and created resistance to market-based solutions in favor of government-directed ones.

Unfortunately, the outcome was a disgrace—sluggish growth, persistent poverty, inefficient industry, and lagging modernization. According to one quip, India suffered from four hundred years of British imperialism and fifty years of the Fabian socialism of the London School of Economics—and it is not clear which did more damage.[12]

However, an economic crisis in 1991 forced reluctant policymakers to undertake a radical shift in policy.[13] India abandoned parts of its

---

[12] In the early and middle twentieth century, the London School of Economics was home to Fabian socialist ideas that influenced generations of Indian policymakers. Moore 2003, 132.

[13] The collapse of Communism and China's success in opening up its economy also helped convince Indian policymakers that state planning was a failure.

_____Figure 6.2

Real per Capita GDP in India, 1950–2004. Major trade reform was initiated in 1991.
Source: Data from Penn World Tables, 6.2. http://pwt.econ.upenn.edu.

central planning system and abolished the requirement of government permission for all industrial investment expenditures, with some exceptions. Indian firms were permitted to borrow on international capital markets, the rupee was devalued and made convertible, quantitative restrictions on imports were abolished, export subsidies were eliminated, and import duties were cut from an average of 87 percent in 1990 to 33 percent in 1994. Nontariff barriers covered 95 percent of all imports in 1988 but just 24 percent in 1999.[14] The "license raj"—the rigid and complex system of import controls and foreign investment restrictions administered by government bureaucrats—was dismantled, unleashing the private sector from red tape but also exposing it to international competition.

The outcome has been astonishing. As figure 6.2 shows, growth in real per capita income in India began to pick up in the mid-1980s, when some tentative steps toward reducing import barriers and investment controls were taken, and accelerated after 1991.[15] The reduction in

[14] Srinivasan and Tendulkar 2003, 33–39.

[15] There is some controversy about the timing of the acceleration in growth and what triggered it. Srinivasan and Tendulkar (2003, 23) argue that "growth performance was distinctly better in the 1980s than in the earlier period" because of a real exchange rate depreciation rather than trade liberalization. "This surge in growth, however, was supported on the demand side by unsustainable fiscal policies, and it ended with an economic crisis in 1991." Rodrik and Subramanian (2004) argue that an attitudinal shift toward a more

trade barriers has also been linked to higher productivity; by one estimate, India experienced a 20 percent increase in aggregate productivity growth and a 30–35 percent increase in intraplant productivity following tariff liberalization.[16] Most important, the poverty rate has fallen from 45 percent in 1983 to 26 percent in 2000, improving the lives of tens of millions of Indians.[17]

The power of economic reform is illustrated by considering seven entrepreneurs who in 1981 started a small business in India with $250 of seed capital. The Indian government created huge obstacles to the setting up of the business. As one of the founders later recalled, "It took us a year to obtain a telephone connection, two years to get a license to import a computer, and 15 days to get foreign currency for travel abroad. . . . The first ten years of our marathon seemed interminable and frustrating. Although we managed to keep our heads above water, we were floundering."

The lifeboat that rescued the firm and allowed it to flourish was India's deregulation and economic liberalization in 1991. That firm is Infosys Technologies Ltd., now one of the largest and most successful software companies in the world, and that entrepreneur is N. R. Narayana Murthy, the chairman and CEO of Infosys. According to Murthy, the economic reforms of 1991 "changed the Indian business context from one of state-centered, control orientation to a free, open market orientation, at least for hi-tech companies." That allowed the company to grow so that it could eventually employ thousands of Indians at relatively high wages. "We at Infosys . . . have never looked back," Murthy says. "The lesson from the Indian experience is a clear clarion call for all who are willing to listen: free trade can bring great benefits to society."[18]

China and India provide dramatic illustrations of the improvement in economic circumstances that can result when poor economic policies are replaced with better ones, particularly with respect to international

---

pro-business stance on the part of the government accounts for the pickup in growth after 1980, prior to economic liberalization, the importance of which they downplay. Panagariya (2008) argues that liberalization in the late 1980s played a crucial role in increasing growth, but that it remained fragile and solidified only after the 1991 economic reforms.

[16] Sivadasan 2003.
[17] World Bank 2003, 7.
[18] Murthy 2001.

trade. Higher incomes translate into tangible improvements in the well-being of millions of people. This improvement in well-being cannot be measured in terms of dollars and cents alone, but in the lives that are saved as a result of moving people away from the knife edge of poverty, where a bad harvest or the loss of a job can spell malnourishment or even death. Hunger and malnutrition, illiteracy, and infant mortality persisted for decades after China adopted central planning in 1949 and India received political independence in 1947. Because of the economic opportunities that opened up after the 1978 and 1991 reforms in China and India, respectively, hundreds of millions of people have a chance to join the middle class.

Thus, the higher income that comes with freer trade is important not just for crass material reasons, but because it can lead to a better life. With higher incomes, families can pay for more and better food, gain access to medicines and better health care, and afford schooling for their children. One study examined the direct connections between trade openness and a society's health outcomes, specifically infant mortality and life expectancy. Even after controlling for a country's per capita income, average years of schooling, number of doctors per capita, and other factors, people in countries with lower tariffs had longer life expectancy and lower infant mortality. For example, an eleven-percentage-point reduction in the tariff rate—a change of about one standard deviation in the sample—is associated with between three and six fewer infants dying per thousand live births.[19] Such findings are a powerful reminder of the life-and-death stakes of good and bad economic policies.

The tragedy of India is that, by delaying economic reforms for so many decades, it contributed to the impoverishment of its people for so long. One Indian businessman writes with dismay:

> Most people remember the Emergency [suspension of
> democracy between 1975 and 1977] because it represented a
> generalized loss of liberty. They do not understand that by
> suppressing economic liberty for forty years, we destroyed
> growth and the future of two generations. For the average
> citizen it was a great betrayal. Lest we forget, we lived under a
> system where a third of the people went hungry and

[19] Wei and Wu 2003.

malnourished, half were illiterate while the elite enjoyed a vast system of higher education, and one of ten infants died at childbirth. Our controls and red tape stifled the entrepreneur and the farmer, and the command mentality of the bureaucrat, which fed the evil system, continues till today to frustrate every effort at reform." [20]

India has paid a very heavy price in human lives for delaying its reforms. But what China and India have accomplished is stunning. Though both countries still have a long way to go, the improvement in human well-being achieved over the past generation is mind-boggling.

Of course, not all of the improved economic performance of China and India can be attributed to more liberal trade policies. China moved away from a system of central planning and collective agriculture, while India freed up bureaucratic obstacles to domestic investment. Nonetheless, trade reforms were a key component of the overall economic reforms. Both countries deliberately shifted from closed economies to ones more open to international trade.

_Trade Policy Reform: Successes and Failures

China and India are dramatic examples of the tangible benefits of economic reform and international trade. On a smaller but no less dramatic scale, other developing countries have changed their economic orientation to the world and have seen improvements in economic performance.

In the mid-1960s, Korea completely changed its trade strategy. The proportion of items automatically approved for import went from zero in June 1964 to 63 percent by December 1965. Korea's currency (the won) was devalued by nearly 50 percent, and a unified exchange rate was adopted. In 1967, many import quotas were abolished and tariffs were sharply reduced. The effective tax on imports fell from nearly 40 percent in 1960 to 8 percent by 1967. Figure 6.3 shows the marked acceleration in Korea's growth of per capita income from around the time of these changes. [21]

[20] Das 2001, 175.
[21] Frank, Kim, and Westphal 1975, 75.

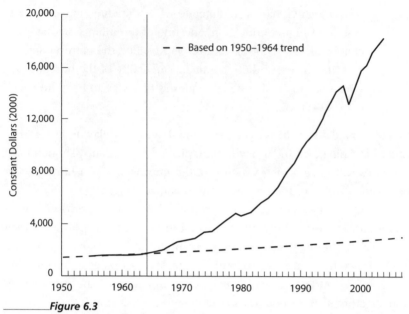

_____Figure 6.3

Real per Capita GDP in South Korea, 1953–2004. . Major trade reforms were initiated between 1963 and 1965.
Source: Data from Penn World Tables, 6.2. http://pwt.econ.upenn.edu.

In the mid-1970s, Chile also sharply changed its trade policy. Between 1975 and 1979, Chile eliminated all quantitative restrictions and exchange controls and reduced import tariffs from over 100 percent to a uniform 10 percent. After suffering a severe economic recession due to a banking crisis in the early 1980s, Chile continued trade liberalization. The payoff materialized in a 7 percent average annual growth rate for more than a decade after 1986.[22]

In the middle and late 1980s, Vietnam adopted economic reforms that helped increase economic growth to an average of more than 7 percent in the late 1990s and early 2000s. As in China, agricultural land reform helped jump-start the growth process. But trade and foreign investment have been important components of Vietnam's success. The poverty rate has been slashed in a remarkably short time. The share of the population living in absolute poverty fell from 75 percent in 1988 to 58 percent in 1993 to 37 percent in 1998 to 29 percent in 2002. The

[22] Edwards and Lederman 2002.

opening of trade contributed directly to this process since exports of rice and labor-intensive manufactured goods are produced by poor households. After the implementation of a U.S.-Vietnamese trade agreement in 2001, Vietnam's exports to the United States doubled in 2002 and again in 2003.[23]

Unfortunately, not all countries that have liberalized their trade policies have enjoyed such dramatic successes. For example, Mexico significantly reduced tariffs and other trade barriers when it joined the GATT in 1985 and signed free trade agreements with the United States and Canada (NAFTA) in 1994 and the European Union in 2000. As a result, Mexico's trade and foreign investment increased significantly. The share of trade (average of exports and imports) in GDP rose from 13 percent in 1985 to 32 percent in 2002. These reforms improved productivity in industries exposed to international competition, as described in chapter 2.

However, Mexico's overall macroeconomic performance has been disappointing since NAFTA. Economic growth has been lackluster, employment is only slightly higher than before the agreement took effect, and real wages are actually lower. NAFTA opponents blame open trade for Mexico's problems. These critics say that NAFTA has harmed farmers and is responsible for the lack of improvement in the standard of living of workers.

The real source of Mexico's malaise is macroeconomic. In December 1994, about a year after NAFTA went into effect, and for reasons not related to the trade agreement, Mexico faced a speculative attack on the peso and was forced to devalue its currency. The peso crisis stemmed from an inconsistency between Mexico's monetary policy and its commitment to maintain a fixed exchange rate. The peso devaluation was a severe setback that slashed real wages overnight and sent the economy into a deep recession.

By keeping trade flows moving, NAFTA helped the Mexican economy through a difficult period. The continued expansion of trade promoted the country's recovery from this traumatic shock. Yet since the initial rebound, the Mexican economy has been weak. The reason for this disappointing performance is not trade related, but a persistent and severe credit crunch, including a deterioration in contract enforceability

[23] Dollar and Ljunggren 1997.

and an increase in nonperforming bank loans. Indeed, Mexico's credit-to-GDP ratio fell from 49 percent in 1994 to 17 percent in 2002, preventing any broad-based economic recovery.[24]

A decade after NAFTA went into effect, a Carnegie Endowment for International Peace study concluded: "Put simply, NAFTA has been neither the disaster its opponents predicted nor the savior hailed by its supporters." The report also noted that "NAFTA has accelerated Mexico's transition to a liberalized economy without creating the necessary conditions for the public and private sectors to respond to the economic, social, and environmental shocks of trading with two of the biggest economies in the world."[25] This suggests that other complementary policies are required if trade liberalization is to succeed in improving welfare, a point that will be discussed below.

Unfortunately, Mexico is not alone. Other developing countries significantly reduced tariffs in the 1990s but also have not performed well. In Latin America, Colombia cut its tariffs by more than half in 1991, while Argentina and Nicaragua reduced them from over 100 percent to just 15 percent in one stroke in 1992. In Africa, Kenya reduced its import duties from over 40 percent in the early 1980s to under 15 percent by the late 1990s.[26] Yet the people of these countries have not seen much improvement in their standard of living.

This disappointing performance is sometimes interpreted as indicating that trade liberalization and increased integration with the world have failed to help developing countries and that therefore the strategy should be abandoned. This is the wrong conclusion to draw. In the case of Argentina, for example, monetary and macroeconomic instability—arising from excessive borrowing abroad and the resulting buildup of foreign debt—have had devastating effects far beyond any good that open trade could bring. Colombia and other countries have had to endure "shock therapy" to end hyperinflation and hemorrhaging budget deficits, forcing the economy through wrenching adjustments that overwhelmed the impact of trade liberalization. Until the mid-1990s, the overvaluation of West African currencies tied to the French franc severely

---

[24] Tornell, Westerman, and Martinez 2004; Kose, Meredith, and Towe 2004; Maurer 2006.

[25] Audley et al. 2003, 6.

[26] World Bank 2001, 51.

constrained the ability of West African countries to stimulate growth through exports.[27]

In its review of the economic reform and growth experience of the 1990s, the World Bank conceded that "the results of trade reforms have varied and sometimes fallen short of expectations."[28] It went on to say: "Trade reforms are most likely to stimulate growth when they are part of a comprehensive strategy. Important elements of an effective growth strategy can include sound macroeconomic management, building of trade-related infrastructure and institutions, economy-wide investments in physical and human capital, greater access to developed- and developing country markets, and maintenance of a sound rule of law. Because these elements are often difficult to implement, there has been excessive emphasis on trade policy alone, rather than as a component of an overall growth strategy."

One recent lesson is that excessive regulation and a poor domestic business environment may prevent trade liberalization from stimulating growth. One study reports that increased openness to trade leads to higher incomes in flexible economies, but not in heavily regulated ones. Specifically, a 1 percent increase in trade is associated with a 1/2 percent rise in per capita income in countries that allow the free entry of firms into sectors that they choose, but has no positive impact on income in countries that restrict business entry.[29] If excessive regulations prevent resources from moving to the economy's most productive sectors and firms, then trade liberalization will fail to improve incomes. A sound domestic environment for business is required for countries to take full advantage of policy reforms that encourage global trade. Highly regulated economies are likely to perform better if they sweep away

---

[27] "Liberalization of trade in Argentina in the 1980s and 1990s, and in Chile in the early 1980s, for example, was accompanied by an appreciation of the real exchange rate, which reduced the competitiveness of domestic industries and incentive to export—with adverse consequences for the balance of payments and real economy. In many countries of the former Soviet Union and some in Eastern Europe in the 1990s, trade was liberalized while property rights were not well defined and the institutional base for a market economy was not well developed. These, and other institutional issues preventing the free movement of resources, often meant that trade reforms did not expand economic opportunities but restricted them instead." World Bank 2005, 137.

[28] World Bank 2005, 131, 137–38.

[29] Freund and Bolaky 2008.

domestic impediments to economic activity before embarking upon trade reforms.[30]

Indeed, in some developing countries, administrative controls and poor infrastructure may be more important obstacles to trade than tariffs alone. Inefficient customs and tax administration have hampered exporters who require imported components and materials for production. For example, a business in the Central African Republic has to take fifty-seven days to complete all the export formalities, submitting eight documents to different government agencies, and spend $4,581 before a container can leave the port in Yaoundé, in neighboring Cameroon. In Angola, a ship arriving in the port of Luanda must wait an average of eight days before landing, a delay that can stretch to fourteen days during the rainy season. It is estimated that each additional day that an export product is delayed reduces exports by more than 1 percent, and the effect on time-sensitive agricultural exports is even more dramatic.[31]

High transport costs and poor infrastructure can prevent trade liberalization from boosting trade in low-income developing countries. Landlocked countries are at a particular disadvantage in world trade since land transport charges have been estimated to be seven times greater than sea transport costs. Studies have found that higher transport costs and weak infrastructure explain much of Africa's poor trade performance.[32] For example, in sub-Saharan Africa, transport costs are five times greater than tariff charges.

Simply chopping import tariffs does not in itself solve these problems. If goods are stranded for weeks at port, or roads are impassable due to the rainy season, cutting tariffs from 20 percent to 10 percent will not make much difference. As formal barriers fall, the quality and reliability of transport infrastructure (including roads, railways, airports,

---

[30] The World Bank has started to examine the high costs of business regulation in developing countries. "It takes two days to start a business in Australia, but 203 days in Haiti and 215 days in the Democratic Republic of Congo. . . . A simple commercial contract is enforced in 7 days in Tunisia and 39 days in the Netherlands, but takes almost 1,500 days in Guatemala. The cost of enforcement is less than 1 percent of the disputed amount in Austria, Canada, and the United Kingdom, but more than 100 percent in Burkina Faso, the Dominican Republic, Indonesia, the Kyrgyz Republic, Madagascar, Malawi, and the Philippines." World Bank 2004, xiii.

[31] World Bank 2007, 44–45.

[32] Limão and Venables 2001.

and seaports) and related services (including telecommunications and business services such as finance and insurance) are increasingly critical to trade.

For this reason, trade facilitation has become a priority in international forums such as the World Trade Organization. Trade facilitation is simply the logistics of moving goods through customs and includes such mundane things as port efficiency, inspections and documentation, transparency of government regulations, and so on. Some policy changes can make a difference. For example, in the early 1990s Argentina began allowing private firms to operate public ports and invest in their infrastructure. As a result, cargo handling increased 50 percent between 1990 and 1995 and labor productivity surged, making Argentine ports among the cheapest in Latin America.[33]

In sum, trade liberalization is not a magic bullet guaranteed to bring about rapid growth in trade and higher incomes. The right conclusion to draw is that the case for free trade requires a caution: other policies in developing countries can prevent the full benefits of trade liberalization from being realized. Many other factors—political conflicts, macroeconomic instability, a poor domestic business environment—can stand in the way of the beneficial effects of trade and can prevent freer trade from yielding the ultimate payoff of higher living standards.

Industrial Policy and the East Asian Miracle

Despite the success that many countries have had with economic liberalization, developing countries still fear the consequences of opening their markets to the world. The old concerns about foreign domination and imports destroying important domestic industries continue to exist. Many people still cling to the view that import substitution and protecting infant industries is the right approach to trade and development.

Import substitution refers to a deliberate policy of encouraging domestic production of manufactured goods in place of imports. Such policies were common in the 1950s and 1960s when industrialization was viewed as the key to economic development. Such policies often succeeded in building up capital-intensive industries and sometimes led to

---

[33] WTO 2004, Box IIB.5.

high rates of output growth. But they often failed to improve standards of living because the high investment rates required to maintain growth in the capital stock detracted from growth in consumption. In the case of Communist China, about a third of national income had to be reinvested to maintain growth in the capital stock, leaving little left over for consumers.[34]

These policies often turned out to be self-inflicted wounds. In many instances, capital-intensive industries were unsuited for developing economies that had a comparative advantage in labor-intensive industries. These industries required ongoing government support to function profitably. By sheltering firms from import competition, protectionist policies inhibited export growth and firms became inward looking, focusing on the domestic rather than the world market. This resulted in small and inefficient firms, since the domestic market was not large enough or competitive enough to promote firms that would be successful on the world market. India is the classic example of a country that built up many manufacturing industries by sheltering them from foreign competition, but failed to deliver a high standard of living to its people.

Although import substitution is widely acknowledged to have failed in comparison to export-promoting policies, export promotion may mean something more than free trade. Many observers point to the stunning growth of several East Asian countries and point to government industrial policies as the key to their success. The economic achievements of Japan in the 1960s and the "four tigers"—South Korea, Taiwan, Singapore, and Hong Kong—in the 1970s have raised new questions about free trade. Many contend that, with the exception of Hong Kong, these countries grew rich not because of free trade, but through wise government use of selective protection and targeted industrial policies.[35]

These countries did many things right—they enjoyed peace and political stability, encouraged high savings and investment rates,

---

[34] "One consequence of this rising capital intensity of production was that gains in per capita consumption were very modest for a country in which per capita output grew relatively rapidly. Between 1957 and 1977, per capita national income rose at an average annual compound rate of 3.4 percent in real terms. Yet, because the share of output that had to be reinvested to sustain that rate of growth rose by fully one-third (from 25 percent in 1957 to an average of 33 percent in the 1970s), improvements in real living standards were quite modest." Lardy 1992, 34.

[35] Wade 2004. For a recent critique of industrial policy, see Pack and Saggi 2006.

emphasized the importance of education and human capital accumulation, provided stable macroeconomic and exchange rate policies, and so on. Korea and Taiwan also pursued important land reforms early in their transition that led to rapid productivity growth in agriculture. In other words, these East Asian countries enjoyed many favorable conditions noticeably absent elsewhere, particularly in Latin America and Africa.

With the exception of Hong Kong, however, these countries did not pursue policies of nonintervention with respect to industry. To varying degrees, governments were involved in the allocation of capital and other resources to promote industrialization, and even employed the tools of trade protectionism. Some observers have concluded that, because the Japanese and Korean governments intervened in their economies to promote certain industries, their economic performance can be attributed to these interventions. In this view, the East Asian experience illustrates how careful industrial policy and protectionism, not free trade, promote economic development.

Yet there are reasons to be skeptical about this conclusion. It is always tempting to reach a conclusion about causality on the basis of correlation: because Japan or Korea intervened in its economy or used protectionist trade measures, the success of the economy is due to that policy. But assessing the contribution of industrial policy to economic growth is a difficult challenge. In a 1993 report on the East Asian miracle, the World Bank noted that

> their interventions did not significantly inhibit growth. But it is
> very difficult to establish statistical links between growth and a
> specific intervention and even more difficult to establish
> causality. Because we cannot know what would have
> happened in the absence of a specific policy, it is difficult to
> test whether interventions increased growth rates.[36]

Thus, when several factors promoting a good outcome exist simultaneously—a stable political environment, a good educational system, high savings and literacy rates, and so on—it becomes difficult to determine the precise contribution of any one specific factor, such as industrial policy, to the outcome. One cannot rule out the possibility that government

[36] World Bank 1993, 6.

intervention actually detracted from the economic success of the country but was more than offset by the other good forces.[37]

In the case of Japan, the country's success after World War II is sometimes attributed to the selective interventions by the Ministry of International Trade and Industry (MITI). MITI used "administrative guidance" to promote investment in and acquire technology for selected industries. Some argue that MITI was involved not just in "picking" winners by diverting resources to selected high-growth industries, but in "making" winners by ensuring their success on international markets.

But the actual evidence on MITI's contributions to Japan's success is weak. The two industries that achieved the most notable success on world markets—automobiles and consumer electronics—did not benefit from extensive government support, unlike some other heavy industries such as chemicals and steel. MITI also had notable failures in promoting its biotechnology and computer industries. In fact, one statistical study of Japanese industrial targeting found that a disproportionate amount of support went to low-growth sectors and sectors with decreasing returns to scale. This study failed to find evidence that productivity was enhanced as a result of industrial policy measures.[38]

Qualitative studies of Japan's policies lend support to this skeptical view. The consulting firm McKinsey concluded that robust domestic competition was a source of Japan's success. In many instances, MITI did not foster but actually tried to reduce competition by forming domestic cartels. (In the case of automobiles, for example, it discouraged Honda from entering the market in the 1950s, thinking that there were already too many firms in the industry.) However, in the case of machine tools, MITI helped standardize tolerances used in machines, thereby allowing large-scale assembly of machine tools and applied electronics technology. As

---

[37] As Adam Smith once opined, "The uniform, constant, and uninterrupted effort of every man to better his condition, the principle from which public and national, as well as private opulence is originally derived, is frequently powerful enough to maintain the natural progress of things towards improvement, in spite both of the extravagance of government and of the greatest errors of administration. . . . But though the profusion of government must, undoubtedly, have retarded the natural progress of England toward wealth and improvement, it has not been able to stop it." Smith 1976, 343, 345.

[38] Beason and Weinstein 1996. Ohashi (2005) finds that there were few intra-industry knowledge spillovers in the case of Japan's steel industry and that export subsidies did not help the industry's growth.

one McKinsey analyst reported, "In all our studies of Japan, this is the only action by MITI that we found to have had a significant beneficial impact on the Japanese economy."[39] If this is MITI's one success, the importance of MITI has been vastly overrated.

South Korea may provide a better example of government industrial policy. Under the military dictatorship of Chung Hee Park, the Korean government employed competent technocrats who were directly involved in economic planning and investment allocation. These bureaucrats were insulated from political decisions and thus did not fall prey to corruption. The principal tool at their disposal was directed credit, which they used to promote capital-intensive industries such as chemicals, steel, and shipbuilding. While the government was involved in strategic decisions about the economy, it did not implement these decisions through state-owned firms or nationalized industries. Rather, once the government and private sector negotiated economic goals and the means to carry them out, the private firms were responsible for executing them. Furthermore, these firms were not insulated from competition; instead, they were encouraged to export and face the full brunt of international competition.

Still, as described earlier in this chapter, what jump-started the Korean economy in the mid-1960s was not industrial policy, but other reforms, including trade and exchange rate policy. One can also question the contribution of the technocrats to Korea's rapid growth since that time. Despite the government's emphasis on building up heavy capital-intensive industries, light labor-intensive industries increased productivity at a more rapid rate during the 1960s and 1970s. Indeed, during the 1970s, the most rapid growth in sectoral shares of value added occurred in lower-wage or low value-added per worker sectors.[40] Furthermore, as in the previously mentioned study of Japan, measures of Korean industrial policy (such as tax incentives and subsidized credit) are not correlated with productivity growth at the industry level.[41] Korea's use of directed credit to promote industrial growth has also led to problems. Korean industry suffers from gross overinvestment and is far too reliant on capital-intensive production methods. Nonperforming loans and

[39] Lewis 2004, 40.
[40] Dollar and Sokoloff 1990; World Bank 1993, 314.
[41] Lee 1996.

weakness in the banking and financial system are related to major economic crises in 1979–81 and 1997–98.

Several points stand out from the Korean experience. First, private firms were not shielded from competition but rather exposed to it and forced to meet the test of international markets. The reforms that put Korea on the path of export-led industrialization "did not achieve this result by the conventionally prescribed approach, which is to reduce greatly (if not eliminate) the domestic market's insulation from import competition."[42] Second, bureaucrats were insulated from political pressures to allocate resources to politically favored projects. The implementation of plans took place by relying on free market institutions and was negotiated with, not imposed on, private firms.

Because of the special historical, political, and cultural circumstances of Korea, even a leading proponent of the view that Korea's economy benefited from government industrial policy has concluded that "one has to be extremely skeptical about the prospects for replicating the Korean government's use of selective intervention."[43] Indeed, the political prerequisites for such judicious intervention are lacking in other Southeast Asian countries, such as Malaysia, Thailand, and Indonesia. The economies of these countries have performed well in recent decades, but corruption and rent seeking have given industrial policy there a bad name. In those countries, industrial policy is virtually synonymous with arbitrary interventions to help out political cronies. In Malaysia and Indonesia, there are "important recent instances of almost capricious selective industrial policy by the executive, with the technocracy having little say in its elaboration. . . . Such efforts did not attempt to achieve international competitiveness or to provide support for other industries seeking to achieve international competitiveness, even in the long run."[44] These countries have welcomed foreign investment in labor-intensive export industries and have not sought to promote investment in heavy industry to the same degree as Japan or Korea.

[42] Rather, it established a "virtual free trade regime for export activity" that also "entailed tremendous openness to imports of raw materials, intermediate inputs, and capital goods." Westphal 1990, 44.

[43] Westphal 1990, 42.

[44] Jomo 2001, 473.

Thus, there is no single East Asian model of economic development. Singapore and Hong Kong are small island states, the latter pursuing an almost pure free market approach. Japan and Korea employed more activist industrial policies, but there is little evidence demonstrating their precise contribution (positive or negative) to the country's development. Malaysia and Indonesia have weaker political institutions that do not keep industrial policy free from corruption and rent seeking. Yet, for the most part, all of these East Asian countries have enjoyed macroeconomic stability, relied on private enterprise and market competition, stressed investment in human capital, and adopted outward-oriented policies rather than import substitution. These are the common elements cutting across the countries' vast differences.

A tentative conclusion regarding government's role in trade is that it should facilitate private sector development. Most developing countries that have shifted from the production of primary products to nontraditional activities have done so with the cooperation of the public sector. The government is not picking the sectors into which resources should move, but should clear obstacles and reduce uncertainties relating to investment—in general, facilitate private sector activities. Whether one considers Chile's diversification away from copper into fruits and salmon, Costa Rica and ecotourism, Bangladesh and garments, Colombia and cut flowers, governments have almost invariably played an important supporting role.[45]

Unfortunately, governments in many developing countries do not facilitate or support the private sector but instead create obstacles for its growth. Even worse, in many countries, particularly but by no means exclusively in Africa, economic success is best achieved by political power and connections rather than by commercial ability or effort.[46] Corrupt regimes that provide no security to economic transactions and throw

---

[45] Hausmann and Rodrik 2003.

[46] The *Economist*'s Africa correspondent argues that personal advancement in Africa is easier to achieve through political success than commercial success. In his view, to become rich, or even minimally prosperous, one must either seek political power or cultivate and become a client of those in power. The more that African bureaucrats and politicians extort and expropriate, the less there is to extort and expropriate, which makes the competition for power even more desperate and violent. Guest 2004.

obstacles in the way of business formation and commerce are perhaps the single greatest problem in promoting economic development.[47]

Recent experience has demonstrated that the economic status of developing countries is not immutably fixed by nature. Neither the geography nor the institutions of China or India or Korea changed when they embarked upon their policy reforms, and yet their economies have been utterly transformed by changes in government policy. Unfortunately, economic policies that stifle development are still pervasive around the world.

Developed Country Trade Policies

While developing countries have yet to reach their full potential in large part because of their own policies, trade barriers and subsidies in the developed world have not helped matters. Development nongovernmental organizations have excoriated the developed countries for keeping their markets closed to imports from developing countries. As an Oxfam report cries out, "the harsh reality is that [developed country] policies are inflicting enormous suffering on the world's poor. When rich countries lock poor people out of their markets, they close the door to an escape route from poverty."[48] This statement is exaggerated but contains some truth. Whether it is closed markets for agricultural goods, high barriers on the importation of labor-intensive manufactures, or efforts to require developing countries to adopt labor standards, many developed country policies are contrary to the interests of developing countries.

In terms of agriculture, the rich countries of the OECD maintain high trade barriers for agricultural products and heavily subsidize their farmers. For every dollar earned by OECD farmers, about 23 cents comes from government policies. In 2007, the OECD subsidized domestic farm producers by $258 billion, of which $126 billion came from high prices

[47] Adam Smith once stated that "Little else is requisite to carry a state to the highest degree of opulence from the lowest barbarism but peace, easy taxes, and a tolerable administration of justice: all the rest being brought about by the natural course of things. All governments which thwart this natural course, which force things into another channel, or which endeavour to arrest the progress of society at a particular point, are unnatural, and to support themselves are obliged to be oppressive and tyrannical." Unfortunately, all too many developing countries lack these three simple requirements. Smith 1980, 322.

[48] Oxfam 2002, 5.

resulting from tariffs and export subsidies and $132 billion was transferred by taxpayers through government payments to farmers.[49] The value of transfers to OECD farmers is greater than the entire GDPs of many developing countries. Because these domestic subsidies and trade barriers have a huge impact on world agricultural markets, they in turn affect developing countries, where agriculture is a very large sector, employing about 60 percent of the labor force and producing about 25 percent of GDP in low-income countries. Indeed, most of the rural poor in developing countries work in the agricultural sector.

Studies have shown that the reduction of agricultural tariffs and trade barriers by OECD and developing countries would produce substantial benefits for both sets of countries. If high-income countries alone opened their markets to imported agricultural goods, their welfare would rise by almost $32 billion and developing country welfare by $12 billion (2001 dollars).[50] Most of the benefits of trade liberalization accrue to the developed countries themselves because their consumers are footing most of the bill. (Similarly, if developing countries reduced their own agricultural trade barriers, which can be much higher than those in developed countries, they too would capture most of the benefits for themselves.)

However, the same mutual benefit does not hold true if industrial countries eliminated domestic and export subsidies to their agricultural producers. Many developing countries are net importers of agricultural goods and actually benefit from these subsidies. Because these subsidies reduce the prices of the goods that they buy on world markets, many developing countries would lose by their elimination. If high-income countries eliminated domestic and export subsidies without touching import barriers, then those countries would gain $3 billion in welfare, but developing countries as a whole would lose nearly $1 billion.[51] The gains from eliminating agricultural subsidies accrue mainly to the country that eliminates the subsidy.

[49] OECD 2008, 12.

[50] Hertel and Keeney 2006.

[51] Hoekman, Ng, and Olarreaga (2004) similarly find that a 50 percent cut in tariffs improves welfare for industrial, developing, and least developed countries alike, but a 50 percent cut in domestic subsidies helps industrial countries but harms developing and least developed countries.

Thus, from the perspective of developing countries, there is a strong stake in reducing barriers to agricultural trade in developed countries and in their own countries as well. (As table 3.1 showed, developing countries impose very high tariffs on agricultural imports.) However, the impact of removing developed country export subsidies has more varied effects on developing countries depending upon whether one is a net importer or net exporter of those goods. If one cares about poor consumers in developing countries, then low prices for agricultural goods is desirable; if one cares about poor agrarian producers in developing countries, then high agricultural prices are desirable. (Developing countries seem to care more about producers given the tight restrictions they impose on agricultural imports.)

However, an overall liberalization of all policy instruments by developed countries would increase household income among the poor in developing countries.[52] The greater market access in rich country markets would compensate the poorer countries for the higher food prices they would have to pay on some products. Indeed, research has shown that eliminating border measures such as tariffs will produce changes in world prices that are many times greater than from eliminating domestic agricultural subsidies.[53] Thus, from the standpoint of agricultural-exporting developing countries, market access (lower import barriers) is much more valuable than domestic subsidy reduction in developed countries.

Still, subsidies to specific crops can impose tremendous hardship on poor farmers in particular developing countries. Cotton is a prime—if exceptional—example. The United States and European Union heavily subsidize domestic cotton growers. In 2004–2005, government subsidies to America's 25,000 cotton farmers amounted to $3.6 billion, double the level a decade earlier. This is more than the entire GDP of the West African country of Burkina Faso. The European Union also subsidizes cotton producers by almost $1 billion per year.

World cotton prices fell by more than half between 1997 and 2002, although they have rebounded since then. The United States accounts for about 20 percent of world cotton production, so any expansion of U.S. production tends to reduce the world price. These subsidies

---

[52] Hertel, Keeney, Ivanic, and Winters 2007.
[53] Hoekman, Ng, and Olarreaga 2004.

have inflicted great harm on cotton producers in Central and West Africa and elsewhere, intensifying poverty in already very poor countries. Cotton exports account for 40 percent of exports in Burkina Faso and Benin and 30 percent of exports in Uzbekistan, Chad, and Mali. Cotton also accounts for over 5 percent of GDP in these countries.[54] Because cotton is such an important source of foreign exchange earnings for these countries, any decline in the world market price—due to subsidies or other reasons—has a tremendous negative ripple effect through their economies. The livelihood of more than 10 million poor farmers is at stake.

Some studies estimate that the elimination of U.S. cotton subsidies would reduce U.S. production by more than 25 percent, reduce U.S. exports by nearly 40 percent, and increase world cotton prices by about 12 percent. This translates into a gain of roughly $80 million in producer surplus for the four key cotton exporting nations in Africa.[55] The case of cotton illustrates the stark impact of the concentrated harm that can be done by agricultural subsidies in the OECD. The United States recently lost a case in the WTO dispute settlement process about the legality of its cotton subsidies, but the 2007 Farm Bill maintains subsidies for cotton. In August 2008, Brazil requested WTO permission to retaliate for this noncompliance by imposing duties on up to $4 billion in U.S. exports.

In the case of manufactured goods, developed countries have low tariffs on average but much higher tariffs on labor-intensive manufactures, particularly textiles and apparel. These are precisely the goods in which developing countries have a comparative advantage. Developing countries have long complained about the Multi-Fiber Arrangement, but even with its abolition they still face very high tariffs. In the United States, for example, the exports of Mongolia, Bangladesh, and Cambodia, among the poorest countries in the world, faced an average tariff of about 15 percent. Meanwhile, the exports of Norway, France, and Singapore faced an average tariff of 1 percent. In 2006, Bangladesh paid $494 million in customs duties to get its goods into the United States; France paid $367 million. Yet Bangladesh exported just $3 billion, while France exported over $37 billion.[56]

[54] Baffes 2005.
[55] Alston, Sumner, and Brunke 2007.
[56] Gresser 2007.

U.S. policy does not deliberately attempt to stifle the trade of developing countries in favor of richer countries, but it does so implicitly by virtue of the tariffs it levies on different goods. Industrial products generally face very low import duties, whereas labor-intensive manufactured goods, such as clothing and consumer products, face much higher tariffs. The developing countries could have much better success in world trade if they did not confront these higher barriers in OECD markets. One study found that recent reductions in trade barriers in developed countries had a pronounced positive impact on export performance and economic growth in developing countries.[57]

Ironically, many in the developed world who are concerned about poverty and economic underdevelopment elsewhere do not focus on U.S. import tariffs as much as they do on working conditions provided by multinational firms in developing countries. This leads us to the controversial question of whether workers in developing countries are being exploited by foreign firms and, if so, what should be done about it.

Sweatshops and Labor Standards

Many multinational corporations have invested in low-wage developing countries to produce labor-intensive goods, such as clothing and shoes. This foreign investment has generated controversy, with companies such as Nike being accused of earning high profits by exploiting cheap labor in Asian sweatshops. Student activists, human rights groups, and other NGOs have decried the poor working conditions and treatment of labor in developing countries, and are sharply critical of multinational corporations for their failure to pay a "living" wage to workers there. Labor unions in the developed countries have long maintained that countries with lower labor standards have an unfair competitive advantage in trade and that they attract jobs and investment at the expense of countries with higher standards.

These groups fault world trade negotiators for neglecting to include labor standards in trade agreements and thus failing to protect the interests of workers. Yet most developing countries strenuously object to any linking of trade policy and labor standards. They fear that if devel-

[57] Romalis 2007.

US = 1.0

___*Figure 6.4*

Labor Costs and Productivity in Manufacturing for 63 Countries, 1995–1999
(United States = 1.0).
Source: World Bank 2000, table 2.6.

oped countries are allowed to restrict imports from countries deemed not
to have adequate labor standards, they will have yet another excuse for
denying low-wage countries access to their markets, thereby preventing
developing countries from taking advantage of their comparative advantage in labor-intensive goods.

Before asking whether trade agreements should include provisions on labor standards, it is worth examining the perennial claim that
low wages give a country an unfair advantage in trade. The key economic lesson is that low wages reflect low labor productivity. Workers in
developed countries enjoy high wages and benefits because of their high
productivity. Figure 6.4 illustrates the strong relationship between labor
costs per worker (a measure of wages and benefits that firms must pay)
and value added per worker (a measure of productivity) in manufacturing for sixty-three countries during 1995–99. The correlation is striking:

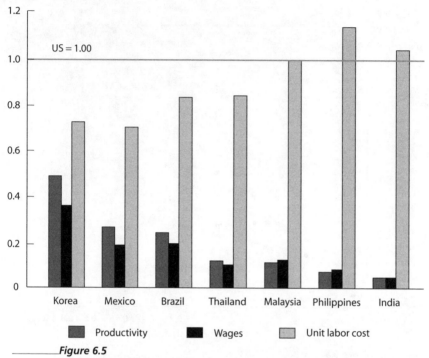

_____*Figure 6.5*
Labor Productivity, Wages, and Unit Labor Costs in Selected Developing
Countries, 1990 (United States = 100).
Source: Golub 1999, 23.

the higher a country's average productivity, the higher the country's average wages. Econometric evidence has regularly shown that labor productivity alone explains about 70–80 percent of the cross-country variation
in average wages in manufacturing. After also accounting for differences
in per capita GDP and in price levels across countries, over 90 percent of
the variation in wages between countries can be explained.[58]

Since average wages reflect average productivity, the cost advantage of low wages is generally offset by the cost disadvantage of low
productivity. This implies that unit labor costs are roughly comparable
across countries. Figure 6.5 depicts this relationship. In India and the
Philippines, for example, average wages are less than 10 percent of those

[58] Even though these purely economic variables explain almost all of the differences in wage rates across countries, Rodrik (1999) finds that indicators of political freedom
contribute some additional explanatory power.

in the United States. But the average productivity of workers is also less than 10 percent of that in the United States. Thus, the unit labor cost—the effective cost of hiring labor—is roughly comparable between the two countries. And, in fact, multinational corporations searching for cheap labor find that you get what you pay for: low wages imply a less productive workforce. Thus, multinationals generally find it profitable to turn to developing countries only for unskilled labor-intensive activities, particularly those in which the productivity of workers is comparable to that in developed countries but the average wage is much less.[59]

As developing countries improve the productivity of their workers, through the acquisition of better technology or other mechanisms, competitive pressures bid up average wages. As a result, the growth in domestic wages tracks the growth in domestic productivity. Indeed, a country's average wage rate is determined almost exclusively by domestic productivity performance. As figure 6.6 shows, for example, the acceleration of productivity in South Korea in the 1980s was accompanied by a dramatic rise in labor compensation. By contrast, the Philippines has been much less successful at increasing productivity and therefore has not seen a comparable rise in wages. The evidence is clear: countries that successfully increase productivity experience a rise in wages, while countries whose productivity is stagnant see little change in wages.

Countries with low wages tend to specialize in unskilled labor-intensive goods. Beyond this, there is little empirical evidence that low labor standards, in themselves, exert an important influence on trade flows. Several studies have failed to find a strong relationship between measures of labor standards and international trade flows (such as export performance in labor-intensive goods) or direct investment flows (such as whether countries with low standards attract more foreign investment).[60] The OECD has concluded that "empirical findings confirm the analytical result that core labor standards do not play a significant role in shaping trade performance. The view which argues that low-standard

---

[59] Of course, overall productivity depends not just on a worker's output, but the economy's infrastructure, the availability of technical and support personnel, and other factors. There are many examples of multinationals relocating production back in the United States because, despite the availability of inexpensive labor in other countries, the general environment for business made it difficult to make effective use of that labor.

[60] See, for example, Rodrik 1996.

a) South Korea

b) The Philippines

_____Figure 6.6_

Real Wages and Labor Productivity in Manufacturing, South Korea and the
Philippines, 1972–1993 (1987 = 100).
Source: World Bank 1975.

countries will enjoy gains in export market shares to the detriment of
high-standard countries appears to lack solid empirical support."[61]

Low wages and poor working conditions in developing countries have sparked protests from concerned citizens in developed countries. The Worker Rights Consortium, established by students, unions,
and human rights groups, has accused the athletic shoe manufacturer

[61] OECD 1996, 33. The OECD (2000, 33) concluded that "this finding has not
been challenged by the literature appearing since the 1996 study was completed."

Nike and other multinationals of subjecting workers to sweatshop conditions and not paying a living wage. Working conditions in many developing countries are indeed horrible by the standards of developed countries, and everyone wants to see those standards of living improve. These activists have changed working conditions for the better by putting companies in the spotlight of bad publicity if their contractors treat their workers poorly.[62]

Still, the best and most direct way to raise wages and labor standards is to enhance the productivity of the workers through economic development. Trade and investment are important components of that development, and therefore efforts to limit international trade or to shut down the sweatshops are counterproductive. For example, most foreign-owned firms pay substantially higher wages than comparable domestic firms.[63] In Vietnam, for instance, while the general population (mainly employed in agriculture in rural areas) could afford per capita expenditures of $205 in 1998, people working in foreign-owned business spent $420 that year.[64] Poverty rates are much lower for those holding jobs with foreign-owned firms. While 37 percent of the Vietnamese workers were classified as poor in 1998, only 8 percent of those working in foreign-owned businesses were considered poor. And although 15 percent of all workers were classified as "very poor," none of the workers in foreign-owned textile and leather-goods businesses were in that category.

The fact that foreign-owned "sweatshops" in poorer countries pay above-average wages in the local labor market may explain the low turnover (or quit) rate of workers at such firms. It may also explain why these jobs are so desirable that, in some instances, workers must pay one month's salary as a bribe to employment officers at such firms in order to get hired. And even though the wages are low, the savings rate of factory workers is much higher than that of workers elsewhere in the economy— an interesting fact in light of the accusation that such firms are not paying

[62] Elliott, Kar, and Richardson (2006) examine the views of activists in developed countries that are pressing for better treatment of labor in developing countries. See also Harrison and Scorse 2004.

[63] See Aitken, Harrison, and Lipsey (1996) for a study of foreign firms in Mexico, Venezuela, and the United States. Lipsey and Sjöholm (2001) show that foreign-owned firms in Indonesia pay higher wages than locally owned firms.

[64] Glewwe 2000.

a living wage. In fact, in Vietnam and elsewhere, workers often request overtime, as they are seeking to maximize their income. International codes and rules that limit hours of work may interfere with the desire of these individuals to earn more money.

Even if the wages and working conditions in developing countries are dismal by the standards of the present-day United States, these multinational firms are at least providing employment opportunities and incomes that might not otherwise exist, enabling the poor to support their families. Two reporters for *The New York Times* provide a vivid example. When they were first assigned to cover Asia, they, like most people, were outraged at the sweatshop conditions. They later changed their opinion: "In time, though, we came to accept the view supported by most Asians: that the campaign against sweatshops risks harming the very people it is intended to help. . . . Those sweatshops tended to generate the wealth to solve the problems they created. . . . it may sound silly to say that sweatshops offer a route to prosperity, when wages in the poorest countries are sometimes less than $1 per day. Still, for an impoverished Indonesian or Bangladeshi woman with a handful of kids who would otherwise drop out of school and risk dying of mundane diseases like diarrhea, $1 or $2 a day can be a life-transforming wage."[65]

Most of the sweatshop workers are young women, many of whom have gone to industrial cities from rural villages. By Western standards, they endure long hours, low pay, and poor conditions. And yet, despite the monotony of factory work, they found it a vast improvement over the back-breaking monotony of field work, according to a sociologist who lived with migrant factory workers in southern China. Many of these women earned seven to eight times what their fathers earned working in rural agriculture in their home village, and could send money back to their families.[66] Yet the motivation for these young women leaving their homes was much more than financial. They left behind a patriarchal order in which their fathers could marry them off to the village idiot without their say in the matter. With their factory work, they gained freedom and independence, as well as dignity and self-respect. It enabled them to spend their lives and their money the way they wanted, such as shopping,

[65] Kristof and WuDunn 2000, 70–71.
[66] Lee 1998.

going to see a movie, or taking English or computer classes at night—things that would have been impossible in their rural communities.

The fundamental problem facing workers in developing countries is not the existence of sweatshops, but the lack of good alternative employment opportunities. Efforts to stop exports from low-wage countries, to prevent investment there by multinationals, or to impose high minimum wages or benefits beyond the productivity level of the domestic workforce will simply diminish the demand for labor in those countries and take away one of the few opportunities that workers have to better themselves and their families. Opponents of sweatshops have failed to consider what alternative opportunities for employment can be created.

_____*Should Trade Agreements Have Labor Standards?*

Can including labor standards in trade agreements help improve labor conditions in developing countries? The United States has been virtually alone in pressing for such standards in trade negotiations. And yet there is a great deal of ambiguity about which standards should be included, their precise definition, and how they should be enforced.[67] Two categories of labor standards are typically discussed. "Core" standards are related to fundamental human rights and can be universal in their application, such as a prohibition on forced labor. "Economic" labor standards, by contrast, are tied more closely to a country's level of economic development and include minimum wages and working conditions.

Core labor standards have been defined by the International Labor Organization (ILO), an international body created in 1919 and composed of member governments, employers, and workers. In 1996, the ILO issued a Declaration on Fundamental Principles and Rights at Work stating that all countries, regardless of their level of economic development, have an obligation to promote the following principles and rights: freedom of association and the effective recognition of the right to collective bargaining; elimination of all forms of forced or compulsory labor; effective abolition of child labor; and elimination of discrimination in respect of employment and occupation.

[67] Bhagwati and Hudec 1996.

Although such core labor standards are generally recognized and attract wide support, there is (with the exception of slavery) remarkably little international consensus on the precise definition of these standards and the method of implementing them. The ILO oversees over 180 conventions on various aspects of labor rights and practices, but very few of them have been ratified by all of the ILO members. As of 2008, for example, the United States had ratified just fourteen and had agreed to only two of the core conventions (on the abolition of forced labor and the prohibition of the worst forms of child labor). The United States has ratified few conventions partly because domestic labor law is largely the prerogative of state governments and partly because the language of the conventions may conflict with national policy. For example, convention number 111 seeks to abolish employment discrimination on the basis of sex and race, but has not been ratified by the United States because it might conflict with affirmative action.

Other countries have also failed to adopt ILO conventions because they are perceived to be inflexible or irrelevant to local circumstances. For example, conventions number 87 and 98 deal with the right to organize and collective bargaining. The United States has not ratified these conventions because many states allow the hiring of replacement workers, which under the ILO convention could be viewed as interfering with the right to strike. Many developing countries are simply indifferent to these conventions. As one economist has noted, "for an overwhelming majority of poor workers in developing countries whose dominant mode of employment is self-employment in rural agricultural activities or in the urban informal sector, unionization has little relevance. Even where relevant and where the freedom to form unions has been exercised to a significant extent, namely in the organized manufacturing and public sector in poor countries, labor unions have been promoting the interests of a small section of the labor force at the expense of many."[68]

Child labor has been a particularly controversial issue, and one that illustrates the limits of using ILO conventions and trade policy to reduce this practice. Convention number 182, signed by President Clinton at the WTO summit in Seattle in 1999, aims to eliminate the worst forms of child labor, such as slavery, the sale of children, forced labor, prostitution,

---

[68] Srinivasan 1998, 76.

and illicit activities. The United States prohibits imports of goods made with forced or indentured child labor, but does not have a generic ban on imported goods made with child labor. Indeed, dealing with nonexploitative child labor is a more difficult issue. The ILO charter establishing minimum ages of work has not been ratified by the United States, Canada, or other developed countries because of differing national views on the details. For example, Canada chooses not to prohibit work at night for children under age thirteen.

Of course, child labor is a major issue in developing countries, and some activists have suggested that developed countries should refuse to import any goods made with child labor. But just as trade policy is an inefficient instrument for achieving environmental objectives, as chapter 2 suggested, it is also an inefficient instrument for raising labor standards. An import ban on goods made with child labor might stop the use of children to produce goods for the U.S. market, but it would not put an end to child labor. Only about 5 percent of working children are employed in the export sector in developing countries. An import ban might simply shift them to other sectors of the domestic economy (about 80 percent are employed in the primary agricultural sector). At worst, an import ban could push them into less desirable or more hazardous work, or even leave them without work and thereby condemn them to starvation.[69] Import bans fail to address the root cause of child labor or offer any resolution to the underlying conditions that create it.

The most effective way of eliminating child labor is to attack the fundamental causes, which are poverty and the lack of affordable or adequate educational opportunities. As figure 6.7 indicates, the incidence of child labor is strongly related to per capita GDP. In fact, about 80 percent of the international variation in child labor is explained by this variable alone. Child labor virtually disappears once a country's annual per capita income reaches $5,000. Developing countries can help reduce

[69] "Caroline Lequesne of Oxfam, a British charity, has just returned from Bangladesh, where she visited factories to determine the impact of American retailers' human-rights policies. She reckons that between 1993 and 1994 around 30,000 of the 50,000 children working in textile firms in Bangladesh were thrown out of factories because suppliers feared losing their business if they kept the children on. But the majority of these children have, because of penury, been forced to turn to prostitution or other industries like welding, where conditions pose far greater risks to them." *Economist*, June 3, 1995, 59.

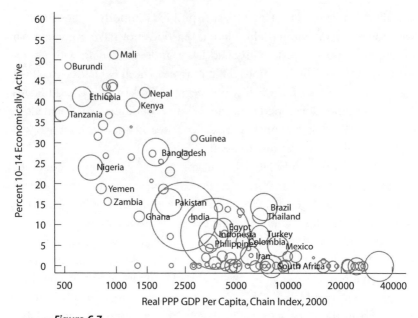

_____Figure 6.7
Child Labor and GDP per Capita, 2000.
Source: Edmonds and Pavcnik 2005.

child labor by raising rural incomes through agricultural price liberalization. Evidence from Vietnam suggests that when the domestic price of
rice rose after the government permitted more rice exports, farmers responded by reducing the use of child labor.[70] Developed countries can
help developing countries raise their income by allowing them to sell
their products more easily in the markets of the richer economies. Compulsory education laws that mandate school attendance have also proven
effective in reducing child labor and are more easily monitored than direct bans on imports.[71]

The WTO is not the proper forum for dealing with the issue of
core labor standards because these standards are not directly related to

[70] Edmonds and Pavcnik 2006.

[71] Rising income and compulsory education accounted for the decline in the employment of children in the United States, and can do so in developing countries as well.
The United States, it should be noted, did not ban child labor until the Fair Employment
Act of 1938, a point when per capita income was well above that in many developing
countries today.

international trade. Even if a country did not engage in international trade but suppressed worker rights, labor standards should still be an issue because of the universality of core labor standards. To put it differently, if a country had a problem with the treatment of child labor but did not use that labor in exported goods, that practice should still be a source of global concern. Furthermore, the WTO lacks the institutional expertise and resources to deal with labor issues. As the WTO membership itself declared at the 1996 ministerial meeting in Singapore, the ILO is the competent body to set and administer labor standards. The effort to push labor standards onto the WTO's lap would undermine the ILO as well as burden the WTO with something it is not well equipped to handle.

The WTO has been tagged with the issue of labor standards primarily because trade sanctions are believed to be the most effective way of enforcing such standards. As we have seen, however, the threat of trade sanctions to enforce labor standards in developing countries risks harming the very workers we are trying to help. As Paul Krugman puts it, "even if we could assure the workers in Third World export industries of higher wages and better working conditions, this would do nothing for the peasants, day laborers, scavengers, and so on who make up the bulk of these countries' populations. At best, forcing developing countries to adhere to our labor standards would create a privileged labor aristocracy, leaving the poor majority no better off."[72] At worst, those export industries would be shut down, causing those workers to lose their jobs. Furthermore, the threat of using trade sanctions to enforce labor standards is precisely why developing countries are so afraid of including them in the WTO. Developing countries adamantly oppose efforts to link trade and labor standards, which is why pressing this issue is asking for a stalemate in the WTO.[73]

[72] Krugman 1998a, 84. Economic development is the only known way to increase wages. The alternatives—massive foreign aid, stronger demands for social justice—are unrealistic or ineffective. As Krugman comments, "As long as you have no realistic alternative to industrialization based on low wages, to oppose [trade and industrialization] means that you are willing to deny desperately poor people the best chance they have of progress for the sake of what amounts to an aesthetic standard—that is, the fact that you don't like the idea of workers being paid a pittance to supply rich Westerners with fashion items."

[73] At the 1996 WTO ministerial meeting in Singapore, the United States pressed for the creation of a working group on labor standards. After sharp opposition by developing countries, the WTO membership agreed that the ILO instead was the appropriate venue

To the extent that international cooperation in the ILO is considered useful, how should ILO charters be enforced? The problem is that if countries lack the political will to adhere to international rules, then the enforcement of those rules is beside the point. "Bad" regimes are unlikely to be moved by trade sanctions. Furthermore, under ILO rules, a government can only bring a complaint against another government if both have ratified the relevant convention. Through its failure to ratify many of the ILO conventions, the United States has effectively forfeited its right to use that organization to enforce labor rights abroad. For those countries that have ratified ILO charters or agree to accords on labor standards, enforcement is best carried out by embedding the ILO commitments in domestic law and enforcing them through civil actions and punitive judgments (such as fines) in the domestic legal system.

If dealing with "core" labor standards is difficult enough, there are political pressures in developed countries to go beyond core standards and into the realm of "economic" standards. Labor unions and other NGOs have pressed for standards that include minimum wages, employment hours, occupational health and safety regulations, minimum age of employment, and so on. Without these economic standards, it is argued, developing countries will attract investment and gain jobs at the expense of developed countries, which will then face pressures to reduce labor standards. Such economic standards, however, have no place in a trade agreement because they are a function of economic development.[74] Labor unions' role in this push is worrisome from the standpoint

---

for considering labor standards. Despite this agreement, the United States again called for an examination of labor standards in the WTO at the 1999 Seattle ministerial meeting. Developing countries were completely hostile, and even Canada failed to support the United States, while the European Union was willing to consider greater cooperation between the WTO and the ILO only if any linkage between labor standards and market access was ruled out. When President Clinton let slip the idea that labor standards should be included in trade agreements and enforced with trade sanctions, developing countries accused the United States of bad faith (ignoring the Singapore declaration) and were galvanized to oppose any new trade round on this basis. The president's statement almost single-handedly ensured the failure of the Seattle meeting.

[74] As Robert Reich (1994), the secretary of labor in the Clinton administration, stated, "It is inappropriate to dictate uniform levels of working hours, minimum wages, benefits, or health and safety standards. The developing countries' insistence that they must grow richer in order to afford American or European labor standards—that they must trade if they are to grow richer is essentially correct."

of developing countries because all too often unions have simply sought to block trade.

As a result, while most advocates of higher labor standards are genuinely motivated by concerns about workers in developing countries, the politics of labor standards are such that attempts will be made to use them to limit the market access of low-wage developing countries. In January 1999, the United States signed an agreement with Cambodia that promised a 14 percent increase in Cambodia's annual quota for textile shipments if the country agreed to meet certain core labor standards. Although the Cambodian garment industry established high minimum wages and agreed to paid vacations, unionization rights, and a ban on child labor, the Union of Needletrades, Industrial and Textile Employees (UNITE) wrote to the U.S. Trade Representative (USTR) opposing any increase in the quota. Following this, and without consulting other views, USTR ruled in December 1999 that Cambodia was not in "substantial compliance" with the agreement and denied the quota increase. The Cambodian government and garment industry were shocked because they believed they had gone beyond the agreement in improving standards. Five months later, USTR agreed to a smaller increase, of 5 percent, after Cambodia and the ILO established a program to monitor work conditions.[75]

Unions such as UNITE, the Teamsters, and the AFL-CIO also opposed legislation that gave African countries the same tariff preferences that the United States had previously extended to Caribbean and other poor developing countries. The African Growth and Opportunity Act of 2000 aimed to help the continent by giving duty-free access to the U.S. market in selected goods. Instead of being viewed as a small way of helping African countries improve their economies, labor-backed opponents dubbed the legislation as "NAFTA for Africa." The proposal to allow African textile producers duty-free access to the U.S. market proved to be quite controversial even though Africa's share of U.S. apparel consumption was only 0.45 percent. The U.S. International Trade Commission concluded that the impact of removing the quota on the U.S. apparel industry would be negligible and that, at most, only 676 U.S. jobs would be affected.[76] Other analysts have suggested that the preferences

[75] Cooper 2000.
[76] U.S. International Trade Commission 1997, 3–12.

might have an even smaller domestic impact because it would simply improve the position of Africa at the expense of China. Their staunch opposition to free trade with Africa fuels suspicions that labor unions are not really interested in helping poor African workers deeply mired in poverty, but oppose any measure that promises to increase trade.

Experience has shown that it is all too easy to mask an antitrade agenda with labor and environmental concerns, as is evident by many anticommercial NGOs and anti-import labor unions. This is regrettable because there are deep and legitimate questions about using trade measures to enforce labor and environmental standards, and therefore the possibility of common ground gets lost in the advocacy of extreme positions. Yet there are inherent flaws in giving the WTO a non-trade-related mission, such as enforcing environmental agreements or enforcing labor standards. The risk is that these poorly targeted and indirect instruments for improving environmental and labor conditions will fail to achieve their objective yet at the same time will expand the allowable rationales for trade barriers, thus undermining the liberal trading system without generating compensating benefits.

In conclusion, expanding world trade presents great opportunities for the world's developing countries. While trade policies in developed countries often hinder the ability of developing countries to improve their condition, developing countries cannot blame all of their problems on foreign trade barriers. Trade restrictions and barriers are much more extensive in the developing world than elsewhere. Much of the blame for the lack of development falls not on the people of these countries, but on their governments and their poor policies that inhibit economic activity. As the examples of India and China dramatically demonstrate, not the rest of the world, but their own misguided policies, have been holding them back from achieving higher rates of economic growth and poverty reduction.

7

The World Trading System:
The WTO, Trade Disputes,
and Regional Agreements

For more than sixty years, the General Agreement on Tariffs and Trade (GATT) has provided a system of world trade rules under which international trade has flourished. In 1994, the Uruguay Round of trade negotiations produced sweeping agreements to liberalize trade in agriculture and apparel and to extend trade rules to new areas such as services, investment, and intellectual property. In addition, the World Trade Organization (WTO) was established as a formal multilateral institution with stronger procedures for resolving disputes than in the GATT. While the GATT had a rather quiet existence, the WTO has proven very controversial. This chapter assesses the WTO as an institution and examines the controversies about its dispute settlement rulings, the prospects for the Doha Round of negotiations, and the increasing importance of regional (or preferential) trade agreements.

The Origins of the GATT System

The searing experience of the Great Depression in the 1930s provided the impetus for establishing a formal system of world trade rules. The Great Depression was a worldwide economic disaster. Between 1929 and 1932, the volume of world trade fell 26 percent and world industrial production fell 32 percent. Unemployment in many countries topped 20 percent. As the economic downturn intensified, countries responded by raising tariffs and imposing import quotas in a desperate attempt to insulate themselves from the worldwide economic collapse and boost domestic employment. Widespread protectionism—in the form of tariffs, quotas, foreign exchange restrictions, and the like—materialized overnight.

Yet reducing imports proved to be a futile method of combating the economic downturn because one country's imports were another country's
exports. The combined effect of this global turn toward protectionism
was a collapse of international trade, which merely exacerbated the
problems of the world economy.

The United States bears some responsibility for these developments. In the 1928 election year, prior to the economic downturn, President Herbert Hoover called for increased tariffs on agricultural imports to
help U.S. farmers. Once Congress started considering higher duties, however, things began to spin out of control. Logrolling coalitions pushed
tariff rates higher and higher, resulting in the infamous Hawley-Smoot
tariff of 1930. Warning of the adverse economic consequences of the
high tariffs, more than one thousand American economists signed a petition urging President Hoover not to sign the bill. The warning was not
heeded, and the Hawley-Smoot tariff helped push up the average tariff
on dutiable imports to nearly 50 percent.[1]

While economic historians do not believe that the Hawley-Smoot
tariff caused the Great Depression, the high tariffs certainly played a role
in the downward spiral of U.S. trade and the overall economic decline.
The act also exacerbated world trade tensions and contributed to the
global rise in trade barriers. As the League of Nations noted at the time,
the Hawley-Smoot tariff was "the signal for an outburst of tariff-making
activity in other countries, partly at least by way of reprisals."[2]

Out of the ashes of the Depression emerged a new approach to
U.S. trade policy. At the request of President Franklin Roosevelt, Congress enacted the Reciprocal Trade Agreements Act (RTAA) in 1934. The
initial RTAA authorized the president to enter into tariff agreements with
foreign countries and to reduce import duties by no more than 50 percent. Although the president's authority required regular renewal, an important element of the RTAA was the prior approval by Congress of any
trade agreement reached by the executive. Congress also endorsed the
unconditional most-favored nation (MFN) clause, under which the lower
U.S. tariffs negotiated with one country would be automatically extended
to other countries.

[1] For a discussion of this period, see Irwin 1998a.
[2] League of Nations 1933, 193.

The RTAA was "too little, too late" to have a big effect on protectionism in the 1930s, but it had a lasting impact as a political innovation. The RTAA fundamentally changed American trade politics by tipping the political balance of power in favor of lower tariffs in several ways.[3]

First, when Congress delegated tariff negotiating power to the chief executive, it effectively gave up the ability to legislate duties on specific goods. Congress had always been very responsive to domestic import-competing interests and did not give much thought to exporters, consumers, or the possibility of foreign retaliation. Congressional votes on trade now came to be framed in terms of whether or not, and under what circumstances, the RTAA should be continued. Vote trading among interests that favored various tariffs was no longer feasible. Thus, the RTAA reduced access to legislative mechanisms that supported redistributive bargains and logrolling coalitions that had led to high tariffs.

Second, the RTAA delegated authority and agenda-setting power to the president, who represented a broad-based constituency and was therefore more likely than Congress to favor lower tariffs. The national electoral base of the president is thought to make the executive more apt to favor policies that benefit the nation as a whole, whereas the narrower geographic representative structure of Congress leads its members to have more parochial interests. Furthermore, the president is more likely than Congress to use trade negotiations to advance foreign policy goals.

Third, the RTAA reduced the threshold of political support needed for members of Congress to approve negotiated agreements reducing tariffs. Prior to the RTAA, a minority could block foreign trade agreements because treaties had to be approved by a two-thirds majority in the Senate. Now, renewal of the RTAA required a simple majority in Congress. This shifted the threshold of political support needed to approve trade agreements and made them easier to enact. Whereas protectionist forces in the past had to muster only 34 percent of all senators to block a reciprocity treaty, now they needed 51 percent of senators to kill a renewal of the RTAA.

Finally, the RTAA helped to bolster the bargaining and lobbying position of exporters in the political process. Previously, the main

---

[3] See the analysis of Bailey, Goldstein, and Weingast 1997 and Irwin and Kroszner 1999.

trade-related special interest groups on Capitol Hill were domestic producers facing import competition. Exporters were harmed by high tariffs on imports, but only indirectly. The cost to exporters of any particular import duty was minute, and therefore exporters failed to organize an effective political opposition. The RTAA explicitly linked foreign tariff reductions that were beneficial to exporters to lower tariff protection for producers competing against imports. This fostered the development of exporters as an organized group opposing high domestic tariffs because they wanted to secure lower foreign tariffs on their products. In addition, the lower tariffs negotiated under the RTAA increased the size of export sectors and decreased the size of sectors that competed with imports, and thereby increased the political clout of interests supporting renewals of the RTAA.

These features of the RTAA reduced the costs and increased the benefits of organization and lobbying by free trade interests.

_____The General Agreement on Tariffs and Trade

To officials at the time, the lesson of the 1930s was absolutely clear: like appeasement in the realm of diplomacy, protectionism in the field of economic policy was a serious mistake that helped make the decade of the 1930s a political and economic disaster. World leaders therefore agreed that, after World War II, cooperative actions must be taken to reduce barriers to international trade. Even as World War II raged, American and British officials began exploring postwar trade arrangements. The United States aimed to convert the piecemeal, bilateral RTAA approach into a broader, multilateral system based on nondiscrimination and the reduction of trade barriers.[4]

After several preliminary meetings, representatives from twenty-three countries met in Geneva in 1947 and agreed on tariff reductions and on the text of a General Agreement on Tariffs and Trade (GATT). The tariff reductions were negotiated on a bilateral, product-by-product basis under the "reciprocal mutual advantage" principle, ensuring that no country would be forced to make unilateral concessions. If a bilateral agreement on specific commodity tariffs were reached, the lower negoti-

---

[4]On the origins of the GATT, see Irwin, Mavroidis, and Sykes 2008.

_____*Table 7.1*
Major Provisions of the General Agreement on Tariffs and Trade

Provision	Description
Article 1	General Most Favored Nation Treatment
Article 2	Schedule of Tariff Concessions
Article 3	National Treatment on Internal Taxes and Regulation
Article 6	Antidumping and Countervailing Duties
Article 10	Transparency of Trade Regulations
Article 11	General Elimination of Quantitative Restrictions
Article 12	Restrictions to Safeguard the Balance of Payments
Article 14	Exceptions to Rule of Non-Discrimination
Article 16	Subsidies
Article 17	State Trading Enterprises
Article 19	Emergency Action on Imports of Particular Products (Safeguards)
Article 20	General Exceptions
Article 21	Security Exceptions
Article 23	Nullification and Impairment
Article 24	Customs Unions and Free Trade Areas

ated rates would then be applied to all other members, through the most-favored nation clause, and considered bound at those rates. The United States reduced its tariff about 20 percent in the first GATT round.[5] Precise estimates of the degree to which other countries reduced their tariffs are unavailable, but major European countries reduced their import tariffs significantly between the early 1930s and the early 1950s, although quantitative restrictions and exchange controls persisted in many of these countries.[6]

The text of General Agreement on Tariffs and Trade set out principles for the conduct of commercial policy. The main provisions of the GATT are summarized in table 7.1.[7] First and foremost, Article 1 declared that all GATT signatories would extend unconditional most favored nation (MFN) treatment to all other contracting parties. The MFN clause

[5] But as figure 1.4 illustrated, average U.S. tariffs dropped sharply from about 45 percent in 1933 to just over 10 percent in the early 1950s. Most of this reduction was not the result of negotiated reductions in tariff rates, but the result of the effect of inflation on specific duties. Because these duties were unchanged in terms of nominal amounts, inflation during and after World War II dramatically eroded the ad valorem equivalent of these duties. See Irwin 1998b.

[6] See WTO 2006.

[7] Hoekman and Kostecki (2009) provide an excellent overview of world trade system rules.

forbids countries from using trade measures to discriminate against other GATT partners. Governments would have discretion in choosing the terms on which they permitted foreign goods into their country, but as a matter of principle (if not always practice) they would not be allowed to treat the goods from one signatory of the GATT differently from the same goods from another.[8]

Similarly, Article 3 requires that countries imposing domestic taxes and regulations adhere to the standard of "national treatment." National treatment is another form of nondiscrimination by which domestic and imported goods should face the same regulatory standards. Under this provision, governments were prevented from setting one standard for domestic products and then imposing a more stringent standard for similar imported products.

The other articles of the GATT deal with more specific trade policy issues. Article 6 condemns dumping if it causes or threatens material injury to an established industry and sets out very general standards for imposing antidumping and countervailing duties. Article 16 mandates that countries avoid the use of subsidies for primary products and proposes that countries limit subsidies. Article 11 is a sweeping prohibition on the use of quantitative restrictions, although Article 12 permits the imposition of import quotas when countries have balance-of-payments difficulties. Article 18 is a general exemption for developing countries from GATT rules to give them flexibility to support infant industries and protect their balance of payments. Other articles of the GATT address such mundane details as the valuation of merchandise for customs purposes, marks of origin, and the transparency of trade regulations.

Unlike the World Bank and International Monetary Fund (IMF), the GATT was not a formal international institution. The countries signing the GATT were "contracting parties" and not members because the GATT was simply an agreement between governments, not an organization. The GATT as an institution consisted of an extremely small secretariat in

---

[8] The MFN clause in Article 1 simply reads: "With respect to customs duties and charges of any kind imposed on or in connection with importation or exportation . . . any advantage, favour, privilege or immunity granted by any contracting party to any product originating in or destined for any other country shall be accorded immediately and unconditionally to the like products . . . of all other contracting parties." But Article 24 permits countries to deviate from unconditional MFN in the case of free trade agreements and customs unions. The text of the 1947 GATT is available in World Trade Organization 1999.

_____***Table 7.2***
GATT Negotiating Rounds

Negotiating Round	Dates	Major Accomplishments
Geneva	1947	GATT established. About 20 percent tariff reduction negotiated.
Annecy	1949	Accession of 11 new contracting parties. Minor tariff reduction (about 2 percent).
Torquay	1950–51	Accession of 7 new contracting parties. Minor tariff reduction (about 3 percent).
Geneva	1955–56	Minor tariff reduction (about 2.5 percent).
Dillon Round	1960–61	Negotiations involving external tariff of European Community. Minor tariff reduction (4 percent).
Kennedy Round	1964–67	About 35 percent tariff reduction.
Tokyo Round	1973–79	About 33 percent tariffs reduction. Six codes negotiated (e.g., subsidies, technical barriers, etc.).
Uruguay Round	1986–94	WTO established. Additional tariff reductions. New agreements on dispute settlement, agriculture, clothing, services, investment, and intellectual property.
Doha Development Round	2001–	To be determined.

Geneva, but its official standing was precarious. The advantage of this situation was that the GATT remained a small body devoted to a single mission: promoting further attempts to liberalize trade and establishing broad rules for commercial policy. In contrast to the World Bank and IMF, the GATT had a narrow focus rather than a multifaceted agenda.

After the establishment of the GATT, the contracting parties met on a regular basis to negotiate further reductions in trade barriers. Table 7.2 lists these negotiating "rounds," as they are called, and their major accomplishments. In the 1950s, more countries acceded to the GATT, but further tariff reductions were negligible. In 1958, six European countries agreed to eliminate all tariffs on each others' goods, thus forming a common market, the precursor to today's European Union. U.S. exporters were concerned that their sales would suffer because American goods would still be subject to import duties in Europe. To reduce the margin of preference on intra-European trade, Congress took a serious interest in reducing trade barriers between the United States and Europe and authorized the president to undertake new negotiations. The Kennedy

Round, begun in 1962 and concluded in 1967, resulted in a 35 percent reduction in tariffs, on average. These cuts were generally across the board, with each country receiving exemptions for sensitive sectors. The across-the-board approach proved to be more efficient and less cumbersome than the product-by-product negotiations used in previous rounds, although this was not obvious from the length of the negotiations.

The Tokyo Round negotiations (from 1973 to 1979) sliced tariffs by another third. By this time, tariffs on manufactured goods for the major industrialized countries had generally fallen to low levels. As a result, the Tokyo Round began the trend toward even more difficult negotiations about nontariff barriers. The Tokyo Round resulted in several codes dealing with nontariff issues such as subsidies, technical barriers, import licenses, government procurement, customs valuation, and anti-dumping procedures. These codes substantially broadened the scope of trade rules in certain areas, but also contained wide-ranging exceptions. In addition, countries could pick and choose which, if any, of the codes it wished to adopt, an approach that became known as "GATT á la carte." A majority of GATT members, including most developing countries, chose not to sign the codes. Indeed, developing countries were given "special and differential" treatment, meaning that they were not required to cut their trade barriers and adhere to GATT rules to the same extent as the industrialized countries.

The Trade Act of 1974, which authorized U.S. participation in the Tokyo Round, also included a provision called "fast track," or what today is sometimes called "trade promotion authority." Because trade agreements now involve much more than just reducing tariff rates, such as dealing with nontariff barriers and government regulations, they require changes in domestic legislation. Rather than have Congress meddle with the outcome of the multilateral negotiations by making amendments, which would essentially bring the negotiating process to an end, Congress agreed to give trade agreements expedited consideration and vote them up or down with no possibility of amendment to facilitate the process. If the president does not have such negotiating authority, it is more difficult—but not impossible—for U.S. negotiators to conclude international trade agreements.[9]

[9] The president's current negotiating authority expired in June 2007.

The Uruguay Round (1986–94) turned out to be the most successful and comprehensive since the formation of the GATT. This round not only liberalized trade in areas that had eluded previous negotiators, notably agriculture and clothing, but extended rules to new areas such as services, investment, and intellectual property. The Uruguay Round also brought about important institutional changes, both creating the World Trade Organization and strengthening the dispute settlement process.[10] At the same time, these far-reaching agreements produced controversy the likes of which the GATT had never seen.

As in previous negotiations, participating countries agreed to reduce tariffs on merchandise goods. Developed countries reduced tariffs on industrial products (excluding petroleum) by about 40 percent on a trade-weighted average basis. This brought average tariff levels in these countries down from 6.3 percent to 3.8 percent. Developing countries reduced their tariffs by 20 percent on average, bringing their average rates down from 15.3 percent to 12.3 percent.[11]

More important, the Uruguay Round began to incorporate trade in agricultural goods and in textiles and apparel into the GATT system. Since the 1950s, the agricultural policies of many countries had been exempt from the GATT rules. The Multi-Fiber Arrangement (MFA) in textiles and apparel set quantitative limits on trade, product by product, country by country, in a way that GATT rules did not generally permit. The Uruguay Round sought to normalize trade in these sectors, so that protection could only take the form of bound, nondiscriminatory tariffs and not be cloaked in special export restraint deals or country-specific quotas operating outside of GATT disciplines.

Reform of agricultural trade had also eluded negotiators ever since the GATT's formation because of the political sensitivity of domestic support for farmers. A key problem facing negotiators in the Uruguay Round was that countries protected agricultural producers through a complex host of measures, including tariffs, import quotas, domestic price supports, and export subsidies. The Uruguay Round agreement limits the use of export subsidies and internal price supports by capping and reducing these outlays from a given base period. The agreement also

[10] See Hoekman and Kostecki (2009) for an overview of the accomplishments of the Uruguay Round and the substance of WTO agreements.
[11] Preeg 1995, 191.

seeks to ensure greater market access by requiring countries to convert all nontariff barriers (variable import levies, import quotas and prohibitions, voluntary export restraints, etc.) into a single import tariff. After this "tariffication" of existing restrictions, the tariffs are to be reduced over ten years by an average one-third for developed countries and by one-quarter for developing countries.

The resulting tariffs, however, are incredibly high. Table 7.3 reveals just how imposing the remaining restrictions are. Many countries used the process of converting the complex trade barriers into tariffs as an opportunity to cheat, raising tariffs above the existing combination of nontariff restrictions. This practice, known as "dirty tariffication," means that the actual liberalization in agriculture was slight.[12] In addition, quantitative restrictions and export subsidies that are generally not permissible with manufactured goods persist in agricultural trade.

Subsidies have also persisted. In 2007, OECD countries provided $258 billion in support to agricultural producers, mainly through price supports. The European Union's farm policy, called the Common Agricultural Policy, involves a bewildering array of subsidies and other programs that take up nearly half of the EU's budget. France and other countries with powerful farm lobbies have fiercely resisted efforts to change the policy. In addition, any rollback of U.S. subsidies was prevented in 2002 and 2008 when new farm bills expanded rather than contracted support for agricultural producers, a big step backward in terms of reforming agricultural policies.[13]

---

[12] Ingco 1996.

[13] One leading agricultural economist wrote of the 2002 farm bill: "America's farm trade policy has become a four-dimensional disaster. It attempts to hide huge subsidy increases behind semantic claims of 'non-product specificity' in order to keep them GATT-legal, effectively insulating U.S. producers from global markets. It sends exactly the wrong signal to those in Europe and developing countries who have struggled for trade liberalization, undercutting progress made in the Uruguay Round to reduce protectionism and expand agricultural markets for all farmers—notably U.S. farmers. Because these huge subsidies will quickly be capitalized into farmland values, U.S. producers will face higher costs, and younger and less landed farmers will be denied entry, aggravating disturbing trends toward an aging farm population and fueling division between a landed elite and their tenants. And despite increases in authorized funding for conservation, the massive infusions of subsidies to row crop production are likely seriously to aggravate soil and water degradation as the United States continues to pay the agricultural polluter." Runge 2003, 93.

Table 7.3
Border Protection for Selected Agricultural Goods, 1986–88, 1995, and 2000 (in percent)

Country/ Region	Wheat Actual Protection 1986–88	Wheat As Bound in Uruguay Round 1995	Wheat As Bound in Uruguay Round 2000	Sugar Actual Protection 1986–88	Sugar As Bound in Uruguay Round 1995	Sugar As Bound in Uruguay Round 2000	Dairy Actual Protection 1986–88	Dairy As Bound in Uruguay Round 1995	Dairy As Bound in Uruguay Round 2000	Meat Actual Protection 1986–88	Meat As Bound in Uruguay Round 1995	Meat As Bound in Uruguay Round 2000
European Union	106	170	82	234	297	152	177	289	178	96	96	76
United States	20	6	4	131	197	91	132	144	93	3	31	26
Japan	651	240	152	184	126	58	501	489	326	87	93	50
Brazil	98	45	45	—	55	35	−21	53	46	−52	25	25
Mexico	−1	74	67	−58	173	156	−3	66	54	42	50	45
Other Latin America	−17	34	34	41	85	80	—	75	69	—	51	47
Sub-Saharan Africa	10	—	133	44	—	100	—	—	100	—	—	100

Source: Ingco 1996, 437.

Still, the WTO's 1994 agreement on agriculture constitutes a critical first step. Although these tariffs are high and severely distort production and trade, they are finally on the negotiating table. Because of the difficult political interests involved, however, the reform of agricultural trade policies will be an objective for many years to come.

The Uruguay Round also abolished the Multi-Fiber Arrangement, the complex web of bilateral export restraints and import quotas that clogs trade in textiles and apparel. The MFA was phased out over ten years, ending in January 2005, and the elimination of these quantitative restrictions has been a major step toward freer trade in clothing. Yet the United States and other developed countries will continue to protect their textile and apparel producers with high tariffs. In addition, antidumping and safeguard laws remain a vehicle for blocking textile and apparel imports with the MFA no longer around.

The Uruguay Round made little progress in regulating the use of antidumping laws, but countries did pledge not to "see, take or maintain any voluntary export restraints, orderly marketing arrangements or any other similar measures on the export or the import side."[14] Previously, the so-called gray measures had been used by countries to restrict trade without explicitly violating GATT rules. They are now eliminated, at least in principle. When countries seek to protect domestic industries from foreign competition, they are obligated to follow existing procedures and rules regarding safeguards and escape clauses. If adhered to, this provision also constitutes a major improvement in discipline.

The Uruguay Round also produced a General Agreement on Trade in Services (GATS) and established rules regarding trade-related investment measures (TRIMs) and trade-related intellectual property (TRIPs). Although these agreements are weak by the standards of the GATT, they constitute the first attempt to extend the principle of nondiscrimination to new areas of international commerce. The core obligations in the GATS are set around three principles: most favored nation treatment, market access, and national treatment. The main sectors include telecommunications, financial services, air and maritime transport, and construction. Although the agreement contains specific commitments to

---

[14] Article 1:1(b) of the Agreement on Safeguards, in WTO 1999, 280.

liberalization, coverage is incomplete because the important provisions of the GATS apply only to the sectors specified by the member countries. In general, trade in services was freed only slightly, but a framework was established in which liberalization could be pursued in the future.

The TRIMs agreement was even more modest in making national treatment the standard for regulating foreign investment. The agreement aims to eliminate quantitative restrictions on investment, including limits on the share of foreign ownership in certain industries. Because of opposition from developing countries, there was no attempt to consider such issues as the right of firms to establish enterprises in other countries, or the elimination of trade-related performance requirements on foreign investment.

The TRIPs agreement is one of the most controversial elements of the Uruguay Round. It consolidates previous international accords protecting copyrights, trademarks, patents, and industrial designs, and provides for the enforcement of these agreements within the WTO. But many economists believe that the protection of intellectual property is not a trade issue that should be under the purview of the WTO, especially given the existence of the World Intellectual Property Organization. Many developing countries complain that, unlike mutually beneficial tariff reductions, the TRIPs agreement merely transfers income from developing to developed countries by strengthening the ability of multinational corporations to charge higher prices in poorer countries.[15] In addition, using instruments of trade policy to protect intellectual property makes it harder to reject demands to use them to enforce other non-trade-related objectives, such as environmental or labor standards. It opens the door to many interests who want to use the threat of trade sanctions to achieve their own nontrade objectives, and thus puts the WTO in the business of enforcing behavior in areas only tangentially related to trade. This dilutes the institution's focus on the reduction of trade barriers.

The Uruguay Round was a "single undertaking," meaning that all participants and future members of the WTO are bound to follow all of the agreements reached. The Uruguay Round was the first round of

---

[15] Maskus (2000) estimates that the full implementation of the TRIPS agreement would transfer $5.8 billion from developing countries to the United States, and another $2.5 billion to five other developed countries.

multilateral trade negotiations in which developing countries played an active role, and their participation helped shape the outcome. Developed countries agreed to abolish the MFA's clothing quotas and to reform agricultural trade, increasing trade in sectors where developing countries have a comparative advantage. In return, developing countries accepted rules in the new areas of trade where developed countries have a comparative advantage. This exchange of market access came to be known as the "grand bargain."

However, developing countries came to view the grand bargain as a major disappointment: they took on many new obligations in services, investment, and intellectual property, and yet developed countries have yet to grant significant access to markets in agriculture and clothing. The developing countries are now more suspicious about the benefits of multilateral negotiations, particularly if developed countries force them to consider labor standards in future negotiations, as discussed in chapter 6. As developing countries such as India, Brazil, and China have become more assertive in the WTO, the developed countries have had to be more sensitive to their concerns; otherwise, developing countries could block any new deals.

As a result, the new round of trade negotiations, launched in Qatar in November 2001, was named the Doha Development Round with the specific goal of using trade to further the development goals of the poorest countries. The formal agenda originally included six broad areas: agriculture, nonagricultural market access, services, the so-called Singapore issues (transparency in government procurement, trade facilitation, investment, and competition policy) and rules (trade remedies), TRIPs, and development-related issues.

The negotiations have been extremely difficult. Each of these areas presents difficulties—agricultural policy reform is a political challenge in the United States and European Union, developing countries objected to negotiations on investment and competition (which were then dropped), and the TRIPs agreement remains contentious. As a result, the Doha Round, which was supposed to have been completed by 2005, has been marred by recriminations and missed deadlines. (Past trade negotiations rarely met such deadlines, which is why the GATT was sometimes referred to as the "General Agreement to Talk and Talk.") A mini-ministerial meeting in July 2008 managed to narrow differences on many issues, but ended when India and China insisted upon special safeguards that would allow them to raise tariffs on agricultural imports.

The failure of the Doha Round after many years of negotiation has led many to question the usefulness of the WTO as a negotiating forum. The WTO is much different than the GATT, particularly in the more active participation of developing countries.[16] Stating that the round would be for "development" gave developing countries a sense that they were entitled to unreciprocated trade concessions, that is, that developed countries would open their markets completely to developing countries, which would not have to do anything in return. Unfortunately for them, this is not the way multilateral trade negotiations work. Yet, despite many gloomy prognostications about the fate of the negotiations, it is still likely that the Doha Round will be completed at some point, even if the results are meager.

What might be the economic effects of a Doha agreement? One study calculates the possible economic consequences of a 50 percent reduction in import tariffs in agriculture and manufacturing, export subsidies, border measures in services, domestic agricultural support in OECD countries, and improvements in trade facilitation. The study found that the world gains would amount to $158 billion (in 2001 prices), or an increase of 0.5 percent to global income.[17] About 0.1 percentage points of the gains come from liberalizing trade in agriculture, manufacturing, and services each, 0.2 percentage points of the gains come from improving trade facilitation. Much of the gains accrue to developing countries (about 1 to 2 percent for some countries, such as South Africa and India).

Another study of various possible Doha Round outcomes, focusing on agricultural tariffs and subsidies and industrial tariffs, put the possible gains in the $40 to $80 billion range, and as high as $120 billion (0.3 percent of world income).[18] However, this study assumes no liberalization of trade in services, where barriers tend to be high and the potential gains relatively large, and no improvement in trade facilitation. Although the numbers are not enormous, they are understated because they do not take into account the productivity and other benefits of trade described in chapter 2.

[16] See Collier 2005 for an analysis of the gridlock at the WTO.
[17] Francois, van Meijl, and van Tongeren 2005.
[18] Anderson, Martin, and van Mensbrugghe 2006.

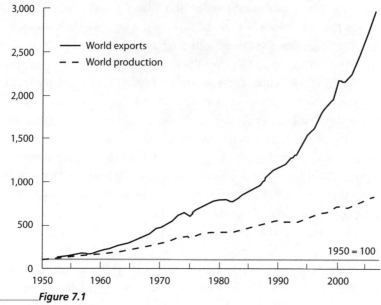

_____Figure 7.1

Volume of World Trade and World Production, 1950–2006.
Source: WTO 2008, table A.1.

_____Is the GATT a Success?

Before considering the WTO as an institution, let us pause to consider a basic question: has the GATT been a success? The answer is clearly yes. The architects of the postwar world trading system desperately wanted to avoid a repeat of the interwar trade policies after World War II. They not only accomplished this goal, but succeeded in eliminating most of the high barriers that arose during the 1930s. The reduction in trade barriers and the stability of tariff policy in most countries in the decades after 1947 has permitted the expansion of world trade to proceed unchecked. As figure 7.1 indicates, world trade has grown much more rapidly than world output over the postwar period.

This figure alone does not prove that the GATT was responsible for much or all of this expansion. But statistical evidence indicates that the GATT can take credit for a good deal of the growth in world trade. A detailed study of bilateral trade flows during the half century since 1946 reveals that countries that participated in the GATT enjoyed trade that is

43 percent greater than a pair of nonparticipating countries.[19] However, this overall effect has not been constant over time. The stimulus to trade arising from participation in the GATT was greatest early on (at over 80 percent in the 1950s) but has diminished to only about 11 percent by the 2000s. This is partly because so few countries now remain outside of the GATT/WTO system.

Similarly, another study has found that the WTO has had a strong and positive impact on world trade, finding that industrial country bilateral imports are 65 percent greater as a result of the GATT.[20] However, GATT participation by developing countries did not increase their trade nearly as much, perhaps because they were given "special and differential" treatment for so long and were not required to liberalize their trade policies. Finally, this analysis shows that bilateral trade for GATT participants is not higher in the case of clothing, footwear, and agriculture, precisely the sectors of trade that have been largely exempt from liberalization.[21]

Granting that the GATT and WTO have succeeded in increasing world trade, another question is why multilateral trade agreements have been politically successful in liberalizing trade. From a strictly economic point of view, the GATT's system of reciprocity in tariff reductions and rules for commercial policy is unnecessary because countries are better off pursuing a policy of free trade regardless of the trade policies pursued by others. As set out in chapter 2, the case for free trade is a unilateral one: as the economist Joan Robinson once put it, a country should not throw rocks in its harbors simply because other countries have rocks in theirs. The mercantilist language of international trade negotiations—that

[19] Goldstein, Rivers, and Tomz 2007.

[20] Subramanian and Wei 2007.

[21] In fact, according to the study, imports by new developing country members of the WTO are greater by virtue of their membership, but imports by old developing country members of the GATT are not. This is because new members are required to liberalize their trade policies before joining the WTO, whereas long-standing members were protected from changing their policies because of special and differential treatment. Rose (2004) originally questioned whether the GATT had any significant impact on trade and, in his examination of the bilateral trade data, he failed to find much of an effect of GATT participation. However, in his table 1 benchmark regressions, when country fixed effects are included in the analysis (which is generally considered to be the most appropriate specification), GATT participation is indeed related to more trade. See also Tomz, Goldstein, and Rivers 2007.

a reduction in one's own trade barriers is a "concession" to others—is wrong from an economic standpoint.

The reason that reciprocity via multilateral trade agreements has worked well since 1947 is that such agreements have both economic and political value for governments seeking to contain protectionist pressures. When countries choose their tariffs alone, the outcome can be inefficient economically because governments are pressured by import-competing producers into maintaining trade restrictions.[22] In addition, the gains from trade are magnified if other countries also reduce their trade barriers. Multilateral tariff cooperation is a way to avoid an economically ineffi- cient result. Trade agreements are also beneficial politically because they enhance domestic support for open trade. Such agreements make ex- porters more politically active, counterbalancing the power of interests opposed to imports and thus facilitating trade liberalization.[23] Although unilateral free trade is beneficial, not all unilateral policies are free trade, as our discussion of trade politics in chapter 3 described.

The GATT's economic and political value is demonstrated in countries' adherence to its provisions even though the agreement has no direct mechanism to enforce them. Under Article 23, if any contracting party fails to carry out its obligation or undertakes an action that "nullifies or impairs" a benefit due to another party, other countries can ask the GATT to allow them to suspend their concessions or waive their obliga- tions to the offending country. In other words, if one country fails to ad- here to the rules, then other countries are not obligated to adhere to the rules with respect to it. They can retaliate by raising tariffs against the rule-breaker's goods. In the "chicken war" of 1962, the United States im- posed tariffs on $26 million in European goods because Europe violated GATT rules by imposing a high variable levy on poultry imports.

Thus, the countries that have signed the GATT contract are re- sponsible for enforcing the agreement; no independent power resides with the GATT itself, which essentially relies on the goodwill of the sig- natories. Countries appear to be concerned about their reputation for ad- hering to agreements. Reputation can be a powerful device for prevent-

[22] If tariff policies are interdependent, such that an increase in one country's tariff leads to an increase in another country's tariff, then a noncooperative equilibrium will in- clude relatively high tariffs and be inefficient. See Bagwell and Staiger 2002.

[23] Hillman and Moser (1996) provide a theoretical analysis of this point.

ing the erosion of agreements because a country that fails to abide by the rules forfeits the right to insist that other countries do so, and thus risks discrimination against its exports.[24] Evidence suggests that countries try to cultivate good reputations and fear retaliation for noncompliance with the agreed-upon rules.[25]

For all of these reasons, most countries that were not a part of the GATT have wanted to become members of the WTO. Although the obligations are extensive, they are less than the costs of remaining outside the agreement and losing the benefits of MFN treatment by other countries. As a result, membership in the WTO has become increasingly attractive. At the start of the Uruguay Round in 1986, the GATT consisted of 91 contracting parties. The WTO was established in 1995 with nearly 130 members, and by December 2008 the membership had risen to 153 nations, accounting for over 90 percent of world trade. Several other countries, notably Russia, are negotiating to join the organization.

Despite its success, the GATT legal framework has several notable defects. The agreement is written broadly, often with several exceptions for every rule. These exceptions give countries the flexibility to deal with unexpected contingencies and to maneuver through politically difficult decisions on policy. But they also provide loopholes and excuses for evading the basic principles of the agreement. For example, Article 1 contains the MFN clause, but Article 14 is entitled "Exceptions to the Rule of Nondiscrimination," and Article 24 permits countries to form customs unions and free trade areas, which are inherently discriminatory. Article 11 generally forbids the use of import quotas and quantitative restrictions, but Article 13 states that when they are imposed, they should be administered in a nondiscriminatory way, a provision that would be unnecessary if Article 11 were fully effective.

Despite these deficiencies, over the past half century the multilateral trading system has achieved many of its original goals. Countries

---

[24] In Hudec's view, "other governments interested in maintaining the integrity of legal commitments are willing to go to considerable lengths to expose the defendant government to criticism for not keeping its word . . . To be caught not performing one's own obligation is to lose the right to enforce the obligations on others, thereby losing specific trade opportunities as well as imperiling the entire liberal trading system. Rarely, if ever, does the gain from a violation of GATT obligations make it worth jeopardizing the benefits of the existing trade order" (1998, 36).

[25] Bown 2004b.

that are party to the GATT have generally adhered to the rules. Nondiscrimination has been established as a benchmark for commercial policy, and tariff barriers have been significantly reduced in successive negotiating rounds. In addition, overall trade relations have been good: specific disputes have been contained and policies have been stable, providing an environment in which international commerce has flourished. To be sure, discriminatory policies remain, antidumping actions and some nontariff barriers have surfaced, and disputes still arise and sometimes fester. But on the whole, the postwar system must be judged a great success. This outcome is a formidable and enduring achievement of the architects of the postwar economic order.

Two other factors have made this outcome possible. First, the postwar economic expansion has been relatively smooth, punctuated only by a few recessions but free of major depressions. This experience has muted demands for protection and reduced the burdens of adhering to the rules. Economic growth and rising income mitigate the pain associated with structural shifts, due to international trade or other factors, by creating new opportunities for those displaced. In short, the economic shocks confronting the trading system have not been strong enough to bring about a systemic collapse, although the system was tested during the severe recession of the early 1980s.

Second, the bipartisan consensus forged in the United States during the 1940s in favor of reciprocal trade agreements has stayed largely intact. The initially tepid Republican support for trade liberalization faded as the postwar economic boom continued and as business interests continued to take an interest in opening up foreign markets for U.S. goods. By the early 1970s, on the other hand, several important Democratic constituencies had become less comfortable with liberalization efforts. Many labor unions, some of which had earlier supported reciprocal trade agreements, now began pressing for limits on trade as competition from imports intensified. As noted in chapter 1, trade issues have become an increasingly contentious political issue in the United States, which has frayed the bipartisan consensus to some extent. Yet both Republican and Democratic administrations have continued to press for trade-liberalizing measures and have passed them through Republican- and Democratic-controlled Congresses. The leaders of both parties recognize that a return to widespread protectionism would damage the economy, even if there is dispute over the wisdom of new trade agreements.

_____The World Trade Organization

The WTO was established in 1995 as a result of the Uruguay Round. The WTO has been a much more visible and controversial organization than the GATT, so it is important to get a sense of what the organization is all about, particularly its dispute settlement mechanism.[26]

The World Trade Organization is something more, but not much more, than the GATT. While the GATT was simply an intergovernmental agreement overseen by a small secretariat, the WTO is an international organization. But like the GATT, it has virtually no independent power and strives to be a neutral party among all the member countries. The director-general of the WTO has no policymaking authority and cannot comment directly on members' policies. The power to make trade policy and to write the rules governing it resides specifically with the member governments, not with the WTO. For this reason, the WTO is often called a "member-driven" organization. In negotiating the rules and running the organization, the WTO operates on the basis of a consensus among its members. Of course, reaching any consensus is extremely difficult, and very easy to block. A former director-general has likened the WTO to a car with one accelerator and 150 handbrakes.[27]

The scope of the WTO is broader than that of the GATT because it oversees multilateral agreements relating not just to goods, but also to services, investment, and intellectual property. The WTO provides the forum for consultations and negotiations on these matters, assists with the interpretation of the legal texts, arranges for the arbitration of disputes, and conducts fact-finding surveillance reviews of members' policies, but

[26] For a general overview of the WTO, see Jones 2004 and Hoekman and Kostecki 2009.

[27] Moore 2003, 110. Of course, not all 153 members have equal input on the negotiations. The United States and European Union carry the most weight. And many small developing countries cannot afford representation in Geneva and hence designate a country, such as India, to represent its interests. For a skeptical view of whether the WTO can serve the interests of developing countries, and an inside look at how negotiations are conducted, see Jawara and Kwa 2003.

ultimately the accords are intergovernmental agreements. The WTO has no power to force countries to obey the agreements or to comply with its rulings.

Because it is a forum for the discussion of trade policy more than anything else, the WTO as an institution is extremely small. The support staff and budget are limited in comparison to other international organizations. The WTO secretariat in Geneva consists of only 629 employees, about a quarter of whom are translators. The WTO's budget in 2008 was about $160 million.[28] These figures are paltry in comparison to other international economic organizations, and even some nongovernmental organizations.[29] Yet these small figures do not reflect the true importance of the organization as the cornerstone of the world trading system. Indeed, resources may be misallocated among the international economic organizations: the WTO's mission—to keep the international trading system functioning smoothly—is more clearly defined and perhaps even more important than the World Bank's more diffused mission of promoting economic development, but the WTO's budget is a tiny fraction of the bank's. Despite its heavy workload and the importance of its mission, the WTO makes do with relatively few resources.

What most distinguishes the WTO from the GATT, aside from the new agreements, is the dispute settlement process. The original GATT agreement made little provision for settling disputes between member countries. When conflicts arose, the Secretariat developed an informal and ad hoc process to help resolve disputes through negotiation. The Uruguay Round agreement established a dispute settlement mechanism that largely formalized existing practices. But it also strengthened the process by providing for specific time tables to expedite cases and, perhaps most important, by preventing countries from blocking the establishment of a panel or the adoption of a panel report.[30]

[28] World Trade Organization 2008a, 108.
[29] For example, the World Bank employs about 10,000 people and has an administrative budget of about $1.2 billion, the IMF employs 2,600 people and has a budget of $840 million, and the Food and Agriculture Organization (FAO) of the United Nations employs 3,500 people with a budget of $750 million. Many nongovernmental organizations have budgets that rival that of the WTO, such as the World Wildlife Fund ($102 million) and Greenpeace ($140 million).
[30] Why was the dispute settlement process strengthened in the Uruguay Round? Largely because Congress insisted on it. Frustrated with the GATT system, Congress wanted

How does the new dispute settlement mechanism work? Countries may file "violation" complaints, alleging that a specific rule (such as nondiscrimination) has been broken, or "nonviolation" complaints, alleging that a government action "nullifies or impairs" a previous concession even if no specific rule has been broken. If initial consultations to resolve the dispute are not successful, a three-member panel is appointed to determine whether WTO rules have been violated. If it establishes a violation, the panel suggests that the disputed policy be brought into conformity with the rules, but generally leaves to the parties themselves the task of working out a solution. The panel decision can be appealed to an Appellate Body, which rules on matters of law and legal interpretation in the panel report.

As under the GATT, if the policy in question is found to violate the rules, the country can bring its policy into conformity with the rules, or keep the policy in place and offer compensation (lower tariffs) on other goods exported from the complaining country, which then has the option of accepting or rejecting the compensation offer. If neither alternative has been implemented, the complaining country can seek authorization to "suspend the application to the Member concerned of concessions or other obligations in the covered agreements." In other words, the complainant can retaliate by withdrawing previous tariff "concessions" to the country that has chosen not to comply with the finding. Such retaliations occur infrequently because most disputes are settled through negotiations. Some recent high-profile cases in which countries were authorized to retaliate include a U.S. case against the European

---

to improve the speed and effectiveness of the dispute settlement mechanisms and procedures. In 1988, Congress instructed negotiators to seek the opening of foreign markets, the elimination of trade-distorting policies, and the establishment of "a more effective system of international trading disciplines and procedures." U.S. House of Representatives 2003a, 230. As a U.S. Trade Representative (2000, 41) report noted, "Under the GATT, panel proceedings took years, the defending party could simply block any unfavorable judgment, and the GATT panel process did not cover some of the agreements. Under the WTO, there are strict timetables for panel proceedings, the defending party cannot block findings unfavorable to it, and there is one comprehensive dispute settlement process covering all of the Uruguay Round Agreements." When members of Congress complain about the strong dispute settlement system as impinging on U.S. sovereignty, it is helpful to remember that it was the Congress itself that demanded that the GATT approach be strengthened because of its inherent weaknesses.

Union's ban on hormone-treated beef and an EU-led case against the Bush administration's steel safeguard tariffs.

How has the new dispute settlement process worked? In a report to Congress in 2000, the independent General Accounting Office concluded that the dispute settlement process has worked well for the United States. Examining the cases considered by the WTO up to that time, the GAO found that most led to beneficial changes in foreign regulations and practices and that "none of the changes the United States has made in response to WTO disputes have had major policy or commercial impact to date, though the stakes in several were important."[31]

In the first five years of the dispute settlement system, the United States brought many more cases against other countries than were brought against it. Since then, however, many more cases have been brought against the United States. In the first thirteen years of the WTO (1995–2008), the United States filed eighty-six complaints about foreign trade measures and was the subject of one hundred twenty-one complaints. Of the eighty-six complaints, fifty-nine had been resolved by June 2008. Of these cases, twenty-six were resolved to U.S. satisfaction without litigation, twenty-nine received favorable rulings by WTO panels, and in four the United States lost on core issues at the WTO. Of the one hundred twenty-one complaints brought against the United States, sixty-eight had been resolved by mid-2008. Of these cases, nineteen were resolved without litigation, the United States won fifteen, and in thirty-four some aspect of U.S. policy was found inconsistent with WTO rules. This reflects a general tendency: countries that bring a complaint to the WTO tend to win their cases, while the defendant countries tend to lose. This probably reflects the fact that countries will only go through the effort of bringing a case if it is a strong one.

Among the politicians in Washington, there is a tendency to judge the dispute settlement mechanism only on the basis of whether the United States "wins" the cases it files and those brought against it. Clearly the mechanism is more important than that. It was established simply to ensure that the rules that countries agreed upon together and pledged to abide by actually mean something. Sometimes the United States is on the wrong side. For example, in 1995 Costa Rica won a complaint against the

---

[31] U.S. GAO 2000b, 2–3.

United States concerning restrictions on imports of underwear. The fact that small countries can receive fair treatment under the rule of law is a strength of the world trading system.[32] The alternative is that more powerful countries simply dictate outcomes to others.

But even when the United States loses a case, the WTO cannot force change in U.S. laws, regulations, or policies. The WTO cannot strike down any U.S. law, as an American court can. As the General Accounting Office puts it: "The United States maintains that it has the right not to comply with WTO rulings. However, the United States recognizes that it may bear a penalty for not complying with WTO rulings, both in the form of retaliatory duties on U.S. exports and in terms of its reputation as a key player in the world trading system."[33] WTO panels merely determine whether disputed policies conflict with WTO rules and, if they do, recommend that members bring those policies into conformity. The disputing countries must still resolve the matter themselves, often through a negotiated settlement.

Some nonparticipants are disturbed by the closed proceedings during disputes and ask whose interests get represented in the panels. Many NGOs, particularly environmental groups, have complained that the WTO is secretive and antidemocratic in its procedures. Although they are now allowed to file amicus (friends of the court) briefs, NGOs are generally barred from the dispute settlement process. This is because the WTO agreements are strictly government-to-government agreements that deal with governmental policy, and not the behavior of private firms. The appropriate way for commercial and noncommercial domestic interests, which are not parties to the negotiated agreements, to influence the WTO is through their member governments.[34] The GATT and WTO have typically operated under a diplomatic veil rather than as an open forum in the past because commercial negotiations involved reducing tariffs in one sector to secure lower foreign tariffs for another sector, thus trading off various domestic interests. The United States wants the institution to become more open and transparent, but other members have strongly

[32] Bown (2004a) shows how developing countries have received better treatment from WTO dispute settlement than under GATT.

[33] U.S. GAO 2000b, 16.

[34] Robertson (2000) provides an incisive examination of whether so-called civil society should participate more directly in the WTO.

resisted. Because the WTO is a consensual body, the issue is not one to decide unilaterally and against the wishes of the other members.[35]

The dispute settlement process has become one of the most controversial aspects of the WTO. Some legal experts have raised the concern that WTO panels and the Appellate Body have exceeded their mandate to interpret the agreements and have created new rights and imposed new obligations on members. Has the WTO overreached its authority by failing to give sufficient deference to policymakers in member countries? While most legal scholars believe that it has not overreached, with the possible exception of trade remedies, others are concerned that judicial legislation does occur.[36] For example, trade remedies, such as antidumping and safeguard measures, discussed in chapter 5, have come under WTO scrutiny, and these reviews have often found problems with the imposition of remedies by domestic authorities.[37]

_____Environmental Regulations and WTO Rules

Several WTO rulings have also raised questions about whether trade rules take precedence over domestic environmental, health, and safety regulations, thereby impinging on a country's sovereignty. Critics, such as Global Trade Watch, part of Ralph Nader's Public Citizen organization, charge that the WTO has undermined every environmental regulation it

[35] As Sampson notes, "the view of the significant majority of WTO members is that it would be inappropriate to allow NGOs to participate directly even as observers in the proceedings of WTO meetings." If such groups were allowed, difficult questions would have to be answered: "Which groups of civil society should be represented at different meetings, and who would decide? . . . Should farmers' unions be present during negotiations on the reduction of agricultural subsidies that lead to environmental degradation, or should environmental NGOs? Should consumer groups be present during negotiations when trade liberalization leading to lower consumer prices was being discussed, or should it be the sectoral interests that would be adversely affected by a lowering of trade barriers? . . . Is it not preferable to have a democratically elected government represent the diverse interest groups in a given country" (2000, 42–43).

[36] Davey 2001; McRae 2004.

[37] With regard to safeguards, the WTO has found fault with just about every escape clause action undertaken by any member. This creates formidable legal obstacles to using safeguards, which as chapter 5 indicated may be a form of trade intervention superior to antidumping duties. The WTO decisions regarding safeguards sometimes have been unclear and often difficult to implement, particularly regarding how agencies should link increased imports and serious injury to a domestic industry. See Irwin 2003 on safeguards.

has reviewed. For example, Global Trade Watch charges that "in the WTO forum, global commerce takes precedence over everything—democracy, public health, equity, access to essential services, the environment, food safety and more . . . years of experience under the WTO have confirmed environmentalists' fears: the WTO is undermining existing local, national, and international environmental and conservation policies."[38]

Unfortunately, the passionate opposition to certain rulings has given rise to much exaggeration and distortion. The General Accounting Office points out that "WTO rulings to date against U.S. environmental measures have not weakened U.S. environmental protections."[39] As of December 2008, only about a dozen of the 381 disputes brought before the WTO have dealt with environmental or health issues, and most trade disputes are quite banal. And these few environmental cases have mainly focused on whether the regulation in question has been implemented in a nondiscriminatory way, not whether that regulation is justifiable. At the same time, however, some cases illustrate the difficult issues and potential conflicts that can arise when trade and environmental policy intersect.

What precisely are the trade rules that affect environmental measures? The most relevant provision of the GATT is Article 20, entitled "General Exceptions:"

> Subject to the requirement that such measures are not applied
> in a manner which would constitute a means of arbitrary or
> unjustifiable discrimination between countries where the same
> conditions prevail, or a disguised restriction on international
> trade, nothing in this Agreement shall be construed to prevent
> the adoption or enforcement by any contracting party of
> measures . . .
> (b) necessary to protect human, animal or plant life or health . . .
> [or]
> (g) relating to the conservation of exhaustible natural resources
>   if such measures are made effective in conjunction with
>   restrictions on domestic production or consumption.[40]

[38] Wallach and Woodall 2004, 13, 20.
[39] U.S. GAO 2000b, 14.
[40] WTO 1999, 455. The remaining provisions relate to the protection of public morals, protection of national treasures of artistic, historic, or archaeological value, to trade

The key element of Article 20 is the introductory paragraph. This provision allows countries to enact and enforce various measures that may restrict trade in order to achieve various objectives, provided that the measure is nondiscriminatory, does not constitute a disguised restriction on international trade, and is necessary to achieve the stated objective. The subsections of Article 20 specify objectives that would justify measures to constrain trade. The most important subsections, (b) and (g), permit regulatory measures to protect human and animal health and to conserve natural resources.[41]

GATT and WTO decisions affirm that Article 20 allows countries to maintain consistent and nondiscriminatory environmental regulations.[42] But some of the WTO's environmental cases have become notorious and are worth considering because popular discussion of them is often superficial and therefore prone to distortion. For example, the "tuna-dolphin" case is an infamous trade dispute because it suggested that trade remedies for environmental regulations might run afoul of GATT rules. In 1991, a GATT panel ruled that a U.S. ban on imported tuna that had been caught without using dolphin-safe methods was inconsistent with GATT rules. The case is completely moot: it was decided under the old GATT (rather than WTO), did not force any change in U.S. policy, and was later resolved through negotiations. The tuna dispute was resolved in 1992 when the United States, Mexico, and eight other tuna-fishing nations signed an international agreement to regulate the conditions of tuna fishing. Since then, incidental dolphin deaths due to

---

in gold and silver, to products of prison labor, and include other measures such as intergovernmental commodity agreements and customs enforcement.

[41] Wallach and Woodall (2004, 21) complain that the Article 20 exceptions apply only in certain narrowly defined circumstances and that in many cases the "exceptions were so narrowly interpreted as to render them moot." But if this is really the problem, then the members of the WTO should simply amend the Article 20 exceptions to reflect a broader view. After all, those rules are not made up by the WTO as some independent entity, but were agreed upon by the member countries of the WTO, among them the United States and European Union.

[42] For example, in 1994, a GATT panel affirmed that the corporate average fuel economy (CAFE) standards, regulating the fuel efficiency of automobiles sold in the United States, were a perfectly acceptable form of product regulation to protect public health and environment, as long as those standards did not explicitly discriminate on the basis of country of origin. Similarly, a WTO panel in 2000 upheld France's ban on asbestos imports, on the grounds that they were hazardous materials, after Canada had challenged the embargo.

tuna fishing have dropped dramatically, according to the National Oceanic and Atmospheric Administration (NOAA).

But the case gave the GATT dispute settlement system a bad name by introducing the "product-process" doctrine that prevents domestic regulations from considering how tunas are fished. The product-process doctrine has been a source of great difficulty. Never explicitly propounded or endorsed by WTO members, the doctrine emerged from a creative interpretation of a GATT panel and gradually took on a life of its own. The distinction is arbitrary and unsustainable because process-based regulation has already been introduced in the agreement on trade-related intellectual property. For example, original and copied software are similar products, but the process by which they were produced is quite different.

Many people in developed countries care about how products are made: tuna may be tuna, but tuna fished by dolphin-safe methods is not viewed as the same as tuna fished by dolphin-unsafe methods. Furthermore, as set out in the tuna-dolphin case, the product-process doctrine may not even be legally sound. One leading GATT legal scholar has written that "the underlying conceptual foundation based on 'product' focus of Article 3 tends to crumble on analysis" and that "the suggestion that Article 3 does not apply to ('cover') process-based regulation is just plain wrong."[43] Although later rulings weakened the product-process doctrine, it might still pose an obstacle to process-based regulation.[44]

At the same time, there are sound reasons for not allowing any and all process regulations. Developing countries fear that process regulation will open the door to the imposition of standards that other countries cannot afford. They are concerned that if the method of production of a particular good becomes grounds for blocking trade, then labor and environmental conditions of production will be introduced as excuses for keeping out the products of developing countries.[45] The product-process

---

[43] Hudec 2000, 198.

[44] One way of addressing "process" based concerns without banning trade is through product labeling. For example, if consumers do not want to purchase hormone-treated beef or tuna caught with unsafe methods, the product can be labeled as such.

[45] As Sampson points out: "In the view of [developing] nations, permitting discrimination among imports on the basis of production methods would profoundly undermine a principle that lies at the heart of the WTO legal system. This concern manifests itself in a resistance to any attempts to provide for the extension of industrial country production

distinction will be one of the most difficult and important issues that the WTO membership has to work out.

The "turtle-shrimp" case is another high-profile case in which the WTO supposedly struck down U.S. regulations on imported shrimp. In 1989, Congress prohibited imports of shrimp and shrimp products harvested in a way that may harm endangered sea turtles. The prohibition was to be lifted only for countries that the State Department had certified as having a program to prevent accidental drowning of turtles through the use of "turtle excluder devices" (TEDs) (or for countries whose fishermen trawl only in cold waters where there are no such turtles). WTO critics charge that the ruling completely undermined U.S. efforts to require foreign shrimp trawlers to use the TEDs, which helped prevent the accidental drowning of endangered sea turtles. But the WTO ruling did not concern the law itself but rather the way in which the United States implemented the law.[46] The WTO did not require the United States to lift its ban on shrimp imports, but only to implement the ban in a nondiscriminatory way. The import ban was not lifted at any point

---

standards to developing countries in order for their exports to be acceptable for import in industrial countries. The strength of feeling on this matter on the part of many developing countries cannot be overstated" (2000, 18–19).

[46] For some reason, the State Department initially interpreted the U.S. law as applying only to countries in the Caribbean and Atlantic. However, the U.S. Court of International Trade determined that the law applied to imports worldwide. The court rejected a request by the State Department to delay the enforcement of the ruling to allow newly affected countries time to comply, and thus the worldwide embargo went into effect in May 1996, less than six months after the ruling. In September 1996, India, Malaysia, Pakistan, and Thailand, all of which were newly affected by the ban, brought a case to the WTO. They argued that shrimp must be allowed in the U.S. market regardless of the "process" by which they are caught. A WTO panel ruled against the United States, but the Appellate Body overruled most of the panel's decision in 1998. The Appellate Body held that the shrimp certification measure was justified under Article 20(g) relating to the conservation of exhaustible natural resources, but that its implementation was inconsistent with the nondiscrimination requirement. For example, in applying a countrywide standard, the State Department might prohibit all imports of shrimp from a country even if some of its shrimp was caught by trawlers using TEDs. There is little doubt, however, that the initial panel decision was not just legally questionable, but created immense political problems for the WTO. The initial decision left the impression that the GATT and environmental rules are necessarily in conflict and ruled against amicus briefs by NGOs, fueling their hostility toward the WTO. Even though the Appellate Body overruled most of the panel report, the damage was already done.

during the dispute process. The United States continues to impose an embargo against shrimp imports from countries that have not been certified, but is negotiating with countries that desire to become certified as not endangering turtles.

Thus, Article 20 has been the focus of disputes not so much because of the exceptions specified in subsections (b) and (g), but because any environmental trade measure must be implemented in a nondiscriminatory fashion. The United States has long insisted that nondiscrimination be the basis of international trade relations, which is why the most favored nation clause is instituted as Article 1, and national treatment is instituted as Article 3, of the GATT. The United States would be understandably upset if foreign regulations discriminated against American exports. If the United States insists upon receiving fair treatment abroad, it cannot be surprised that other countries demand nondiscriminatory treatment from the United States. This appears to be a noncontroversial proposition. Surprisingly, Public Citizen's most widely trumpeted example of the WTO's weakening of U.S. environmental regulations involves precisely this issue.

The Public Citizen book *Whose Trade Organization?* opens by accusing the WTO of forcing the Environmental Protection Agency (EPA) to weaken its environmental standards on imported gasoline. This case "was the first concrete evidence of the WTO's threat to environmental policy" and "an example of how the WTO could be used to skirt a country's democratic policymaking and judicial systems," bringing "credibility to critics' concerns that the WTO could threaten national sovereignty to set and effectively enforce important policies."[47]

Yet the case did not involve the stringency of the EPA's regulation, but simply the nondiscriminatory implementation of the regulation as required by the introductory paragraph of Article 20. Simply put, the U.S. regulation discriminated against imported gasoline to the benefit of domestically refined gasoline. The EPA was free to demand any standard of cleanliness it chose, but was obligated under Article 20 to apply the same standard to domestic and foreign producers.

In December 1993, the EPA issued a regulation to reduce the amount of contaminants in domestic and imported gasoline. Its purpose

[47] Wallach and Woodall 2004, 25.

was to limit harmful emissions from automobile exhaust. Each domestic refiner was required to meet a new, more stringent standard based on its own 1990 benchmark quality level. This individual standard was permitted because a single industry-wide baseline would make compliance very costly for certain domestic oil refiners, which vary in cleanliness. Imported gasoline, however, was subject to a uniform baseline, and foreign refiners were not offered the option of establishing an individual benchmark. And though this was partly for ease of administration, a less publicized reason was deliberate discrimination. As an EPA administrator later testified before Congress, the agency thought "that it was appropriate, if we had a choice, to lean in the direction of doing something that would favor their competitive position [i.e., that of domestic refiners] vis-à-vis the [foreign producers]."[48] In other words, the EPA built in discrimination to help domestic oil refiners compete against foreign refiners.

In 1995, Venezuela and Brazil brought a complaint to the WTO, charging that the United States was applying a more stringent standard on imported gasoline. A WTO panel ruled against the United States, which then appealed to the Appellate Body. The Appellate Body determined that while such regulations were permitted under Article 20, this regulation involved discrimination and therefore violated the introductory provision of the article. The Appellate Body recommended that the regulation be brought into conformity with WTO obligations, but left it to the United States to determine how it would comply.

At this point, the United States had three options: it could ignore the Appellate Body finding, let the regulation stand but offer compensation to Venezuela and Brazil in the form of lower tariffs on other products, or bring the regulation into conformity with the WTO obligation.[49] It is useful to consider the implications of each option.

If the United States chose to ignore the ruling, Venezuela and Brazil could legally withdraw previous tariff concessions extended to

[48] Quoted in Palmeter 1999.

[49] Public Citizen makes the options appear more draconian, saying that the "WTO's ruling forced the U.S. to make a 'no-win' choice: repeal the regulation and permit imports of gasoline with higher contamination levels . . . , or keep the policy and face $150 million in trade sanctions each year the U.S. failed to comply" (Wallach and Woodall, 2004, 28). The EPA regulation would not have to be "repealed," just modified to eliminate the discrimination. The regulation would not make imports dirtier as long as the domestic regulation was made as stringent as that on imports.

U.S. goods, equivalent in value to their lost gasoline exports. In signing the GATT, the United States agreed to abide by its rules. No authority can force compliance or negotiated settlement, but other countries can retaliate by withdrawing tariff concessions (i.e., raising tariffs) on their imports from the United States.[50] In practice, Venezuela and Brazil might choose not to retaliate against the United States, realizing that such actions would probably fail to accomplish anything. But they might choose this option, which would be permissible under WTO rules.

The second possible U.S. response would be to keep the existing regulation in place, but to compensate Venezuela and Brazil by lowering tariffs against other goods. If this compensation were acceptable to Venezuela and Brazil, the case would be over. But this response requires lowering tariffs on another industry, an unlikely outcome. One trade lawyer pointed to the political difficulty: "Imagine the U.S. Trade Representative explaining to an industry why the United States had agreed to lower tariffs on its products in order to keep in place a discriminatory rule that favored the oil industry."[51]

As a result, the United States chose to bring the regulation into conformity with the WTO nondiscrimination requirement. This could have been accomplished by requiring domestic refiners to meet the same statutory baseline that applied to imports, but the domestic industry did not want this option. Instead, in August 1997 the EPA allowed foreign refiners to use individual baselines, as domestic producers were allowed to do. To ensure that imports of "dirty" gas did not increase, the EPA established a benchmark for imported gasoline quality based on the volume-weighted average of individual benchmarks for domestic refiners. The EPA monitors imported gasoline closely and imposes remedies if imports do not meet that benchmark.[52]

Note that compliance with the WTO rules and resolution of this dispute had nothing to do with whether a more or less stringent standard

---

[50] As Palmeter puts it, "the sole remedy available to a WTO member that wins its case against the measure of another, if that measure is not changed and if adequate compensation is not forthcoming, is, effectively, cancellation of the bargain . . . [In other words,] if some side backs out of its bargain, the other side may do the same" (1999, 90).

[51] Palmeter 1999, 86.

[52] For a full description, see the EPA's notice in the August 28, 1997, issue of the Federal Register (45544–45568), available on-line at http://www.access.gpo.gov.

was applied. It only required that the *same* standard be applied to domestic and foreign sources of gasoline. The EPA could have resolved the case by raising the domestic standard, rather than lowering the standard applied to imports. Thus, the case is far from one in which the WTO "undermines" domestic environmental regulation, as Global Trade Watch and others have made it out to be. In fact, Public Citizen, which decries corporate influence on government policy, put itself in the position of defending a rule that worked to the advantage of the domestic petroleum industry, one of the nation's most politically powerful special interest groups. The United States may have lost this case, but the system worked exactly as the United States wanted it to. The United States can invoke the same rule against discriminatory regulations in other countries.

Finally, it is important to understand the small proportions of this case. Most of the gasoline consumed in the United States is refined in the United States from imported crude petroleum. The United States imports only a small amount of finished motor gasoline, just 3.7 percent of the total U.S. supply (domestic production plus imports) in 1998. By far the largest foreign supplier of gasoline in that year was the Virgin Islands, followed by Venezuela, with Canada a close third. Other countries such as Brazil supply just a tiny amount.[53]

World trade rules do not stand in the way of government action to protect the public health, but a long-standing and unresolved WTO case concerns the United States and European Union trade in beef. When the United States banned imports of livestock and meats from Europe in 2001 because of fears of mad cow and foot and mouth disease, the action was legal according to WTO rules. At the same time, public health is sometimes used as a justification for regulations intended only to protect special interests. International negotiators have attempted to allow health and safety regulations even if they restrict trade, while trying to discourage regulatory protectionism, that is, trade barriers designed to protect domestic producers but cloaked under a health or safety rationale. Distinguishing these two cases, however, can be extremely difficult.

The use of public health as an excuse for protectionist regulations is not a new problem.[54] Today, the United States and other coun-

[53] U.S. Department of Energy 1998, 1:17, 56.

[54] In the late 1880s, for example, many European countries banned the sale of American pork after rumors spread that it was tainted with trichinosis. Even though

tries maintain trade barriers that are ostensibly designed to protect the public health, but upon further examination are actually maintained for the benefit of producers. The Department of Agriculture estimates that questionable foreign regulations cost the United States about $5 billion in agricultural, forestry, and fishery exports in 1996.[55]

The U.S.-EU dispute over hormone-treated beef is a classic example of the extreme difficulty in drawing the line between regulations to protect consumers and regulations to protect producers. The conflict began in 1985, when Europe restricted the use of natural hormones for therapeutic purposes and banned the use of synthetic hormones for growth purposes in cattle and meat sold in the EU. At the same time, the EU prohibited the importation of animals or meat from animals that had been treated with such hormones. Thus, the regulation seemed to be nondiscriminatory because the same standard was applied to domestic and imported meat. In such cases, the regulation cannot be held in violation of Article 1 or Article 20 of the GATT.

Implemented in 1989, the measure wiped out about $100 million in American beef exports to Europe. The United States strenuously objected, arguing that the EU ban was unjustifiable because the hormones had been found safe when used in accordance with good practices of animal husbandry. The safety of the hormones had been accepted not just by the U.S. Food and Drug Administration, but by numerous international scientific panels. Efforts to resolve the dispute under the Tokyo Round's Agreement on Technical Barriers failed because it dealt only with end-product characteristics, and naturally occurring hormones cannot be distinguished from cattle and beef treated with supplemental hormones. As a result, the United States retaliated in 1989 by imposing 100 percent tariffs on $100 million of agricultural imports from Europe.

---

there proved to be no evidence of such a problem, the ban was enormously beneficial to European pork farmers, who had well-known difficulties competing against low-priced American pork. According to one historian of the incident, "the general fear of trichinosis was a godsend for European protectionists." The American consulate in Le Havre reported that French inspectors were instructed to find trichinae in at least 25 percent of American pork that they examined. The Foreign Minister of Austria-Hungary publicly admitted that protection to domestic producers was a determining factor in the exclusion, though it was ostensibly imposed for sanitary reasons. See Gignilliat 1961.

[55] Roberts and DeRemer 1997.

The United States sought to clarify international rules on health and safety regulations during the Uruguay Round, and the result was the Agreement on the Application of Sanitary and Phytosanitary Measures (SPS). The SPS agreement provides that trade-related sanitary measures should be based on scientific principles and maintained with sufficient scientific evidence (Article 2.2) or be based on international standards (if they exist). Sanitary measures should be nondiscriminatory and not be more trade-restrictive than required to achieve the appropriate level of sanitary protection. In addition, Article 5.5 of the SPS states that governments should strive to achieve consistency in the protection of health risks and "shall avoid arbitrary or unjustifiable distinctions in the levels it considers to be appropriate in different situations, if such distinctions result in discrimination or a disguised restriction on international trade."[56]

The United States (supported by Australia, Canada, and New Zealand) used the SPS to challenge the EU ban on beef imports, arguing that the ban failed to meet any of these requirements. The WTO panel convened experts, two chosen by the United States, two chosen by the European Union, and another by those four, to evaluate the scientific evidence regarding the hormones. The five scientists unanimously concluded that there was no public health risk. In 1995 the United Nations Codex Alimentarius Commission and a scientific panel convened by the EU declared that there is no human health risk from the hormones when used in accordance with proper animal husbandry, confirming what other international science bodies had stated.

The record also showed that high levels of several of the hormones occurred naturally in animal products, and yet these products were not regulated. For example, of the six hormones at issue, the one identified as most dangerous by the EU is found from ten times to hundreds of times more concentrated in such products as eggs, cabbage, broccoli, and soybean oil than in hormone-treated beef. If the objective was to protect the public from exposure to specific hormones, then why was the sale of eggs not banned, since there are seventy-five times more naturally occurring hormones in a single egg than in a kilogram of beef?

---

[56] WTO 1999, 62. For an evaluation of the SPS Agreement, see Josling, Roberts, and Orden 2004.

In the view of the U.S. government, these facts made the ban arbitrary and inconsistent. According to the United States, the real motivation for the measure was to protect domestic beef producers from foreign competition and to reduce surplus beef supplies in the EU. If consumer health were the true motivation, then the EU should not have continued to allow the use of growth additives by its competitive pork producers instead of disallowing it just in its less competitive beef industry.[57]

The EU countered by arguing that the ban was justified under Article 20(b) of the GATT and claimed that the United States was simply attacking the "level" of protection provided. The EU maintained that the WTO could not rule on the appropriate level of protection provided by any regulation, but merely whether the measure itself was in conformity with the SPS. The EU argued that the ban was based on the "precautionary" principle, which took the view that if scientific evidence did not establish beyond a doubt that the hormone residues were safe for humans, then a ban was appropriate.[58] The EU stressed that it did not ban all meat imports, and that hormone-free beef could be sold in Europe.

In 1997, the WTO panel ruled that the hormone ban was not based on scientific evidence or a risk assessment and therefore was inconsistent with the EU's obligations under the SPS agreement. The Appellate Body reaffirmed that decision in 1998. In 1999, after the EU failed to implement any changes in policy, the United States imposed 100 percent tariffs on European imports valued at nearly $120 million, the estimated annual amount of lost U.S. beef exports. Proposals to resolve the impasse by replacing the import ban with a labeling requirement, allowing consumers to make the choice about whether to purchase hormone-treated

[57] The United States noted that Europe introduced milk quotas in 1984 to reduce the oversupply of dairy products, and this resulted in an increase in cattle slaughter, which more than doubled the stock of surplus beef (WTO 1997, 20). As Roberts (1998, 394) points out, "It was no coincidence, the United States argued, that EC officials were willing to allow the use of productivity-enhancing inputs in the internationally competitive pork sector, but substantially more conservative about allowing the use of such inputs in a sector which relied on costly domestic price support measures, import protection, and export subsidies to maintain producer profitability."

[58] Article 5.7 of the SPS states, "In cases where relevant scientific evidence is insufficient, a Member may provisionally adopt sanitary or phytosanitary measures on the basis of available pertinent information." The EU did not formally invoke this provision because its ban was permanent, and as the record made clear there was abundant scientific evidence that judicious use of hormones was not harmful.

beef, ran into difficulties. As of 2008, a negotiated settlement had yet to be reached and the tariffs remain in place.

As already noted, Article 20 allows trade restrictions with the proviso that they be imposed in a nondiscriminatory fashion, but also that they are not "a disguised restriction on international trade." Discrimination was never an issue in this case because the use of hormones was forbidden in domestic as well as imported meat. The question is whether the measure was a "disguised restriction" on trade. The problem is that this standard is virtually impossible to determine because it gets to the unobserved motives behind a trade action. If the intention was not disguised, it would be obvious. The head of the European Alliance for Safe Meat, and a member of the European parliament, admitted that "the decision to ban these substances was made for political and commercial reasons and not, as the public was led to believe, for consumer protection."[59] Such admissions only fuel the suspicion that there is no compelling health or safety reason for the ban, but that it was designed to help special interests, namely European beef producers.

The challenge confronting trade policymakers is to distinguish health and safety protection from regulatory protectionism enacted under the name of health and safety. As it turns out, there are tangible benefits to giving many of the existing regulations a hard look. As a result of the SPS agreement, the United States lifted a controversial eighty-three-year ban on Mexican avocados and allowed the importation of uncooked Argentine beef for the first time in eighty years (from regions of Argentina recognized as free of foot and mouth disease). In addition, Japan removed its forty-six-year ban on U.S. tomatoes, New Zealand citizens are now able to purchase Canadian salmon, and Australians are now able to buy cooked poultry meat. In each case, the restriction's public health rationale was questionable.

And yet merely writing rules (such as SPS) is not going to end such trade disputes. Negotiated rules are a useful way of finding common ground, but countries are bound to have different assessments of the risk trade-offs involved in any given regulation. For example, the United States and European Union have different assessments of the risks of genetically modified foods, such as corn and other agricultural crops.

---

[59] Quoted in Aaronson 2001, 153.

In Europe, the food is under suspicion until proven safe, whereas in the United States, the food is acceptable until proven harmful. There is little scientific evidence that such foods are harmful, but Europe invokes the precautionary principle to justify restrictions on its use. These different principles cannot be easily bridged simply by writing down rules. The question is how far WTO members want to go in limiting the ability of governments to adopt trade restrictions when scientific evidence does not exist or is ambiguous about a particular rationale. One approach is to allow countries complete freedom in choosing their own product safety standards because they benefit the most from proper regulation and bear the cost of regulatory protectionism. Governments and the business community, however, appear to benefit from having some common ground, some rules that provide a transparent and stable system for distinguishing appropriate from inappropriate standards.

The WTO may have a limited role in such conflicts. Some trade disputes are not a matter for litigation and a legal solution, but negotiation and a diplomatic solution. As one observer of the WTO has put it: "Too much policy in the WTO is now formulated on the basis of finding legal 'solutions' to problems, often through legal interpretations of the GATT and WTO agreements, instead of through decisions taken by all members after a full-fledged policy debate. Today's WTO is moving toward being a 'House of Litigation,' lost in the intricacies of legal rulings, rather than an institution based on widely accepted principles that have produced time-tested policies."[60] This is a critical issue that the WTO membership will have to confront in coming years.

What are some of the lessons to be learned from these and other trade and environment cases? One lesson is that unilateral trade sanctions are a poor instrument for achieving environmental objectives. Simply keeping foreign goods out of the U.S. market may be viscerally satisfying, but it does not solve the problem. The refusal of the United States to buy fish that have been caught in ways that harm other animals does

---

[60] Sampson 2000, 7. Sampson has also noted that "perhaps [legal] rulings such as this have some short-term political merit in finding immediate 'solutions' to politically sensitive matters, but in the long term, policy choices as important as the legitimacy of the unilateral application of trade measures to enforce domestic societal preferences extraterritoriality should not be left to litigation of this nature, with confusing and uncertain outcomes" (111).

nothing directly to help those other animals. Sanctions do not prevent a country from diverting tuna and shrimp caught with harmful methods away from the U.S. market toward other markets that would accept it. In the end, international agreements on standards are clearly preferable to trade embargoes, and a global approach must be taken in those negotiations because the lack of cooperation by a few key countries can undermine the goal.

While the threat of sanctions can sometimes provide the incentive for countries to join negotiations, it is also true that countries are apt to resent and resist the imposition of U.S. standards. When other nations are reluctant to negotiate about a problem, the carrot of subsidies rather than the stick of sanctions can be used to promote the adoption of safer production methods. For example, a straightforward solution to the dolphin and turtle problem would have been to subsidize the purchase of dolphin-safe nets and turtle excluder devices for use around the world. These technologies are not expensive. Rather than spending millions of dollars on legal fees over many years in an effort to solve the problem through compulsion, a combination of foreign aid, World Bank assistance, and NGO financial resources should have been pooled to give these dolphin- and turtle-saving technologies to fishermen in developing countries.

Because trade controls are usually ineffective and sometimes counterproductive as environmental regulations, the whole issue of whether trade restrictions are a necessary part of the environmental effort should be considered. For example, the Convention on International Trade in Endangered Species (CITES) bans trade in ivory and other products to help save endangered animals. But an ivory trade ban is not the best policy to protect endangered African elephants because it fails to deal with the underlying problem of domestic resource management. The convention hurts countries that manage their resources well, such as Botswana and South Africa, where the number of elephants has risen. The sale of ivory from herd culls in these countries could generate valuable revenue that the cash-starved game reserves could use to improve the situation even more. Meanwhile, the decline in elephant populations in Kenya and Tanzania is not directly due to the ivory trade, but to poor national management that has failed to raise the costs of poaching to locals. Simply banning trade is no substitute for strong domestic measures, and a well-regulated and well-managed trade can prove better than import bans.[61]

The Basel Convention on the Control of Transboundary Movement on Hazardous Wastes and their Disposal bans illegal trade in toxic waste to prevent its dumping in developing countries. But illegal dumping occurred very infrequently in the past, and the ban did nothing to solve the underlying problem: that national laws that already regulated toxic waste dumping were not enforced. According to some analysts, the convention may even have impeded recycling efforts in developing countries.[62]

In the case of trade in ivory and trash, the problem is not that the WTO poses a barrier to effective environmental management, but that trade restrictions are sometimes viewed as substitutes for multilateral solutions that more effectively address the underlying problem. Yet a global consensus could emerge that trade sanctions are an effective component of an international economic agreement. If provisions of an environmental agreement conflict with WTO rules on nondiscrimination, then the governments agreeing to the environmental accord could also form a consensus in the WTO that discrimination in certain products was acceptable for cnvironmental reasons.[63] There should be enough common ground between the trade policy and the environmental community to work out these differences.

---

[61] As Morris puts it, "CITES imposes trade restrictions on trade in certain species. The ostensible ground for such restrictions is that demand for parts of those species outside the territory of the nations in which those species live is encouraging people to poach those species, leading to dwindling stocks. However, this characterization of the problem misses what for most species is the most important factor in determining numbers, namely the opportunity cost of their continued existence to those people who live nearby. Indeed, by reducing the value of various species to the locals, CITES may in fact discourage conservation" (2000, 279).

[62] See Montgomery 1995. Similarly, the Montreal Protocol on Florocarbons seeks to limit the production and use of chlorofluorocarbons (CFCs), but also imposes bans on the export or import of controlled substances and requires trade sanctions against nonsignatory countries. While the protocol has been effective in limiting CFC production, the question is how effective trade sanctions are against countries that choose not to comply with the agreement, since production and not trade is the main problem.

[63] As Sampson (2000, 97) argues, "If the agreed solution involves a loss of rights under the WTO (that is, being discriminated against), then providing all WTO members agree to forgo those rights, it is difficult to see where there could be a problem."

What has become clear is that it will not be acceptable for the world trade community to ignore or undermine environmental concerns when there appears to be a global consensus on those concerns. Effective environmental and safety regulations should not be blocked simply because they reduce international trade. The notion that all trade must be kept free at all costs is simply wrong. As Thomas Babington Macaulay put it in a parliamentary speech in 1845:

> I am, I believe, as strongly attached as any member of this House to the principle of free trade, rightly understood. Trade, considered merely as trade, considered merely with reference to the pecuniary interest of the contracting parties, can hardly be too free. But there is a great deal of trade which cannot be considered merely as trade, and which affects higher than pecuniary interests. And to say that government never ought to regulate such trade is a monstrous proposition, a proposition at which Adam Smith would have stood aghast.[64]

Regional Trade Agreements

Although multilateral trade agreements such as the GATT have been an integral part of the international trade landscape since World War II, they have not been the only—or even the most important—method of liberalizing trade policy. As discussed in chapter 6, many developing countries have unilaterally decided to make big changes in their trade regime, such as China in 1979, India in 1991, among many others.[65]

A third method of reducing trade barriers is through bilateral or regional trade initiatives. Under this approach, which has proven popular in recent years, a distinction should be made between free trade agreements and customs unions. In a free trade agreement (FTA), such as NAFTA, two or more countries agree to eliminate tariffs on each others' goods, but maintain their own tariffs against imports from nonmember countries. In a customs union, such as the European Union, the member

[64] Macaulay 1900, 102.

[65] The World Bank (2005) reports that, of developing country tariff reductions over the period from 1983 to 2003, 65 percent were due to unilateral reforms, 25 percent to multilateral agreements, and 10 percent due to regional agreements. See Bhagwati 2002 for a study of unilateral trade liberalization.

countries eliminate tariffs on each others' goods and impose a common external tariff on imports from nonmembers.

These bilateral and regional agreements come in various shapes and forms. Some of them are substantial, such as the European Union, NAFTA, and the Common Market of the South (MERCOSUR, for Mercado Común del Sur in South America). Others are of modest importance, such as the EU-Mexico or Japan-Mexico free trade agreements. Many are trivial, such as the Taiwan-Guatemala agreement or the Singapore-Jordan accord. Some make sense as regional partnerships, such as the Southern Africa Customs Unions (which includes South Africa, Botswana, Lesotho, Swaziland, and Namibia), whereas other link quite different countries (the Trans-Pacific Strategic Economic Partnership of Chile, New Zealand, Brunei, and Singapore).

The motivations for these agreements vary. In many instances, they are pursued as much for their political importance as for their economic effects. The formation of the European Economic Community in 1958, the precursor to the present-day European Union, was driven by a desire to solidify political and economic ties among western European countries. When Mexico signaled that it was interested in joining the U.S.-Canada FTA to promote closer political ties and economic integration, it would have been nearly impossible for any U.S. administration to reject the opportunity to improve relations. In others cases, countries might want to obtain more secure market access to major markets, to make binding commitments for domestic policy as a signal to foreign investors, or to integrate markets more deeply than is possible through WTO agreements (such as more detailed agreements on trade in services).

Such trade arrangements have proliferated in recent years. The World Trade Organization reports that, whereas the GATT was notified of 124 such agreements between 1948 and 1994, the WTO has been notified of 240 agreements from 1995 to 2008. Figure 7.2 shows the growth in number of these agreements. Yet simply counting the number of bilateral and regional agreements is misleading because many of them are inconsequential. The main reason for the rapid increase in the number of RTAs during the 1990s was the proliferation of bilateral and plurilateral free trade agreements among countries of the former East bloc in Eastern Europe and the former Soviet Union: "the increased number of RTAs in the 1990s and early 2000s was largely driven by a decline in regionalism and

_____Figure 7.2
Number of Regional Trade Arrangements in Force, 1948–2008.
Source: WTO, www.wto.org.

shift toward multilateralism on the part of two dozen formerly centrally planned economies."[66] The breakup of the former Soviet Union, Yugoslavia, and Czechoslovakia has resulted in a huge number of free trade agreements between places that were formally tied together within one nation or through the Eastern bloc's Council of Mutual Economic Assistance.[67] This is the response to regional disintegration and the dissolution of a larger region bloc rather than an increase in regionalism, and most of the new countries embrace the multilateral system.

Still, the spread of more significant bilateral and regional trade arrangements present difficulties for the multilateral trading system of the GATT and WTO. Such agreements depart from the nondiscriminatory, most favored nation treatment set out in Article 1 of the GATT, even though they are permitted under Article 24 of the GATT. There is a tension between the nondiscriminatory, multilateral approach to trade liberalization and the discriminatory, preferential approach taken in bilateral and regional deals. For this reason, they are sometimes referred to as "preferential" trade agreements.[68]

[66] Pomfret 2007, 928.
[67] For example, in 2005, Moldova formalized free trade agreements with Bulgaria, Macedonia, Serbia and Monetenegro, Bosnia and Herzegovina, Croatia, and others.
[68] See Bhagwati 2008 for a spirited attack on preferential trade agreements.

Indeed, many economists have viewed these preferential trade arrangements with skepticism, if not dismay, particularly in comparison to unilateral or multilateral approaches to trade liberalization. The classic analysis of preferential trade arrangements distinguishes two effects: trade creation and trade diversion. When the United States and Mexico eliminated tariffs on each other's goods, for example, prices to consumers fell and trade was created. Indeed, most such agreements substantially increase trade. One study finds that free trade agreements roughly doubled trade between a pair of countries within a decade.[69]

But just because more trade is generated does not mean it is all for the good. U.S. and Mexican exporters, to continue with this example, are also given preference over other countries in each others' markets. This possibly diverts existing trade away from nonmember countries. In other words, trade may grow between partners but decline between the partners and nonpartners. Trade is stimulated not on the basis of economic efficiency, but on the basis of preferential tax treatment that gives an incentive to trade with certain countries and not with others. In the worst case, the tax preference may induce countries to obtain their imports from less efficient but preferred suppliers. This raises the possibility that economic welfare is actually reduced.

In practice, the precise magnitudes of trade creation and trade diversion are hard to determine. In the case of NAFTA, for example, it is extremely difficult to distinguish the effects of the slowly phased-in tariff preferences on U.S.-Mexico trade from those of the peso crisis in December 1994 and the ongoing rise of the maquiladoras.[70] The welfare effects of the preferences are even harder to gauge. Assessment hinges on whether (pretariff) import prices were actually higher than they would have been in the absence of the preferential treatment. There is precious little empirical evidence on this crucial point: some research suggests that preferences harm the welfare of nonmembers by forcing them to reduce their export prices.[71]

But preferential trade arrangements detract from two key components of the multilateral trading system: nondiscrimination and

[69] Baier and Bergstrand 2007.

[70] According to one assessment (Krueger 2000), there is not much empirical support for the concern that NAFTA has resulted in substantial trade diversion.

[71] Winters and Chang 2000.

transparency. Nondiscrimination is desirable not only because it promotes economic efficiency, but because it levels the playing field in terms of power relationships: tiny Jamaica or St. Kitts get the same access to the U.S. market as Canada or the EU. The adverse effect of trade preferences on nonparticipants is damaging to the world trading system. Some small, poorer countries that do not have the clout to merit an FTA agreement with the United States or EU, such as African countries or smaller Caribbean or Asian countries, are excluded and are discriminated against in the larger markets.

While the United States and EU sometimes offer these poor developing countries special trade preferences, these preferences have problems as well.[72] Usually they are granted on just a select group of goods, not all goods like an FTA, and thus reinforce the specialization of the developing countries in certain commodities. The preferences also require frequent renewal, meaning that foreign investors face the uncertainty about whether market access will continue. Finally, once given preferences, developing countries want to preserve them, even resisting any multilateral liberalization that might enhance efficiency but would erode their preferential access. For example, in the 1990s the EU restricted banana imports from Central American countries so that it would import bananas from former colonies in Africa and the Caribbean, even though the latter suppliers were much less efficient. The latter suppliers, particularly small islands in the Caribbean, fiercely resisted Central American efforts to open up the EU banana market on a nondiscriminatory basis.

And preferential trade arrangements undermine transparency by creating complex and conflicting policies governing imports of the same goods from different countries. This fragments the world trading system and increases the cost and uncertainty of trade. One potentially serious distortion to trade that arises in preferential agreements is rules of origin. In an FTA, each member country retains its own tariff schedule that it applies to imports from nonmember countries.[73] This gives rise to transshipment: the incentive to bring imports into the low-tariff country and then

[72] In the U.S. case, the Caribbean Basin Initiative, the African Growth and Opportunity Act (AGOA), the Andean Trade Preferences Act, all give selective preferences to developing country imports.

[73] In a customs union such as the EU, all member countries have a common external tariff.

ship them into the high-tariff country to avoid paying the higher duties. To stop transshipment, NAFTA mandates that duty-free treatment extends only to goods with sufficient "North American" content.

About two hundred pages of the two-thousand-page NAFTA text are devoted to rules of origin, which are stricter than those in the U.S.-Canada Free Trade Agreement. In the Canadian agreement, automobiles must have 50 percent North American content to receive duty-free treatment, but this was raised to 62.5 percent in NAFTA. In the original agreement with Canada, textile and apparel goods must be made from North American fabric to be eligible, but under NAFTA the yarn from which the fabric is woven must also be of North American content. Thus, Mexican garments receive duty-free treatment in the United States only if the yarn is made, the cloth woven, and the cutting and sewing done primarily in North America. Rules of origin can distort trade when exporters strive to raise artificially the North American content so that the goods can qualify for duty-free treatment in the United States.[74]

One of the key issues concerning regional trade arrangements is whether they are stepping stones toward the multilateral liberalization of trade, or stumbling blocks that impede multilateralism and simply create trade blocs that distort commerce into artificial regional patterns. One hope is for "open regionalism" that allows any country that wishes to join an agreement the freedom to do so, or that eventually leads to the merging of the various agreements at a broader level. It is difficult to know, a priori, whether regional and multilateral trade arrangements are complements or substitutes. In practice, open regionalism does not appear to work: the various agreements are not easily harmonized, and accession for interested parties is not easy because insiders often want to continue to discriminate against outsiders. The empirical evidence on stepping stones versus stumbling blocs is mixed. Some studies show that the United States and European Union reduced their tariffs less in the Uruguay Round on goods heavily traded in its existing FTAs, implying that the preferential agreements were stumbling block to multilateral reforms.[75] In contrast, for Latin American countries, FTAs appear to be linked to faster declines in external tariffs, but not in the case of customs unions.[76]

[74] Krueger 1999.
[75] Limao 2006 and Karacaovali and Limao 2008.
[76] Estevadeordal, Freund, and Ornelas 2008.

Prior to 2001, the United States signed very few free trade agreements (with Israel in 1985, Canada in 1989, and NAFTA in 1993). However, the Bush administration made such trade agreements a central part of its trade strategy. Robert Zoellick, the U.S. trade representative under President Bush, argued that bilateral agreements were a part of a "competitive liberalization" strategy that would jumpstart the WTO process in which the most reluctant reformers could slow progress toward dismantling trade barriers. In Zoellick's view, the United States would bypass the WTO and pursue bilateral and regional trade agreements as a way of putting pressure on those reluctant reformers. As he argued:

> If some regions are too slow to open their markets, the
> United States should move on to others. America should
> spur a competitive dynamic for openness and transparency.
> Competition can work wonders: when the United States
> pursued NAFTA and APEC, the EU finally felt the pressure to
> complete the global Uruguay Round trade negotiations. If
> others hold back in the new WTO round, the United States
> should repeat this strategy of regionalism with a global goal in
> order to break the logjam.[77]

As a result, the United States significantly increased the number of bilateral trade negotiations after 2001. As indicated in table 7.4, the United States concluded agreements with Jordan, Australia, Chile, Singapore, Peru, Morocco, Bahrain, South Korea, Colombia, Panama, and five Central American countries (Costa Rica, El Salvador, Guatemala, Honduras, and Nicaragua) and the Dominican Republic (CAFTA-DR, for Central American Free Trade Agreement and the Dominican Republic). Negotiations with other countries are in progress.

Despite the hopes that bilateral agreements would fuel "competitive liberalization," it seemed to trigger more bilateral agreements rather than accelerate the completion of the Doha Round.[78] For example, shortly after the United States signed NAFTA with Mexico, the European Union sought a similar trade agreement with Mexico to keep its exports competitive in the country. Of course, the United States has not been alone

[77] Zoellick 2000.
[78] Evenett and Meier 2008.

_____*Table 7.4*
U.S. Regional and Bilateral Trade Agreements

Country or Region	Status (as of January 2009)
Israel	In effect since 1985
North American Free Trade Agreement (NAFTA)—Canada and Mexico	In effect since 1994
Jordan	In effect since 2001
Singapore	In effect since 2004
Chile	In effect since 2004
Australia	In effect since 2005
Morocco	In effect since 2005
Central American Free Trade Agreement and Dominican Republic (CAFTA-DR)— Costa Rica, El Salvador, Guatemala, Honduras, Nicaragua	In effect since 2006
Bahrain	In effect since 2006
Oman	In effect since 2007
Peru	In effect since 2008
Colombia	Signed November 2006, pending congressional approval
Panama	Signed June 2007, pending congressional approval
Republic of Korea	Signed June 2007, pending congressional approval
Southern African Customs Union (Botswana, Lesotho, Namibia, South Africa, Swaziland)	Negotiations launched June 2003
Thailand	Negotiations launched June 2004
United Arab Emirates	Negotiations launched March 2005
Malaysia	Negotiations launched March 2006

Source: Office of the U.S. Trade Representative.

in negotiating bilateral and regional trade deals. The EU has actively pursued them, and they have spread throughout Asia and Latin America as well. Some have argued that this takes attention away from the multilateral discussions at the WTO, the only forum where agricultural subsidies and trade barriers can be effectively discussed and where the interests of small countries stand a chance for representation.

The formation of competing trade blocs could even fuel great power rivalries. For example, China and the Association of South East Asian nations (ASEAN) reached an FTA to come into force in 2010. This has been a worrisome development for Korea, which is not included, but not as much for Japan, which has an FTA with ASEAN. And American commercial interests could be compromised if China secures preferential access to raw materials and important markets in Asia and elsewhere, putting it at a competitive disadvantage.

Regrettably, the U.S. turn to bilateral FTAs has also made already bad domestic trade politics even worse. Such agreements force Congress to vote frequently on trade bills, which puts most members into uncomfortable political positions. Some agreements were uncontroversial and passed the Congress easily, such as those with Australia, Singapore, Morocco, and Bahrain. Others encountered stiff opposition and required much arm twisting to ensure their passage, such as CAFTA-DR and Oman. The close, partisan nature of these trade votes gives individual members of Congress an incentive to keep their position ambiguous until they obtain a political favor from the president in exchange for their vote. The more times that Congress is required to vote on trade bills, the more difficult the environment becomes for future trade legislation.

The Democrats' capture of the Congress in the 2006 midterm elections spelled the end of the Bush trade agenda. Furthermore, the Obama administration does not view these bilateral agreements as a priority. Many Democrats have been skeptical of measures to expand trade and have resisted FTAs, particularly with developing countries, which they believe should include stronger labor and environmental provisions if pursued at all. Democratic opposition to FTAs, however, is almost purely political and not based on the underlying economic stakes in these agreements. For example, in its investigation of the U.S.-Colombia FTA, the International Trade Commission concluded that the agreement would have a small, positive impact on U.S. exports, which face tariffs in the 10–20 percent range in Colombia, and almost no impact on U.S. imports because more than 90 percent of Colombia's goods (which account for 0.5 percent of all imports) already enter the U.S. market duty-free.[79] Thus, the agreement would have been a "tax cut on exports" with virtually no impact on American jobs, but nonetheless it was considered controversial. In early 2008, the House decided to postpone its consideration of the agreement.

Although preferential trade agreements have been subject to many valid criticisms, such agreements have some countervailing bene-

[79] U.S. International Trade Commission 2006.

fits. The concerns about trade creation and trade diversion take a purely static view of trade, ignoring the beneficial effects on productivity as a result of greater competition. Trade diversion may not be a serious concern if tariff levels are already low and rules of origin are liberal. Developing countries may be able to lock in greater access to richer, developed markets, although they also may take on burdensome requirements in intellectual property and other areas. And sometimes regional trade agreements can provide templates that later can be adopted at the multilateral level, as was the case with the U.S.-Canada agreement on services trade.

Despite these benefits, the political effort vested in these schemes probably could be better deployed at the multilateral level. And because of their overlapping nature, to say nothing of their complexity, preferential trade arrangements detract from the simplicity that was part of the multilateral system's design. Large regional trade arrangements are generally concluded no more quickly than multilateral initiatives, and therefore the advantages of pursuing them are questionable. Thus, despite these regional diversions, the world has a much greater stake in strengthening the multilateral system of the WTO.

No nation was ever ruined by trade, even seemingly the most disadvantageous.
—George Whaley, 1774

Conclusion

In a recent speech at Dartmouth College, former senator George Mitchell said that he had drawn two conclusions from his role as mediator in the conflict in Northern Ireland: that economic opportunity is a prerequisite for peace, and that America's vision of that economic opportunity is the basis of its influence in the world.

These simple lessons have some connection to trade policy. For nearly three-quarters of a century, the United States has nurtured a rules-based world trading system centered on the principle of nondiscrimination and the goal of gradually reducing trade barriers. The United States is admired around the world as a place of economic opportunity, where individuals are given a chance to succeed regardless of their background. (The election of Barack Obama as president of the United States has underscored this fact.) America's free and competitive markets, and its willingness to accept goods and services from all over the world, is one reason it is so highly regarded. The United States is expected to set an example for the world, and people everywhere look to it for leadership. If the United States weakens its commitment to a system of open world trade, other countries will inevitably follow. The choices that the United States makes in its own trade policies have ramifications far beyond America's shores and have implications well beyond economics.

The open world trading system has faced many challenges in the past and will continue to face challenges in the future. In the 1970s and 1980s, the major threat to open trade was protectionism in developed countries. Protectionist pressures are always present because, as this book has noted many times, economic interests that are adversely affected by trade always seek to limit it. Painful recessions and structural change led to an increase in trade barriers in those decades. In the United States and elsewhere, industry after industry, from footwear and apparel to automobiles and steel to semiconductors and consumer electronics, received protection from foreign competition through antidumping duties, import quotas, voluntary export restraints, so-called orderly market arrangements, and other trade barriers.[1] Fortunately, these import restrictions proved temporary and most of them had lapsed by the early 1990s.

There is always a chance that protectionist pressures will reappear and pose a threat to the open trading system. Those supporting the liberal trading system should always remain vigilant with respect to the demands for protectionist policies. Yet, given the rapid increase in trade integration over the past few decades, it is remarkable that those pressures have been so weak in recent years.[2] Why have protectionist demands been so muted? Postwar economic growth and macroeconomic stability have tempered such demands by creating new opportunities for those displaced by imports. Transfer payments and social insurance have also mitigated the cost to those adversely affected by economic change. Businesses that depend upon imported intermediate goods have become a countervailing force against those that demand new trade restrictions. Finally, many industries facing foreign competition have found that international diversification or joint ventures with foreign partners are a more profitable way of coping with global competition than simply stopping goods at the border.

For example, the world's economic and financial crisis of 2008–09—marked by plummeting stock markets, sharply rising unemployment rates, and the threat of deflation—has prompted many comparisons to the Great Depression of the 1930s. Some have even raised the specter that the recession will lead to a resurgence of protectionism, as seen in the 1930s. Yet the trade policy environment is very different now than it was back then. First, countries today have many more policy

---

[1] See Krueger (1996) for a collection of industry case studies on U.S. trade policy during this period.

[2] Pastor (1983) analyzes what he calls the "cry and sigh" cycle that has routinely exaggerated the threat of protectionism over the past half century. The cry is the consistent refrain that protectionist pressures are on the rise and the sighing is when these pressures are diffused and markets are opened even further.

instruments for addressing the economic crisis than they did in the 1930s. Governments then took no responsibility for supporting financial institutions and were unable to pursue reflationary monetary policies because of fixed exchange rates under the gold standard. Countries resorted to draconian import restrictions in the 1930s because they lacked other macroeconomic policy instruments, mainly monetary policy, to stabilize the financial system and improve economic conditions.

Second, in the 1930s, countries could impose higher trade barriers without violating any international agreements or expecting much of a foreign reaction. Today, WTO agreements restrict the use of such discretionary trade policy. Countries that are tempted to violate WTO agreements can have no illusion that they will avoid swift foreign retaliation if they choose that path. When a country is certain that its exports will be slapped down by other countries if it chooses to impose WTO-inconsistent import restrictions, that country will think twice about doing so.

Third, unlike the early 1930s, foreign investment has transformed the world economy. Leading firms around the world have become so multinational in their production operations and supply chains that they have a vested interest in resisting protectionism. Many domestic industries no longer have a strong incentive to demand import restrictions because foreign rivals now produce in the domestic market, thereby erasing the benefits of trade barriers for domestic firms. For example, unlike the early 1980s, U.S. automakers are not asking for trade protection because it would not solve any of their problems; they are diversified into other markets with equity stakes in foreign producers, and foreign firms operate large production facilities in the United States.

Fourth, unlike the early 1930s, the United States and other leading nations accept their international responsibilities and appear prepared to prevent an outbreak of protectionism. Determined to avoid the mistakes of the past, the Group of 20 leaders have pledged to avoid imposing new restrictions on international trade. "We underscore the critical importance of rejecting protectionism and not turning inward in times of financial uncertainty," they declared in November 2008. They also agreed to "refrain from raising new barriers to investment or to trade in goods and services, imposing new export restrictions, or implementing World Trade Organization inconsistent measures to stimulate exports."

All of these factors have sustained political support for an open trading system and have prevented a globalization backlash. As a result, the political appeal of economic nationalism, with protectionism as a central part of its program, has not been as strong as one might have thought. A century ago, protectionism was associated with industrial strength and independence.[3] But today, protectionism is taken as a sign of weakness. As Senator John McCain once put it, building walls is for cowards.

During the 1990s and 2000s, the main challenge facing the world trading system was not protectionism driven by interest groups, but the antiglobalization movement. This new challenge came from nongovernmental organizations (NGOs) that do not represent sectional interests, but stood for particular causes. These "public interest" groups include "consumer associations, conservation and environmental groups, societies concerned with development in poor countries, human rights groups, movements for social justice, humanitarian societies, organizations representing indigenous people, and church groups from all denominations." Together, they are said to comprise "civil society."[4]

In many instances, these groups oppose the current system of world trade. "With some exceptions, they are hostile to, or highly critical of, capitalism, multinational corporations, freedom of cross-border trade and capital flows, and the idea of a market economy," notes David Henderson, the former chief economist of the OECD. "They are a force on the side of interventionism."[5] The antagonism of these groups goes well beyond international trade to include most forms of market-based commerce. Despite differences of interest and emphasis among these groups, the more radical elements "share a vision of the world in which past history and present-day market-based economic systems are portrayed in terms of patterns of oppression and abuses of power. Free markets and capitalism are seen as embodying and furthering environmental destruction, male dominance, class oppression, racial intolerance, imperialist coercion and colonial exploitation."[6]

---

[3] As the robust Theodore Roosevelt once quipped, "Thank God I am not a free-trader. In this country pernicious indulgence in the doctrine of free trade seems inevitably to produce fatty degeneration of the moral fibre." Quoted in Viner 1991, 246.

[4] From Henderson (2001, 19), whose incisive analysis I have drawn upon here. See also Robertson 2000.

[5] Henderson 2001, 20.

[6] Henderson 2001, 30.

The recent books of the prominent Canadian journalist Naomi Klein are examples of this view. Her 2000 book *No Logo* was a spirited attack on multinational corporations and the policies of the WTO.[7] In her 2007 book, *The Shock Doctrine: The Rise of Disaster Capitalism*, Klein argues that natural disasters, wars, and coups are welcomed (if not organized by) by those who favor neoliberal economic policies because they provide an opportunity to implement privatization and free trade. These policies, she continues, have produced catastrophic results, including economic depressions and mass poverty. She likens free market shock therapy to electroshock torture.

The charges made by Klein and these groups against the world economy are wide-ranging and serious. "If the critics were right," Martin Wolf points out, "supporters of the global market economy would be in favour of mass poverty, grotesque inequality, destruction of state-provided welfare, infringement of national sovereignty, subversion of democracy, unbridled corporate power, environmental degradation, human rights abuses and much more."[8] Of course, this is not true. As chapters 2 and 6 have argued, growing world trade can improve growth prospects and thereby help reduce poverty, can check corporate power through greater competition, can improve the environment by allowing the spread of new, cleaner technologies, and may even unleash a process that promotes democracy, as we have seen in Chile, Mexico, South Korea, Taiwan, and elsewhere. Economic fragmentation, on the other hand, would exacerbate rather than ameliorate many of the problems that the critics identify.

Although these antiglobalization groups have not been represented in the corridors of power, they cannot be dismissed as insignificant. The more radical groups have gained respectability by positioning themselves with mainstream organizations, such as moderate NGOs, UN agencies, labor unions, and some political leaders and other public figures. They have been able to achieve a broader appeal by focusing on human rights, corporate responsibility, and sustainable development, all of which are agreeable in principle but behind which are very different views of policy.[9] As a result, these groups have not only been politically

---

[7] See Segerstrom 2003 for a level-headed critique.

[8] Wolf 2004, 23. See also Bhagwati 2004.

[9] "All three appear, and are presented, as proof against doubt and objections: who could want to oppose, deny or restrict human rights, to prefer that corporations

active, but have become an increasingly influential part of the public debate.

International agencies, national governments, and even corporations that in the past have had a stake in promoting markets have begun to acquiesce to their demands. Yet reconciling their interests with much of the NGO agenda is difficult because there is often a fundamental incompatibility in outlook. For many of the more militant NGOs, the attack on trade is simply an attack on the most visible part of the market economy. They are just starting with the easiest target, but the objective is much bigger. As the *Economist* put it several years ago:

> It is no coincidence that the keenest economic reformers among the developing and ex-communist countries are the new champions of free trade. It is also no coincidence that those in the industrial countries who are most fearful about the future seek to lessen the rich world's reliance on the market economy, and have made it their first goal to smash the GATT and the other institutions of liberal trade. Both sides, in their different ways, are right. Each has recognized that the market economy is ultimately inseparable from a liberal order of international trade.[10]

Still, the antiglobalization movement, which seemed to gain strength after the "Battle of Seattle" protests against the WTO in 1999, began to lose steam after 9/11. Since then, it has not posed as strong a threat to the open trading system as many had anticipated.

As we approach the 2010s, the major challenge facing the world trading system is likely to be "green protectionism." As the United States and other countries debate legislation to limit greenhouse gas emissions, they are also considering imposing new taxes on imports to prevent "carbon leakage." In other words, if the United States creates a "cap-and-trade" system for CO_2 emissions or imposes a carbon tax on domestic industry, it will also limit imports of carbon-producing goods from countries such as China. But how high should such "green tariffs" be? Will they be

---

should act non-responsibly, or to advocate development that was unsustainable? Yet all these virtuous-seeming notions, as now interpreted, bear a collectivist message" (Henderson 2001, 31).

[10] "Battle Lines," *Economist*, December 24, 1994, 14.

compatible with WTO rules and other international agreements? Article 3.5 of the United Nations Framework Convention on Climate Change states that: "Measures taken to combat climate change, including unilateral ones, should not constitute a means of arbitrary or unjustifiable discrimination or a disguised restriction on international trade."

Still, this issue could severely complicate international trade policy. For example, the United States might want to impose penalties on imports of Chinese goods produced using dirty manufacturing methods. But China might respond by saying that the overall U.S. production process releases more carbon because, although the American factory might be cleaner, U.S. workers drive to and from work and live in large homes and therefore have a much bigger carbon footprint than their Chinese counterparts. Then they could justify imposing green taxes on imports from the United States.

Such a situation could lead to absolute chaos in the world trading system. It could also open the door to all sorts of trade protectionism under the guise of environmental protection. In a worse-case scenario, retaliatory and counter-retaliatory import restrictions, as each country tries to impose its environmental standards on others, would shut down world trade. Even Ralph Nader has warned that "runaway environmental protectionism—which Washington's K Street lobbyists would be only too happy to grease—would almost certainly lead to a collapse of the multilateral trading system."[11]

Perhaps the best solution would be an international agreement on a global tax on CO_2 emissions. Such an agreement, although difficult to reach and to implement, would address the root source of greenhouse gas emissions, provide for a uniform treatment of producers across different countries, and thereby preserve the open world trading system and all the benefits that it creates. In any event, the difficult policy choices at the intersection of trade policy and climate change policy may be where the key battles over the world trading system are fought in coming years.[12]

To conclude, trade policy has always been one of the most contentious areas of economic policy and is therefore the subject of a never-

---

[11] Ralph Nader and Toby Heaps, "We Need a Global Carbon Tax." *Wall Street Journal*, December 3, 2008, A17.

[12] For a recent analysis, see Houser et al. 2008.

ending debate. Though the post–World War II period has been marked by a concerted reduction in trade barriers, the matter is not settled because the pressures to weaken the commitment to open markets never abate. The world trading system is far from perfect, and many reforms and changes in rules should be under discussion. Yet, in so doing, we should always keep in mind the manifold benefits of world trade and the contribution of trade liberalization to the welfare and prosperity of billions of people around the world.

References

Aaronson, Susan A. 2001. *Taking Trade to the Streets: The Lost History of Public Efforts to Shape Globalization*. Ann Arbor: University of Michigan Press.

Acharya, Ram C., and Wolfgang Keller. 2007. "Technology Transfer through Imports." NBER Working Paper No. 13086.

Addison, John T., Douglas A. Fox, and Christopher J. Ruhm. 1995. "Trade and Displacement in Manufacturing." *Monthly Labor Review* 118 (April): 58–67.

Ades, Alberto, and Rafael Di Tella. 1999. "Rents, Competition, and Corruption." *American Economic Review* 89 (September): 982–93.

Aitken, Brian, Ann Harrison, and Robert E. Lipsey. 1996. "Wages and Foreign Ownership: A Comparative Study of Mexico, Venezuela, and the United States." *Journal of International Economics* 40 (May): 345–71.

Alston, Julian, M., Daniel A. Sumner, and Henrich Brunke. 2007. "Impacts of Reductions in U.S. Cotton Subsidies on West African Cotton Producers." Oxfam Research Paper, June.

Amiti, Mary, and Josef Konings. 2007. "Trade Liberalization, Intermediate Inputs, and Productivity: Evidence from Indonesia." *American Economic Review* 97:1611–38.

Anderson, Kym. 1992. "Effects on the Environment and Welfare of Liberalizing World Trade: The Cases of Coal and Food." In Kym Anderson and Richard Blackhurst (eds.), *The Greening of World Trade Issues*. Ann Arbor: University of Michigan Press.

———. 1998. "Agricultural Trade Reforms, Research Initiatives, and the Environment." In E. Lutz (ed.), *Agriculture and the Environment: Perspectives on Sustainable Rural Development*. Washington D.C.: World Bank.

Anderson, Kym, Will Martin, and Dominique van der Mensbrugghe. 2006. "Doha Merchandise Trade Reform: What Is at Stake for Developing Countries?" *World Bank Economic Review* 20:169–95.

Anderson, James, and Eric van Wincoop. 2003. "Gravity with Gravitas: A Solution to the Border Puzzle." *American Economic Review* 93 (March): 170–92.

———. 2004. "Trade Costs." *Journal of Economic Literature* 42:691–751.

Anderson, Thomas. 2008. "U.S. Affiliates of Foreign Companies: Activities in 2006." *Survey of Current Business* 88:186–203.

Antweiler, Werner, Brian R. Copeland, and M. Scott Taylor. 2001. "Is Free Trade Good for the Environment?" *American Economic Review* 91 (September): 877–908.

Arkolakis, Costas, Svetlana Demidova, Peter Klenow, and Andrés Rodríguez–Clare. 2008. "Endogenous Variety and the Gains from Trade." *American Economic Review* 98:444–50.

Audley, John J. 1997. *Green Politics and Global Trade: NAFTA and the Future of Environmental Politics.* Washington, D.C.: Georgetown University Press.

Audley, John J., Demetrios G. Papademetriou, Sandra Polaski, and Scott Vaughan. 2003. *NAFTA's Promise and Reality: Lessons from Mexico for the Hemisphere.* Carnegie Endowment for International Peace.

Autor, David H., Lawrence F. Katz, and Melissa S. Kearney. 2008. "Trends in U.S. Wage Inequality: Revising the Revisionists." *Review of Economics and Statistics* 90:300–323.

Baffes, John. 2005. "The Cotton Problem." *World Bank Research Observer* 20:109–44.

Bagwell, Kyle, and Robert W. Staiger. 2002. *The Economics of the World Trading System.* Cambridge: MIT Press.

Baicker, Katherine, and Marit Rehavi. 2004. "Trade Adjustment Assistance." *Journal of Economic Perspectives* 18 (Spring): 239–56.

Baier, Scott L., and Jeffrey H. Bergstrand. 2001. "The Growth of World Trade: Tariffs, Transport Costs, and Income Similarity." *Journal of International Economics* 53 (February): 1–27.

———. 2007. "Do Free Trade Agreements Actually Increase Members' International Trade?" *Journal of International Economics* 71:72–95.

Baily, Martin Neil, and Robert Z. Lawrence. 2004. "What Happened to the Great U.S. Job Machine? The Role of Trade and Electronic Offshoring." *Brookings Papers on Economic Activity* 2:211–70.

Bailey, Michael, Judith Goldstein, and Barry Weingast. 1997. "The Institutional Roots of American Trade Policy: Politics, Coalitions, and International Trade." *World Politics* 49 (April): 309–38.

Baldwin, Robert E. 1988. "The Inefficacy of Trade Policy." In *Trade Policy in a Changing World Economy.* Chicago: University of Chicago Press.

Balke, Norman, and Robert J. Gordon. 1989. "The Estimation of Prewar Gross National Product: Methodology and New Evidence." *Journal of Political Economy* 97 (February): 38–92.

Barbier, Edward B., Nancy Bockstael, Joanne C. Burgess, and Ivar Strand. 1995. "The Linkage Between the Timber Trade and Tropical Deforestation—Indonesia." *The World Economy* (May): 411–42.

Barfield, Claude. 2003. *High Tech Protectionism: The Irrationality of Antidumping Laws.* Washington, D.C.: AEI Press.

Barringer, William H., and Kenneth J. Pierce. 2000. *Paying the Price for Big Steel: $100 Billion in Trade Restraints and Corporate Welfare.* Washington, D.C.: American Institute for International Steel.

Beason, Richard, and David Weinstein. 1996. "Growth, Economies of Scale, and Targeting in Japan (1955–1990)." *Review of Economics and Statistics* 78 (May): 286–95.

Beghin, John C. et al. 2003. "The Cost of the U.S. Sugar Program Revisited." *Contemporary Economic Policy* 21 (January): 106–16.

Berman, Eli, John Bound, and Zvi Griliches. 1994. "Changes in the Demand for Skilled Labor within U.S. Manufacturing: Evidence from the Annual Survey of Manufacturers." *Quarterly Journal of Economics* 109 (May): 367–97.

Bernard, Andrew B., and J. Bradford Jensen. 1999. "Exceptional Exporter Performance: Cause, Effect, or Both?" *Journal of International Economics* 47 (February): 1–26.

Bernard, Andrew, J. Bradford Jensen, Stephen Redding, and Peter Schott. 2007. "Firms in International Trade." *Journal of Economic Perspectives* 21:105–30.

Bernard, Andrew, Brad Jensen, and Peter Schott. 2006. "Survival of the Best Fit: Exposure to Low-Wage Countries and the (Uneven) Growth of U.S. Manufacturing Plants." *Journal of International Economics* 68:219–37.

Bernhofen, Daniel M., and John C. Brown. 2005. "Estimating the Comparative Advantage Gains from Trade: Evidence from Japan." *American Economic Review* 95:208–25.

Bhagwati, Jagdish (ed.). 2002. *Going Alone: The Case for Relaxed Reciprocity in Freeing Trade.* Cambridge: MIT Press.

———. 2004. *In Defense of Globalization.* New York: Oxford University Press.

———. 2008. *Termites in the Trading System: How Preferential Agreements Undermine Free Trade.* New York: Oxford University Press.

Bhagwati, Jagdish, and Robert Hudec. 1996. *Fair Trade and Harmonization: Prerequisites for Free Trade?* Cambridge: MIT Press.

Bhagwati, Jagdish, and Arvind Panagariya. 1996. "Preferential Trading Areas and Multilateralism: Strangers, Friends, or Foes?" In Jagdish Bhagwati and Arvind Panagariya (eds.), *The Economics of Preferential Trading Areas.* Washington, D.C.: AEI Press.

Bhagwati, Jagdish, and T. N. Srinivasan. 2002. "Trade and Poverty in Poor Countries." *American Economic Review* 92:180–83.

Blinder, Alan. 2006. "Offshoring: The Next Industrial Revolution?" *Foreign Affairs* 85:113–28.

Blonigen, Bruce A. 2006. "Evolving Discretionary Practices of U.S. Antidumping Activity." *Canadian Journal of Economics* 39:874–900.

Blonigen, Bruce A., and Thomas J. Prusa. 2003. "Antidumping." In E. Kwan Choi and James Harrigan (eds.), *Handbook of International Trade.* Oxford: Blackwell.

Bordo, Michael D., Barry Eichengreen, and Douglas A. Irwin. 1999. "Is Globalization Today Really Different From Globalization a Hundred Years Ago?" In Susan Collins and Robert Z. Lawrence (eds.), *Brookings Trade Forum, 1999.* Washington, D.C.: Brookings Institution.

Borjas, George J., Richard B. Freeman, and Lawrence F. Katz. 1997. "How Much Do Immigration and Trade Affect Labor Market Outcomes?" *Brookings Papers on Economic Activity.*1–67.

Bovard, James. 1991. *The Fair Trade Fraud.* New York: St. Martin's Press.

Bown, Chad P. 2004a. "Developing Countries as Plaintiffs and Defendants in GATT/WTO Trade Disputes." *World Economy* 27 (January): 59–80.

———. 2004b. "Trade Disputes and the Implementation of Protection under the GATT: An Empirical Assessment." *Journal of International Economics* 62 (March): 263–94.

Bradsher, Keith. 2008. "Investors Seek Asian Options to Costly China." *New York Times*, June 18.

Brander, James A. 1995. "Strategic Trade Policy." In Gene M. Grossman and Kenneth Rogoff (eds.), *Handbook of International Economics*, Vol. 3. New York: Elsevier.

Branstetter, Lee G. 2001. "Are Knowledge Spillovers International or Intranational in Scope? Microeconometric Evidence from the U.S. and Japan." *Journal of International Economics* 53 (February): 53–80.

Broda, Christian, Nuno Limão, and David Weinstein. 2008. "Optimal Tariffs and Market Power: The Evidence." *American Economic Review* 98:2032–2065.

Broda, Christian, and David Weinstein. 2006. "Globalization and the Gains from Variety." *Quarterly Journal of Economics* 121:541–585.

Brown, Andrew G., and Robert M. Stern. 2008. "What Are the Issues in Using Trade Agreements for Improving International Labor Standards?" *World Trade Review* 7:331–58.

Brown, Sherrod. 2006. *Myths of Free Trade: Why American Trade Policy Has Failed.* New York: New Press.

Buchanan, Patrick. 1998. *The Great Betrayal: How American Sovereignty and Social Justice Are Being Sacrificed to the Gods of the Global Economy.* Boston: Little, Brown.

Bureau of Labor Statistics. 2004. "Extended Mass Layoffs Associated with Domestic and Overseas Relocations, First Quarter 2004, Summary." June 10.

Burtless, Gary, and Robert Z. Lawrence, Robert E. Litan, Robert J. Shapiro. 1998. *Globaphobia: Confronting Fears about Open Trade.* Washington, D.C.: Brookings Institution, Progressive Policy Institute, & Twentieth Century Fund.

Ceglowski, Janet, and Stephen Golub. 2007. "Just How Low Are China's Labour Costs?" *World Economy* 30:597–617.

Collier, Paul. 2005. "Why the WTO Is Deadlocked: And What Can Be Done About It." *World Economy* 29:1423–49.

Collins, Susan (ed.). 1998. *Exports, Imports, and the American Worker.* Washington, D.C.: Brookings Institution.

Congressional Budget Office. 1994. *How the GATT Affects U.S. Antidumping and Countervailing Duty Policy.* Washington, D.C., September.

———. 1998. *Antidumping Action in the United States and Around the World: An Analysis of International Data.* Washington, D.C., June.

———. 2004. "Economic Analysis of the Countervailing Duty and Subsidy Offset Act of 2000." Washington, D.C., March 2.

———. 2007. "Cost Estimate: H.R. 3920: Trade and Globalization Assistance Act of 2007." Washington, D.C., October 29.

———. 2008. "How Changes in the Value of the Chinese Currency Affect U.S. Imports." Washington, D.C., July.

Cooper, Helene. 2000. "A Trade Deal Helps Cambodian Workers, But Payoff Is Withheld." *Wall Street Journal,* February 28, p. A1.

Corden, W. Max. 1974. *Trade Policy and Economic Welfare.* Oxford: Clarendon Press.

Council of Economic Advisers. 2004. Economic Report of the President, February. Washington, D.C.: GPO.

———. 2009. Economic Report of the President, February. Washington, D.C.: GPO.

Dai, Xiudian, Alan Cawson, and Peter Holmes. 1996. "The Rise and Fall of High Definition Television: The Impact of European Technology Policy." *Journal of Common Market Studies* 34 (June): 149–66.

Das, Gurcharan. 2001. *India Unbound.* New York: Knopf.

Dasgupta, Susmita, Benoit Laplante, Hua Wang, and David Wheeler. 2002. "Confronting the Environmental Kuznets Curve." *Journal of Economic Perspectives* 16:147–68.

Davey, William J. 2001. "Has the WTO Dispute Settlement System Exceeded Its Authority?" *Journal of International Economic Law* 4: 79–110.

Davis, Steven J., John C. Haltiwanger, and Scott Schuh.1995. *Job Creation and Destruction.* Cambridge: MIT Press.

de Melo, Jaime, and David Tarr. 1992. *A General Equilibrium Analysis of U.S. Foreign Trade Policy.* Cambridge: MIT Press.

de Melo, Jaime, and David Tarr. 1993. "Industrial Policy in the Presence of Wage Distortions: The Case of the U.S. Auto and Steel Industries." *International Economic Review* 34 (November): 833–51.

Dean, Judith, and Mary E. Lovely, 2008. "Trade Growth, Production Fragmentation, and China's Environment." In Robert C. Feenstra and Shang-Jin Wei (eds.), *China's Growing Role in World Trade.* Chicago: University of Chicago Press.

Decker, Paul T., and Walter Corson. 1995. "International Trade and Worker Displacement: Evaluation of the Trade Adjustment Assistance Program." *Industrial and Labor Relations Review* 48 (July): 758–74.

Destler, I. M. 1998. "Trade Politics and Labor Issues, 1953–1995." In Susan Collins (ed.), *Imports, Exports, and the American Worker.* Washington, D.C.: Brookings Institution Press.

Dew-Becker, Ian, and Robert J. Gordon. 2005. "Where Did the Productivity Growth Go? Inflation Dynamics and the Distribution of Income." *Brookings Papers on Economic Activity* 2: 67–150.

Dickens, William T. 1995. "Do Labor Rents Justify Strategic Trade and Industrial Policy?" NBER Working Paper No. 5137, May.

Dollar, David, and Aart Kraay. 2004. "Trade, Growth, and Poverty." *Economic Journal* 114 (February): F22–F49.

Dollar, David, and Borje Ljunggren. 1997. "Vietnam." In Padma Desai (ed.), *Going Global: Transition from Plan to Market in the World Economy.* Cambridge: MIT Press.

Dollar, David, and Kenneth Sokoloff. 1990. "Patterns of Productivity Growth in South Korean Manufacturing Industries, 1963–1979." *Journal of Development Economics* 33 (October): 309–27.

Eaton, Jonathan, and Samuel Kortum. 2001. "Trade in Capital Goods." *European Economic Review* 45:1195–1235.

Edmonds, Eric, and Nina Pavcnik. 2005. "Child Labor in the Global Economy." *Journal of Economic Perspectives* 18:199–220.

———. 2006. "International Trade and Child Labor: Cross-Country Evidence." *Journal of International Economics* 68:115–40.

Edwards, Sebastian, and Daniel Lederman. 2002. "The Political Economy of Unilateral Trade Liberalization: The Case of Chile." In Jagdish Bhagwati (ed.), *Going Alone: The Case for Relaxed Reciprocity in Freeing Trade.* Cambridge: MIT Press.

Elliott, Kimberly Ann, and Richard Freeman. 2001. "White Hats or Don Quixotes? Human Rights Vigilantes in the Global Economy." NBER Working Paper No. 8102, January.

Elliott, Kimberly Ann, Debayani Kar, and J. David Richardson. 2006. "Assessing Globalization's Critics: 'Talkers Are No Good Doers???'" Working Paper, Peterson Institute for International Economics.

Estevadeordal, Antoni, Brian Frantz, and Alan M. Taylor. 2003. "The Rise and Fall of World Trade, 1870–1939." *Quarterly Journal of Economics* 118:359–407.

Estevadeordal, Antoni, Caroline Freund, and Emanuel Ornelas. 2008. "Does Regionalism Affect Trade Liberalization towards Non-members?" Centre for Economic Performance Working Paper No. 868, London School of Economics.

Estevadeordal, Antoni, and Alan M. Taylor. 2008. "Is the Washington Consensus Dead? Growth, Openness, and the Great Liberalization 1970s–2000s." NBER Working Paper No. 14264, August.

Evenett, Simon J., and Michael Meier. 2008. "An Interim Assessment of the US Trade Policy of 'Competitive Liberalization'." *World Economy* 31:31–66.

Feenstra, Robert C. 1984. "Voluntary Export Restraint in U.S. Autos, 1980–81." In Robert Baldwin and Anne Krueger (eds.), *The Structure and Evolution of Recent U.S. Trade Policy.* Chicago: University of Chicago Press.

Feenstra, Robert C. (ed.). 2000. *The Impact of International Trade on Wages.* Chicago: University of Chicago Press.

———. 2006. "New Evidence on the Gains from Trade." *Review of World Economics* 142:617–41.

Feenstra, Robert C., and Gordon H. Hanson. 2003. "Global Production and Rising Inequality: A Survey of Trade and Wages." In E. Kwan Choi and James Harrigan (eds.), *Handbook of International Trade.* New York: Basil Blackwell.

Feenstra, Robert C., James R. Markusen, and William Zeile. 1992. "Accounting for Growth with New Inputs." *American Economic Review* 82 (May): 415–21.

Feinberg, Robert A., and Kara Reynolds. 2008. "Friendly Fire: The Impact of U.S. Antidumping Enforcement on U.S. Exporters." *Review of World Economics* 144:366–78.

Feldstein, Martin. 2008. "Did Wages Reflect Productivity Growth?" *Journal of Policy Modeling* 30:591–94.

Fernandes, Ana M. 2007. "Trade Policy, Trade Volumes and Plant-level Productivity in Colombian Manufacturing Industries." *Journal of International Economics* 71:52–71.

Fernandez, Raquel, and Dani Rodrik. 1991. "Resistance to Reform: Status Quo Bias in the Presence of Individual–Specific Uncertainty." *American Economic Review* 81 (December): 1146–55.

Ferreira, Pedro C., and Jose L. Rossi. 2003. "New Evidence from Brazil on Trade Liberalization and Productivity Growth." *International Economic Review* 44 (November): 1383–1405.

Ferreira, Susana. 2004. "Deforestation, Property Rights, and International Trade." *Land Economics* 80 (May): 174–93.

Feyrer, James. 2008. "Trade and Income—Exploiting Time Series in Geography." Unpublished working paper, Dartmouth College.

Field, Alfred J., and Edward M. Graham. 1997. "Is There a Special Case for Import Protection for the Textile and Apparel Sectors Base on Labour Adjustment?" *World Economy* 20 (March): 137–57.

Finger, J. Michael (ed.). 1993. *Antidumping: How It Works and Who Gets Hurt.* Ann Arbor: University of Michigan Press.

———. 1996. "Legalized Backsliding: Safeguard Provisions in GATT." In Will Martin and L. Alan Winters (eds.), *The Uruguay Round and Developing Countries.* New York: Cambridge University Press.

Finger, J. Michael, Merlinda D. Ingco, and Ulrich Reincke. 1996. *The Uruguay Round: Statistics on Tariff Concessions Given and Received.* Washington, D.C.: World Bank.

Fitzgerald, Terry J. 2008. "Where Has All the Income Gone?" Federal Reserve Bank of Minneapolis Region, September, 24–29.

Flam, Harry. 1985. "A Heckscher-Ohlin Analysis of the Law of Declining International Trade." *Canadian Journal of Economics* 18 (August): 602–15.

Flamm, Kenneth. 1996. *Mismanaged Trade? Strategic Policy and the Semiconductor Industry.* Washington, D.C.: Brookings Institution.

Foer, Franklin. 2002. "Fabric Softener." *New Republic.* March 4 and 11, 19–21.

Food and Agriculture Organization. 2002. *FAO Annual Yearbook: Fertilizer 1999.* Rome: FAO, 2002.

Francois, Joseph F., and Laura M. Baughman. 2001. "Estimated Economic Effects of Proposed Import Relief Remedies for Steel." Washington, D.C.: The Trade Partnership, December.

Francois, Joseph F., Hans van Meijl, and Frank van Tongeren. 2005. "Trade Liberalization in the Doha Development Round." *Economic Policy* 20:349–91.

Frank, Charles R., Jr., Kwang S. Kim, and Larry E. Westphal. 1975. *Foreign Trade Regimes and Economic Development: South Korea.* New York: National Bureau of Economic Research.

Frankel, Jeffrey. 2000. "Globalization of the Economy." In Joseph Nye and John Donahue (eds.), *Governance in a Globalizing World.* Washington, D.C.: Brookings Institution.

Frankel, Jeffrey A., and David Romer. 1999. "Does Trade Cause Growth?" *American Economic Review* 89:379–99.

Frankel, Jeffrey A., and Andrew K. Rose. 2002. "An Estimate of the Effect of Currency Unions on Trade and Income." *Quarterly Journal of Economics* 117:437–66.

———. 2005. "Is Trade Good or Bad for the Environment? Sorting out the Causality." *Review of Economics and Statistics* 87:85–91.

Freeman, Richard B., and Morris M. Kleiner. 2005. "The Last American Shoe Manufacturers: Changing the Method of Pay to Survive Foreign Competition." *Industrial Relations* 44:307–30.

Freund, Caroline, and Bineswaree Bolaky. 2008. "Trade, Regulations, and Income." *Journal of Development Economics* 87:309–21.

Gallaway, Michael P., Bruce A. Blonigen, and Joseph E. Flynn. 1999. "Welfare Costs of the U.S. Antidumping and Countervailing Duty Laws." *Journal of International Economics* 49:211–44.

Gates, Scott, Torbjørn Knutsen, and Jonathon Moses. 1996. "Democracy and Peace: A More Skeptical View." *Journal of Peace Research* 33 (February): 1–10.

Gawande, Kishore, and Pravin Krishna. 2003. "The Political Economy of Trade Policy: Empirical Approaches." In E. Kwan Choi and James Harrigan (eds.), *Handbook of International Trade*. Oxford: Blackwell.

Gignilliat, John L. 1961. "Pigs, Politics, and Protection: The European Boycott of American Pork." *Agricultural History* 35:3–24.

Giridharadas, Anand. 2007. "Outsourcing Works, So India Is Exporting Jobs." *New York Times*, September 25.

Glewwe, Paul. 2000. "Are Foreign Owned Businesses in Vietnam Really Sweatshops?" Agricultural Economist Newsletter, University of Minnesota Extension Service, No. 701. Summer.

Goldberg, Penny, and Nina Pavcnik. 2007. "Distributional Effects of Globalization in Developing Countries." *Journal of Economic Literature* 45:39–82.

Goldin, Claudia, and Lawrence F. Katz. 2007. "Long-Run Changes in the Wage Structure: Narrowing, Widening, Polarizing." *Brookings Papers on Economic Activity* 2:135–65.

Goldstein, Judith L., Douglas Rivers, and Michael Tomz. 2007. "Institutions in International Relations: Understanding the Effects of the GATT and WTO on World Trade." *International Organization* 61:37–67.

Goldstein, Morris, and Nicholas Lardy. 2008. *Debating China's Exchange Rate Policy*. Washington, D.C.: Peterson Institute for International Economics.

Golub, Stephen S. 1999. *Labor Costs and International Trade*. Washington, D.C.: AEI Press.

Golub, Stephen S., and Chang-Tai Hsieh. 2000. "Classical Ricardian Theory of Comparative Advantage Revisited." *Review of International Economics* 8 (May): 221–34.

Greenspan, Alan. 2004. "The Critical Role of Education in the Nation's Economy." Speech at Greater Omaha Chamber of Commerce Annual Meeting, February 20.

Gresser, Edward. 2002a. "America's Hidden Tax on the Poor: The Case for Reforming U.S. Tariff Policy." Progressive Policy Institute Policy Report, March.

———. 2002b. "Toughest on the Poor: America's Flawed Tariff System." *Foreign Affairs* 81 (November/December): 9–14.

Gresser, Edward. 2007. *Freedom from Want: American Liberalism and the Global Economy*. Brooklyn, N.Y.: Soft Skull.

Groombridge, Mark A. 2001. "America's Bittersweet Sugar Policy." Trade Briefing Paper, Center for Trade Policy Studies, Cato Institute, December.

Groshen, Erica L., Bart Hobijn, and Margaret M. McConnell. 2005. "U.S. Jobs Gained and Lost through Trade: A Net Measure." Current Issues in Economics and Finance, Federal Reserve Bank of New York, August.

Grossman, Gene M., and Alan B. Krueger. 1993. "Environmental Impacts of a North American Free Trade Agreement." In Peter Garber (ed.), *The Mexico-U.S. Free Trade Agreement*. Cambridge: MIT Press.

Grossman, Gene M., and Giovanni Maggi. 1998. "Free Trade vs. Strategic Trade: A Peak into Pandora's Box." In R. Sato, R. V. Ramachandran, and K. Mino (eds.), *Global Competition and Integration*. Boston: Kluwer Academic Publishers.

Guest, Robert. 2004. *The Shackled Continent: Power, Corruption, and African Lives*. London: Macmillan.

Hansen, Wendy L., and Thomas J. Prusa. 1996. "Cumulation and ITC Decision-Making: The Sum of the Parts Is Greater Than the Whole." *Economic Inquiry* 34 (October): 746–69.

Harrison, Ann E. 1994. "Productivity, Imperfect Competition and Trade Reform: Theory and Evidence." *Journal of International Economics* 36 (February): 53–73.

Harrison, Ann E., and Jason Scorse. 2004. "Moving Up or Moving Out? Anti-Sweatshop Activists and Labor Market Outcomes." NBER Working Paper No. 10492, May.

Hart, Jeffrey A. 1993. "The Antidumping Petition of the Advanced Display Manufacturers of America: Origin and Consequences." *World Economy* 16 (January): 85–109.

———. 1994. "The Politics of HDTV in the United States." *Policy Studies Journal* 22 (Summer): 213–28.

Hausmann Ricardo, and Dani Rodrik. 2003. "Economic Development as Self-Discovery." *Journal of Economic Development* 72 (December): 603–33.

Heckman, James. 1999. "Doing It Right: Job Training and Education." *Public Interest* 135 (Spring): 86–107.

Henderson, David. 2001. *Anti-Liberalism 2000: The Rise of New Millennium Collectivism*. London: Institute of Economic Affairs.

Hertel, Thomas W., and Roman Keeney. 2006. "What Is at Stake: The Relative Importance of Import Barriers, Export Subsidies, and Domestic Support." In Kym Anderson and Will Martin (eds.), *Agricultural Trade Reform and the Doha Development Agenda*. Washington, D.C.: World Bank.

Hertel, Thomas W., Roman Keeney, Maros Ivanic, and L. Alan Winters. 2007. "Distributional Effects of WTO Agricultural Reform in Rich and Poor Countries." *Economic Policy* 50:1–49.

Hillman, Arye, and Peter Moser. 1996. "Trade Liberalization as Politically Optimal Exchange of Market Access." In Matthew Canzoneri, Wilfred Ethier, and Vittorio Grilli (eds.), *The New Transatlantic Economy.* New York: Cambridge University Press.

Hiscox, Michael. 2007. "Through a Glass and Darkly: Framing Effects and Individuals' Attitudes Towards International Trade." *International Organization* 60:755–80.

Hoekman, Bernard, and Michel Kostecki. 2009. *The Political Economy of the World Trading System: The WTO and Beyond.* 3rd ed. New York: Oxford University Press.

Hoekman, Bernard, Francis Ng, and M. Olarreaga. 2004. "Reducing Agricultural Tariffs versus Domestic Support: What Is More Important for Developing Countries?" *World Bank Economic Review* 18:175–204.

Houser, Trevor et al. 2008. *Leveling the Carbon Playing Field: International Competition and US Climate Policy Design.* Washington, D.C.: Peterson Institute for International Economics.

Hudec, Robert. 1990. *The GATT Legal System and World Trade Diplomacy.* 2nd ed. Salem, N.H.: Butterworth Legal Publishers.

———. 1998. "Does the Agreement on Agriculture Work? Agricultural Disputes After the Uruguay Round." International Agricultural Trade Research Consortium orking Paper No. 98–2. April. http://www.umn.edu/iatrc.

———. 2000. "The Product-Process Doctrine in GATT/WTO Jurisprudence." In Marco Bronckers and Reinhard Quick (eds.), *New Directions in International Economic Law: Essays in Honour of John H. Jackson.* Boston: Kluwer Law International.

Hufbauer, Gary C., and Kimberly A. Elliott. 1994. *Measuring the Costs of Protection in the United States.* Washington, D.C.: Institute for International Economics, January.

Hufbauer, Gary C., and Jeffrey J. Schott. 2005. *NAFTA Revisited: Achievements and Challenges.* Washington, D.C.: Institute for International Economics.

Hummels, David. 2007. "Transportation Costs and International Trade in the Second Era of Globalization." *Journal of Economic Perspectives* 21:131–54.

Hummels, David, Jun Ishii, and Kei Mu Yi. 2001. "The Nature and Growth of Vertical Specialization in World Trade." *Journal of International Economics* 54:75–96.

Hummels, David, and Peter Klenow. 2005. "The Variety and Quality of a Nation's Exports." *American Economic Review* 95, 704–723.

Hummels, David, Dana Rapoport, and Kei-Mu Yi. 1998. "Vertical Specialization and the Changing Nature of World Trade." *Federal Reserve Bank of New York Economic Policy Review* 79–99.

Ianchovichina, Elena, and Will Martin. 2004. "Impacts of China's Accession to the World Trade Organization." *World Bank Economic Review* 18:3–37.

Ikenson, Dan. 2004. "Zeroing In: Antidumping's Flawed Methodology under Fire." Center for Trade Policy Studies, Cato Institute, Free Trade Bulletin No. 11, April 27.

Ingco, Merlinda D. 1996. "Tariffication in the Uruguay Round: How Much Liberalization?" *World Economy* 19:425–46.

International Monetary Fund. 2000. *International Financial Statistics Yearbook 2000.* Washington, D.C.: IMF.

Irwin, Douglas A. 1996a. *Against the Tide: An Intellectual History of Free Trade.* Princeton: Princeton University Press.

———. 1996b. "Trade Politics and the Semiconductor Industry." In Anne O. Krueger (ed.), *The Political Economy of American Trade Policy.* Chicago: University of Chicago Press.

———. 1998a. "From Smoot-Hawley to Reciprocal Trade Agreements: Changing the Course of U.S. Trade Policy in the 1930s." In Michael Bordo, Claudia Goldin, and Eugene White (eds.), *The Defining Moment: The Great Depression and the American Economy.* Chicago: University of Chicago Press.

———. 1998b. "Changes in U.S. Tariffs: The Role of Import Prices and Commercial Policies." *American Economic Review* 88 (September): 1015–26.

———. 2003. "Causing Problems? The WTO Review of Causation and Injury Attribution in U.S. Section 201 Cases." *World Trade Review* 2 (November): 297–325.

———. 2005a. "The Rise of U.S. Antidumping Actions in Historical Perspective." *World Economy* 28:651–68.

———. 2005b. "Welfare Effects of Autarky: Evidence from the Jeffersonian Embargo of 1807–1809." *Review of International Economics* 13:631–45.

Irwin, Douglas A., and Peter J. Klenow. 1994. "Learning-by-Doing Spillovers in the Semiconductor Industry." *Journal of Political Economy* 102:1200–1227.

Irwin, Douglas A., and Randall S. Kroszner. 1999. "Interests, Institutions, and Ideology in Securing Policy Change: The Republican Conversion to Trade Liberalization after Smoot-Hawley." *Journal of Law and Economics* 42:643–73.

Irwin, Douglas A., Petros C. Mavroidis, and Alan O. Sykes. 2008. *The Genesis of the GATT.* New York: Cambridge University Press.

Irwin, Douglas A., and Nina Pavcnik. 2004. "Airbus versus Boeing Revisited: International Competition in the Aircraft Market." *Journal of International Economics* 64:223–45.

Jacks, David, Christopher Meissner, and Dennis Novy. 2008. "Trade Costs, 1870–2000." *American Economic Review* 98:529–34.

Jacobson, Louis. 1998. "Compensation Programs." In Susan Collins (ed.), *Imports, Exports, and the American Worker*. Washington, D.C.: Brookings Institution.

Jaffe, Adam B. et al. 1995. "Environmental Regulation and the Competitiveness of U.S. Manufacturing: What Does the Evidence Tell Us?" *Journal of Economic Literature* 33 (March): 132–63.

Jawara, Fatoumata, and Aileen Kwa. 2003. *Behind the Scenes at the WTO: The Real World of International Trade Negotiations*. New York: Zed Books.

Jefferson, Gary H., Albert G. Z. Hu, and Jian Su. 2006. "The Sources and Sustainability of China's Economic Growth." *Brookings Papers on Economic Activity*:1–60.

Jensen, J. Bradford, and Lori G. Kletzer. 2008. "'Fear' and Offshoring: The Scope and Potential Impact of Imports and Exports of Services." Policy Brief No. 08-1. Washington, D.C.: Peterson Institute for International Economics.

Jomo, K. S. 2001. "Rethinking the Role of Government Policy in Southeast Asia." In Joseph Stiglitz and Shahid Yusuf (eds.), *Rethinking the East Asian Miracle*. New York: Oxford University Press.

Jones, Charles I. 2001. "Comment on Rodríguez and Rodrik." In Ben S. Bernanke and Kenneth Rogoff (eds.), *NBER Macroeconomics Annual, 2000*. Cambridge: MIT Press.

Jones, Kent. 2004. *Who's Afraid of the WTO?* New York: Cambridge University Press.

Josling, Timothy, Donna Roberts, and David Orden. 2004. *Food Regulation and Trade: Toward a Safe and Open Global System*. Washington, D.C.: Institute for International Economics.

Kahn, Matthew. 2003. "The Geography of U.S. Pollution Intensive Trade: Evidence from 1958 to 1994." *Regional Science and Urban Economics* 33, 383–400.

Kaivanto, Kim. 2007. "Trade-Related Job Loss, Wage Insurance and Externalities: An Ex Ante Efficiency Rationale for Wage Insurance." *World Economy* 30:962–71.

Karacaovali, Baybars, and Nuno Limao. 2008. "The Clash of Liberalizations: Preferential vs. Multilateral Trade Liberalization in the European Union." *Journal of International Economics* 74:299–327.

Kasahara, Hiroyuki, and Joel Rodrigue. 2008. "Does the Use of Imported Intermediates Increase Productivity? Plant-level Evidence." *Journal of Development Economics* 87:106–18.

Katz, Lawrence F., and Lawrence H. Summers. 1989. "Industry Rents: Evidence and Implications." *Brookings Papers on Economic Activity: Microeconomics*.

Kee, Hiau Looi, Alessandro Nicita, and Marcelo Olarreaga. 2009. "Estimating Trade Restrictiveness Indices." *Economic Journal* 119:172–199.

Kee, Hiau Looi, Alessandro Nicita, and Marcelo Olarreaga. 2008. "Import Demand Elasticities and Trade Distortions." *Review of Economics and Statistics* 90:666–82.

Kehoe, Timothy J., and Kim J. Ruhl. 2002. "How Important Is the New Goods Margin in International Trade?" Working Paper, University of Minnesota, October.

Keller, Wolfgang. 2004. "International Technology Diffusion." *Journal of Economic Literature* 42:752–83.

Kim, Euysung. 2000. "Trade Liberalization and Productivity Growth in Korean Manufacturing Industries: Price Protection, Market Power, and Scale Efficiency." *Journal of Development Economics* 62 (June): 55–83.

King, Neil. 2002. "Trade Imbalance: Why Uncle Same Wrote a Big Check to a Sparkler Maker." *Wall Street Journal*, December 5.

Kitano, Taiju, and Hiroshi Ohashi. 2007. "Did U.S. Safeguard Resuscitate Harley Davidson in the 1980s?" Working Paper, Department of Economics, University of Tokyo.

Klenow, Peter, and Andrés Rodríguez–Claire. 1997. "Quantifying Variety Gains from Trade Liberalization." Working Paper, University of Chicago, September.

Kletzer, Lori G. 1998a. "Job Displacement." *Journal of Economic Perspectives* 12 (Winter): 115–36.

———. 1998b. "Trade and Job Displacement in U.S. Manufacturing: 1979–1991." In Susan Collins (ed.), *Imports, Exports, and the American Worker*. Washington, D.C.: Brookings Institution.

———. 2000. "Trade and Job Loss in U.S. Manufacturing, 1979–1994." In Robert Feenstra (ed.), *The Impact of International Trade on Wages*. Chicago: University of Chicago Press for the NBER.

———. 2001. *Job Loss from Imports: Measuring the Costs*. Washington, D.C.: Institute for International Economics.

———. 2004. "Trade-related Job Loss and Wage Insurance: A Synthetic Review." *Review of International Economics* 12:724–48.

Koopman, Robert, Zhi Wang, and Shang-jin Wei. 2008. "How Much of Chinese Exports Is Really Made in China? Assessing Domestic Value Added when Processing Trade Is Pervasive." NBER Working Paper No. 14109, June.

Kose, M. Ayhan, Guy Meredith, and Christopher Towe. 2004. "How Has NAFTA Affected the Mexican Economy? Review and Evidence." IMF Working Paper 94/59.

Krishna, Pravin, and Devashish Mitra. 1998. "Trade Liberalization, Market Discipline and Productivity Growth: New Evidence from India." *Journal of Development Economics* 56 (August): 447–62.

Kristof, Nicholas D., and Sheryl WuDunn. 2000. "Two Cheers for Sweatshops." *New York Times Magazine*, September 24, pp. 70–71.

Krueger, Anne O. 1990. "Free Trade is the Best Policy." In Robert Z. Lawrence and Charles L. Schultze (eds.), *An American Trade Strategy: Options for the 1990s.* Washington, D.C.: Brookings Institution.

———. (ed.). 1996. *The Political Economy of American Trade Policy.* Chicago: University of Chicago Press.

———. 1997. "Trade Policy and Economic Development: How We Learn." *American Economic Review* 87 (March): 1–22.

———. 1999. "Free Trade Agreements as Protectionist Devices: Rules of Origin." In James R. Melvin, James C. Moore, and Raymond Reizman (eds.), *Trade, Theory and Econometrics: Essays in Honor of John S. Chipman.* New York: Routledge.

———. 2000. "NAFTA's Effects: A Preliminary Assessment." *World Economy* 23 (June): 761–75.

Krugman, Paul R. 1990. *The Age of Diminished Expectations.* Cambridge: MIT Press.

———. 1994. "Competitiveness: A Dangerous Obsession." *Foreign Affairs* 73:28–44.

———. 1995. "Dutch Tulips and Emerging Markets." *Foreign Affairs* 74:28–44.

———. 1998a. "Ricardo's Difficult Idea: Why Intellectuals Don't Understand Comparative Advantage." In Gary Cook (ed.), *The Economics and Politics of International Trade.* London: Routledge.

———. 1998b. *The Accidental Theorist.* New York: Norton.

———. 2008. "Trade and Wages, Reconsidered." *Brookings Papers on Economic Activity* 1:103–54.

Kull, Steven. 2000. *Americans on Globalization.* University of Maryland, Program on International Policy Attitudes, March 28.

———. 2004. *Americans on Globalization, Trade, and Farm Subsidies.* University of Maryland, Program on International Policy Attitudes, January 22.

Lardy, Nicholas. 1992. *Foreign Trade and Economic Reform in China, 1978–1990.* New York: Cambridge University Press.

Lawrence, Robert Z. 2008. *Blue Collar Blues: Is Trade to Blame for Rising U.S. Income Inequality?* Washington, D.C.: Peterson Institute for International Economics.

Lawrence, Robert Z., and Robert E. Litan. 1986. *Saving Free Trade: A Pragmatic Approach.* Washington, D.C.: Brookings Institution.

League of Nations. 1933. *World Economic Survey.* Geneva: League of Nations.

Lee, Ching Kwan. 1998. *Gender and the South China Miracle: Two Worlds of Factory Women.* Berkeley: University of California Press.

Lee, Jong-Wha. 1995. "Capital Goods Imports and Long-Run Growth." *Journal of Development Economics* 48 (October): 91–110.

———. 1996. "Government Interventions and Productivity Growth." *Journal of Economic Growth* 1 (September): 391–414.

Lerner, Abba P. 1936. "The Symmetry between Import and Export Taxes." *Economica* 3:306–13.

Lett, Erin, and Judith Banister. 2006. "Labor Costs of Manufacturing Employees in China: An Update to 2003–04." *Monthly Labor Review* 129: 40–44.

Levinsohn, James. 1993. "Testing the Imports-as-Market-Discipline Hypothesis." *Journal of International Economics* 35 (August): 1–22.

Levinsohn, James. 1999. "Employment Responses to International Liberalization in Chile." *Journal of International Economics* 47 (April): 321–44.

Levinsohn, James, and Wendy Petropoulos. 2001. "Creative Destruction or Just Plain Destruction?: The U.S. Textile and Apparel Industries since 1972." NBER Working Paper No. 8348.

Levinson, Arik. 2007. "Technology, International Trade, and Pollution from U.S. Manufacturing." NBER Working Paper No. 13616, November.

Levy, Frank, and Ari Goelman. 2005. "Offshoring and Radiology." *Brookings Trade Forum*:411–23.

Lewis, William W. 2004. *The Power of Productivity: Wealth, Poverty, and the Threat to Global Stability.* Chicago: University of Chicago Press.

Limão, Nuno. 2006. "Preferential Trade Agreements as Stumbling Blocks for Multilateral Trade Liberalization: Evidence for the U.S." *American Economic Review* 96:896–914.

Limão, Nuno, and Anthony Venables. 2001. "Infrastructure, Geographical Disadvantage, Transport Costs and Trade." *World Bank Economic Review* 15:451–79.

Linden, Greg, Kenneth L. Kraemer, and Jason Dedrick. 2007. "Who Captures the Value in a Global Innovation System? The Case of Apple's iPod." Personal Computing Center, University of California at Irvine.

Lindsey, Brink. 2001. "Poor Choice: Why Globalization Didn't Cause 9/11." *New Republic* 225 (November 12).

———. 2004. "Job Losses and Trade: A Reality Check." Trade Policy Briefing Paper No. 19, Center for Trade Policy Studies. Washington, D.C.: Cato Institute, March 17.

Lindsey, Brink, Daniel T. Griswold, and Aaron Lukas. 1999. "The Steel 'Crisis' and the Costs of Protectionism." Trade Briefing Paper, Center for Trade Policy Studies. Washington, D.C.: Cato Institute, April 16.

Lindsey, Brink, and Daniel J. Ikenson. 2003. *Antidumping Exposed: The Devilish Details of Unfair Trade Law.* Washington, D.C.: Cato Institute.

Lipsey, Robert E., and Fredrik Sjöholm. 2001. "Foreign Direct Investment and Wages in Indonesian Manufacturing." NBER Working Paper No. 8299, May.

Lizza, Ryan. 2000. "Silent Partner: The Man Behind the Anti–Free Trade Revolt." *New Republic* 222 (January 10): 22–25.

Lopez-Cordova, J. Ernesto, and Christopher Meissner. 2004. "Globalization and Democracy, 1870–2000." Working Paper, Cambridge University, United Kingdom.

Low, Patrick. 1993. *Trading Free: The GATT and U.S. Trade Policy.* New York: Twentieth Century Fund.

Lowe, Jeffrey H. 2004. "An Ownership-Based Framework of the U.S. Current Account, 1992–2002." *Survey of Current Business* 84 (January): 66–68.

Macaulay, Thomas Babington. 1900. *The Complete Writings of Lord Macaulay.* Volume 18: Speeches and Legal Studies. Boston: Houghton, Mifflin.

Madsen, Jakob. 2007. "Technology Spillover through Trade and TFP Convergence: 135 Years of Evidence for the OECD Countries." *Journal of International Economics* 72:464–80.

Mansfield, Edward D., Helen V. Milner, and B. Peter Rosendorff. 2000. "Free to Trade: Democracies, Autocracies, and International Trade." *American Political Science Review* 94 (June): 305–21.

Mansfield, Edward, D., and Brian M. Pollins. 2003. *Economic Interdependence and International Conflict: New Perspectives on an Enduring Debate.* Ann Arbor: University of Michigan Press.

Marshall, Alfred. 1926. *Official Papers of Alfred Marshall.* Edited by J. M. Keynes. London: Macmillan.

Martin, Will, and Elena Ianchovichina. 2001. "Trade Liberalization in China's Accession to the World Trade Organization." *World Bank Policy Research Working Paper No. 2623.* Washington, D.C.: World Bank.

Maskus, Keith. 1997. "Should Core Labor Standards Be Imposed Through International Trade Policy?" World Bank Policy Research Paper No. 1817, August.

———. 2000. *Intellectual Property Rights in the Global Economy.* Washington, D.C.: Institute for International Economics.

Mataloni, Ray. 2008. "Operations of U.S. Multinational Corporations." *Survey of Current Business* 88:26–47.

Maurer, Noel. 2006. "Was NAFTA Necessary? Trade Policy and Relative Economic Failure since 1982." Harvard Business School Working Paper, No. 06-043.

Mayda, Anna Maria, and Dani Rodrik. 2005. "Why Are Some Individuals (and Countries) More Protectionist than Others?" *European Economic Review* 49:1393–1430.

Mayer, Jane, and Jose de Cordoba. 1991. "Sweet Life: First Family of Sugar Is Tough on Workers, Generous to Politicians." *Wall Street Journal,* July 29.

Mayer, Wolfgang. 1984. "Endogenous Tariff Formation." *American Economic Review* 74 (December): 970–85.

Mazumdar, Joy. 2001. "Imported Machinery and Growth in LDCs." *Journal of Development Economics* 65 (June): 209–24.

McLean, Ian, and Kris Mitchener. 1999. "U.S. Economic Growth and Convergence, 1880–1980." *Journal of Economic History* 59 (December): 1016–42.

McKinsey Global Institute. 1993. *Manufacturing Productivity.* Washington, D.C.: McKinsey & Co.

McRae, Donald. 2004. WhatIs the Future of WTO Dispute Settlement? *Journal of International Economics Law* 7 (March): 3–21.

Messerlin, Patrick A. 2001. *Measuring the Costs of Protection in Europe.* Washington, D.C.: Institute for International Economics, May.

Milazzo, Matteo. 1998. *Subsidies in World Fisheries: A Reexamination.* World Bank Technical Paper No. 406. Washington, D.C.: World Bank.

Mill, John Stuart. 1909. *Principles of Political Economy.* London: Longmans.

———. 1982. *On Liberty.* New York: Penguin.

Montesquieu. 1989. *The Spirit of the Laws,* translated by A. M. Cohler, B. C. Miller, and H. S. Stone. New York: Cambridge University Press.

Montgomery, Mark. 1995. "Reassessing the Waste Trade Crisis: What Do We Really Know?" *Journal of Environment and Development* 4:1–28.

Moore, Michael O. 1996. "Steel Protection in the 1980s: The Waning Influence of Big Steel?" In Anne O. Krueger (ed.), *The Political Economy of American Trade Policy.* Chicago: University of Chicago Press.

———. 1999. "Antidumping Reform in the United States: A Faded Sunset." *Journal of World Trade* 33 (August): 1–17.

———. 2005. "VERs vs. Price Undertakings Under the WTO." *Review of International Economics* 13:298–310.

———. 2007. "Antidumping Reform in the Doha Round: A Pessimistic Assessment." *Pacific Economic Review* 12:335–79.

Moore, Michael. 2003. *A World Without Walls: Freedom, Development, Free Trade, and Global Governance.* New York: Cambridge University Press.

Morris, Julian. 2000. "International Environmental Agreements: Developing Another Path." In Terry L. Anderson and Henry I. Miller (eds.), *The Greening of U.S. Foreign Policy.* Stanford: Hoover Institution Press.

Murthy, N. R. Narayana. 2001. "Reflections of an Entrepreneur." Commencement address at the Wharton School of Business, University of Pennsylvania. May 20. Available at: http://knowledge.wharton.upenn.edu/india/article.cfm?articleid=4004/

Mussa, Michael. 1982. "Government Policy and the Adjustment Process." In Jagdish Bhagwati (ed.), *Import Competition and Response.* Chicago: University of Chicago Press.

Nader, Ralph (ed.). 1993. *The Case Against Free Trade: GATT, NAFTA, and the Globalization of Corporate Power.* San Francisco: Earth Island Press.

Nelson, Douglas. 2006. "The Political Economy of Antidumping." *European Journal of Political Economy* 22:554–90.

Ohashi, Hiroshi. 2005. "Learning by Doing, Export Subsidies, and Industry Growth: Japanese Steel in the 1950s and 60s." *Journal of International Economics* 66:297–323.

Oneal, John, and Bruce Russett. 2000. *Triangulating Peace: Democracy, Interdependence, and International Organizations.* New York: Norton.

Organization for Economic Cooperation and Development. 1994. *The OECD Jobs Study: Facts, Analysis, Strategy.* Paris: OECD.

———. 1996. *Trade, Employment, and Labour Standards: A Study of Core Workers' Rights and International Trade.* Paris: OECD.

———. 2000. *International Trade and Core Labour Standards.* Paris: OECD.

———. 2008. *Agricultural Policies in OECD Countries, 2008.* Paris: OCED.

Orme, William A., Jr. 1996. *Understanding NAFTA: Mexico, Free Trade, and the New North America.* Austin: University of Texas Press.

Oxfam. 2002. *Rigged Rules and Double Standards: Trade, Globalisation, and the Fight Against Poverty.* London: Oxfam.

Pack, Howard, and Kamal Saggi. 2006. "Is There a Case for Industrial Policy? A Critical Survey." *World Bank Research Observer* 21:267–97.

Palmeter, N. David. 1999. "National Sovereignty and the World Trade Organization." *Journal of World Intellectual Property* 2 (January): 77–91.

Panagariya, Arvind. 2004. "Miracles and Debacles: In Defense of Trade Openness." *World Economy* 27, 1149–72.

———. 2005. "Agricultural Liberalisation and the Least Developed Countries: Six Fallacies." *World Economy* 28:1277–99.

———. 2008. *India: the Emerging Giant.* New York: Oxford University Press.

Panagariya, Arvind, Shekhar Shah, and Deepak Mishra. 2001. "Demand Elasticities in International Trade: Are They Really Low?" *Journal of Development Economics* 64 (April): 313–42.

Pareto, Vilfredo. 1971. *Manual of Political Economy.* Translated by Ann S. Schwier. New York: Augustus M. Kelley.

Pastor, Robert. 1983. "The Cry-and-Sigh Syndrome: Congress and Trade Policy." In Allen Shick (ed.), *Making Economic Policy in Congress.* Washington, D.C.: American Enterprise Institute.

Pavcnik, Nina. 2002. "Trade Liberalization, Exit, and Productivity Improvements: Evidence from Chilean Plants." *Review of Economic Studies* 69 (January): 245–76.

Pierce, Richard J. 2000. "Antidumping Law as a Means of Facilitating Cartelization." *Antitrust Law Journal* 67:725–43.

Pomfret, Richard. 2007. "Is Regionalism an Increasing Feature of the World Economy?" *World Economy* 30:923–47.

Preeg, Ernest H. 1995. *Traders in a Brave New World: The Uruguay Round and the Future of the International Trading System.* Chicago: University of Chicago Press.

Prusa, Thomas J. 1998. "Cumulation and Antidumping: A Challenge to Competition." *World Economy* 21 (November): 1021–33.

———. 2001. "On the Spread and Impact of Antidumping Duties." *Canadian Journal of Economics* 34 (August): 591–611.

Read, Robert. 2005. "The Political Economy of Trade Protection: The Determinants and Welfare Impact of the 2002 US Emergency Steel Safeguard Measures." *World Economy* 28:1119–37.

Reich, Robert B. 1994. "Keynote Address." In *International Labor Standards and Global Economic Integration: Proceedings of a Symposium.* Washington, D.C.: U.S. Department of Labor.

Reid, Peter C. 1990. *Made Well in America: Lessons From Harley-Davidson on Being the Best.* New York: McGraw-Hill.

Renaud, Jean-Paul. 2004. "Steep Cost Overruns, Delays Plague Efforts to Rebuild Bay Bridge." *Los Angeles Times,* May 29.

Revenga, Ana L. 1992. "Exporting Jobs? The Impact of Import Competition on Employment and Wages in U.S. Manufacturing." *Quarterly Journal of Economics* 107 (February): 255–84.

Reynolds, Kara. 2006. "Subsidizing Rent-Seeking: Antidumping Protection and the Byrd Amendment." *Journal of International Economics* 70:490–502.

Richards, Bill. 1997. "Shaky Numbers: Layoffs Not Related to NAFTA Can Trigger Special Help Anyway." *Wall Street Journal,* June 30, p. A1.

Roberts, Donna. 1998. "Preliminary Assessment of the Effects of the WTO Agreement on Sanitary and Phytosanitary Measures Trade Regulations." *Journal of International Economic Law* 2 (December): 377–405.

Roberts, Donna, and Kate DeRemer. 1997. *An Overview of Technical Barriers to U.S. Agricultural Exports.* Economic Research Service, U.S. Department of Agriculture, Staff Paper AGES-9705, March.

Roberts, Mark J., and James R. Tybout. 1996. *Industrial Evolution in Developing Countries: Micro Patterns of Turnover, Productivity, and Market Structure.* New York: Oxford University Press for the World Bank.

Robertson, David. 2000. "Civil Society and the WTO." *World Economy* 23 (September): 1119–34.

Rodríguez, Francisco. 2007. "Openness and Growth: What Have We Learned?" In José Antonio Ocampo, K. S. Jomo, and Rob Vos (eds.), *Growth Divergences: Explaining Differences in Economic Performance.* London: Zed Books.

Rodríguez, Francisco, and Dani Rodrik. 2001. "Trade Policy and Economic Growth: A Skeptic's Guide to Cross-National Evidence." In Ben S. Bernanke and Kenneth Rogoff (eds.), *NBER Macroeconomics Annual, 2000.* Cambridge: MIT Press.

Rodrik, Dani. 1989. "Optimal Trade Taxes for a Large Country with Non-atomistic Firms." *Journal of International Economics* 26 (February): 157–67.

———. 1995. "Political Economy of Trade." In Gene M. Grossman and Kenneth Rogoff (eds.), *The Handbook of International Economics*, Vol. 3. Amsterdam: Elsevier.

———. 1996. "Labor Standards in International Trade: Do They Matter and What Do We Do About Them?" In Robert Lawrence et al., *Emerging Agenda for Global Trade: High Stakes for Developing Countries*. Washington, D.C.: Overseas Development Council.

———. 1999. "Democracies Pay Higher Wages." *Quarterly Journal of Economics* 114 (August): 707–38.

Rodrik, Dani, and Arvind Subramanian. 2004. "From 'Hindu Growth' to Productivity Surge: The Mystery of the Indian Growth Transition." NBER Working Paper No. 10376, March.

Roland-Holst, David, Kenneth Reinhart, and Clinton Schiells. 1992. "North American Trade Liberalization and the Role of Non-Tariff Barriers." In U.S. International Trade Commission, *Economy-Wide Modeling of the Economic Implication of an FTA with Mexico and a NAFTA with Canada and Mexico*. USITC Publication 20436. Washington, D.C.: USITC.

Romalis, John. 2007. "Market Access, Openness and Growth." NBER Working Paper No. 13048, April.

Romer, Paul. 1994. "New Goods, Old Theory, and the Welfare Costs of Trade Restrictions." *Journal of Development Economics* 43 (February): 5–38.

Rose, Andrew K. 2004. "Do We Really Know that the WTO Increases Trade?" *American Economic Review* 94 (March): 98–114.

Rosenberg, Nathan. 1960. "Some Institutional Aspects of the 'Wealth of Nations.'" *Journal of Political Economy* 68 (December): 557–70.

Rosenthal, Elisabeth. 2002. "Buicks, Starbucks and Fried Chicken. Still China?" *New York Times*, February 25.

Ruffin, Roy J. 2002. "David Ricardo's Discovery of Comparative Advantage." *History of Political Economy* 34 (Winter): 727–48.

Runge, C. Ford. 2003. "Agri-vation: The Farm Bill from Hell." *National Interest* 72 (Summer):85–93.

Rutherford, Thomas F., and David G. Tarr. 2002. "Trade Liberalization, Product Variety, and Growth in a Small Open Economy: A Quantitative Assessment." *Journal of International Economics* 56 (March): 247–72.

Rutkowski, Aleksander. 2006. "Withdrawals of Anti-dumping Complaints in the EU: A Sign of Collusion." *World Economy* 30: 470–503.

Sampson, Gary P. 2000. *Trade, Environment, and the WTO: The Post-Seattle Agenda*. Washington, D.C.: Overseas Development Council.

Samuelson, Paul A. 1972. *The Collected Scientific Papers of Paul A. Samuelson*. Vol. 3. Cambridge: MIT Press.

Sanchez, Julian. 2003. "Lou's Blues: Lou Dobbs and the New Mercantilism." http://www.reason.com, October 30.

Saunders, Caroline, Andrew Barber, and Greg Taylor. 2006. "Food Miles: Comparative Energy/Emissions Performance of New Zealand's Agricultural Industries." Research Report No. 285. Christchurch: Lincoln University, New Zealand.

Sazanami, Yoko, Shujiro Urata, and Hiroki Kawai. 1995. *Measuring the Costs of Protection in Japan.* Washington, D.C.: Institute for International Economics, January.

Scheiber, Noam. 2004. "As a Center for Outsourcing, India Could Be Losing Its Edge." *New York Times,* May 2.

Scheve, Kenneth F., and Matthew J. Slaughter. 2001a. *Worker Perceptions and Pressures in the Global Economy.* Washington, D.C.: Institute for International Economics, March.

————. 2001b. "What Determines Individual Trade-Policy Preferences?" *Journal of International Economics* 54 (August): 267–92.

Schoepfle, Gregory K. 2000. "U.S. Trade Adjustment Assistance Policies for Workers." In Alan V. Deardorff and Robert M. Stern (eds.), *Social Dimensions of U.S. Trade Policies.* Ann Arbor: University of Michigan Press.

Schott, Peter K. 2008. "The Relative Sophistication of China's Exports." *Economic Policy* 23, 5–49.

Scott, Robert E. 1999. "NAFTA's Pain Deepens: Job Destruction Accelerates in 1999 with Losses in Every State." Washington, D.C.: Economic Policy Institute Briefing Paper, November.

————. 2008. "The China Trade Toll: Widespread Wage Suppression, 2 Million Jobs Lost in the U.S." Washington, D.C.: Economic Policy Institute Briefing Paper No. 219, July 30.

Segerstrom, Paul. 2003. "Naomi Klein and the Anti-Globalization Movement." In Mats Lundahl (ed.), *Globalization and Its Enemies.* Stockholm: Economic Research Institute.

Shin, Hyun Ja. 1998. "Possible Instances of Predatory Pricing in Recent U.S. Antidumping Cases." In Robert Z. Lawrence (ed.), *Brookings Trade Forum, 1998.* Washington, D.C.: Brookings Institution.

Shirk, Susan L. 1994. *How China Opened Its Door: The Political Success of the PRC's Foreign Trade and Investment Reforms.* Washington, D.C.: Brookings Institution.

Sivadasan, Jagadeesh. 2003. "Barriers to Entry and Productivity: Micro-evidence from Indian Manufacturing Sector Reforms." Working paper, University of Chicago Graduate School of Business, November.

Smith, Adam. 1976. *An Inquiry into the Nature and Causes of the Wealth of Nations.* Oxford: Clarendon Press.

————. 1977. *Correspondence of Adam Smith.* Oxford: Clarendon Press.

————. 1978. *Lectures on Jurisprudence.* Oxford: Clarendon Press.

————, 1980. *Essays on Philosophical Subjects.* Oxford: Clarendon Press.

Specter, Michael. 2008. "Big Foot." *New Yorker.* February 25.

Spinanger, Dean. 1999. "Textiles Beyond the MFA Phase-Out." *World Economy* 22 (June): 455–76.

Srinivasan, T. N. 1998. *Developing Countries and the Multilateral Trading System.* Boulder, Colo.: Westview Press.

Srinivasan, T. N., and Suresh Tendulkar. 2003. *Reintegrating India with the World Economy.* Washington, D.C.: Institute for International Economics.

Stolper, Wolfgang F., and Paul A. Samuelson. 1941. "Protection and Real Wages." *Review of Economic Studies* 9 (November): 58–73.

Subramanian, Arvind, and Shang-Jin Wei. 2007. "The WTO Promotes Trade, Strongly But Unevenly." *Journal of International Economics* 72:151–75.

Sumner, Daniel A. 2006. "Reducing Cotton Subsidies: The DDA Initiative." In Kym Anderson and Will Martin (eds.), *Agricultural Trade Reform and the Doha Development Agenda.* Washington, D.C.: World Bank.

Suomela, John W. 1993. *Free Trade versus Fair Trade: The Making of American Trade Policy in a Political Environment.* Turku, Finland: Institute for European Studies.

Swagel, Phillip. 2000. "Union Behavior, Industry Rents, and Optimal Policies." *International Journal of Industrial Organization* 18 (August): 925–47.

Sykes, Alan O. 1998. "Antidumping and Antitrust: What Problems Does Each Address?" In Robert Z. Lawrence (ed.), *Brookings Trade Forum, 1998.* Washington, D.C.: Brookings Institution.

———. 2003. "The Safeguards Mess: A Critique of WTO Jurisprudence." *World Trade Review* 2 (November): 261–96.

Taylor, Christopher T. 2004. "The Economic Effects of Withdrawn Antidumping Investigations: Is There Evidence of Collusive Settlements?" *Journal of International Economics* 62 (March): 295–312.

Tempest, Rohn. 1996. "Barbie and the World Economy." *Los Angeles Times,* September 22, p. A-1.

Thorton, John L. 2008. "Long Time Coming: The Prospects for Democracy in China." *Foreign Affairs* 87:17–26.

Tomz, Michael, Judith L. Goldstein, and Douglas Rivers. 2007. "Do We Really Know that the WTO Increases Trade? Comment." *American Economic Review* 97:2005–2018.

Tonelson, Alan. 1994. "Beating Back Predatory Trade." *Foreign Affairs* 73: 123–35.

Tornell, Aaron. 1991. "Time Inconsistency of Protectionist Programs." *Quarterly Journal of Economics* 106:963–74.

Tornell, Aaron, Frank Westermann, and Lorenza Martinez. 2004. "NAFTA and Mexico's Less-than-Stellar Performance." NBER Working Paper No. 10289, February.

Trefler, Daniel. 1993. "Trade Liberalization and the Theory of Endogenous Pro-
    tection: An Econometric Study of U.S. Import Policy." *Journal of Politi-
    cal Economy* 101 (February): 138–60.

———. 2004. "The Long and Short of the Canada-U.S. Free Trade Agreement."
    American Economic Review 94 (September): 870–95.

Tybout, James R. 2000. "Manufacturing Firms in Developing Countries: How
    Well Do They Do, and Why?" *Journal of Economic Literature* 38
    (March): 11–44.

———. 2003. "Plant and Firm Level Evidence on 'New' Trade Theories." In
    E. Kwan Choi and James Harrigan (eds.), *Handbook of International
    Trade*. New York: Basil Blackwell.

Tybout, James R., and M. Daniel Westbrook. 1995. "Trade Liberalization and the
    Dimensions of Efficiency Change in Mexican Manufacturing Indus-
    tries." *Journal of International Economics* 39 (August): 53–78.

United Nations. 1962. *Yearbook of International Trade Statistics 1960.* New
    York: United Nations.

United Nations Development Program. 2002. Arab Human Development Report,
    2002: Creating Opportunities for Future Generations. New York:
    United Nations.

U.S. Bureau of the Census. 1975. *Historical Statistics of the United States, From
    Colonial Times to 1970.* Washington, D.C.: GPO.

———. 2009. *Statistical Abstract of the United States, 2009.* Washington, D.C.:
    GPO.

U.S. Department of Commerce, Office of Inspector General. 1993. "Import Ad-
    ministration's Investigations of Steel Industry Petitions," Report No.
    TTD-5541-4-0001, December.

U.S. Department of Commerce, International Trade Administration. 2006.
    "Employment Changes in U.S. Sugar Manufacturing: The Impact of
    Sugar Prices." March. Available at: http://www.ita.doc.gov/media/
    Publications/pdf/sugar06.pdf.

U.S. Department of Energy, Energy Information Administration. 1998. *Petroleum
    Supply Annual 1998.* Washington, D.C.: GPO.

U.S. General Accounting Office. 1993. *Sugar Program: Changing Domestic and
    International Conditions Require Program Changes.* RCED/93/84.
    Washington, D.C.: GAO.

——— 2000a. *Sugar Program: Supporting Sugar Prices Has Increased Users'
    Costs While Benefiting Producers.* RCED/00/126. Washington, D.C.:
    GAO, June.

——— 2000b. *World Trade Organization: Issues in Dispute Settlement.* NSIAD-
    00-210. Washington, D.C.: GAO, August.

———. 2003. *World Trade Organization: Standard of Review and Impact of
    Trade Remedy Rulings.* GAO-03-824. Washington, D.C.: GAO, July.

U.S. General Accountability Office. 2005. *Issues and Effects of Implementing the Continued Dumping and Subsidy Offset Act.* GAO-05-979. Washington, D.C.: GAO, September.

U.S. House of Representatives, Committee on Ways and Means. 1994. *Hearings: North American Free Trade Agreement (NAFTA) and Supplemental Agreements to the NAFTA.* Washington, D.C.: GPO.

———. 2003a. *Overview and Compilation of U.S. Trade Statues: 2003 Edition.* Washington, D.C.: GPO, June.

———. 2003b. *Greenbook.* Washington, D.C.: GPO.

U.S. International Trade Commission. 1995. *The Economic Effects of Antidumping and Countervailing Duty Orders and Suspension Agreements.* Investigation No. 332-344. Publication 2900. Washington, D.C.: USITC, June.

———. 1997. *Likely Impact of Providing Quota-Free and Duty-Free Entry to Textiles and Apparel from Sub-Saharan Africa.* Investigation 332-379. Publication 3056. Washington, D.C.: USITC, September.

———. 1999. *Production Sharing: Use of U.S. Components and Materials in Foreign Assembly, Operations 1995–1999.* USITC Publication 3265. Washington, D.C.: USITC, December.

———. 2003. *Steel Consuming Industries: Competitive Conditions with Respect to Steel Safeguard Measures. Volume III: Executive Summaries.* Investigation No. 332-452. Publication 3632. Washington, D.C.: USITC, September.

———. 2006. *U.S.-Colombia Trade Promotion Agreement: Potential Economy-wide and Selected Sectoral Effects.* Publication 3896. Washington, D.C.: USITC, December.

———. 2007a. *The Economic Effects of Significant U.S. Import Restraints.* Fifth Update 2007. Investigation No. 332-325. Publication 3906. Washington, D.C.: USITC.

———. 2007b. *Steel Wire Garment Hangers from China.* Investigation No. 731–TA–1123 (Preliminary). Publication 3951. Washington, D.C.: USTIC.

U.S. Trade Representative. 2000. *2000 Trade Policy Agenda and 1999 Annual Report.* Washington, D.C.: USTR.

Vandenbussche, Hylke, and Maurizio Zanardi. 2008. "What Explains the Proliferation of Antidumping Laws?" *Economic Policy* 23:93–138.

Viner, Jacob. 1991. *Essays on the Intellectual History of Economics.* Princeton: Princeton University Press.

Wacziarg, Romain. 2001. "Measuring the Dynamic Gains from Trade." *World Bank Economic Review* 15 (October): 393–429.

Wacziarg, Romain, and Karen H. Welch. 2008. "Trade Liberalization and Growth: New Evidence." *World Bank Economic Review* 22:187–231.

Wade, Robert. 2004. *Governing the Market: Economic Theory and the Role of Government in East Asian Industrialization.* Princeton: Princeton University Press.

Wallach, Lori, and Patrick Woodall. 2004. *Whose Trade Organization?* New York: New Press.

Watkins, Kevin. 2002. "Cultivating Poverty: The Impact of US Cotton Subsidies on Africa." Oxfam Briefing Paper No. 30, September.

Watkins, Ralph. 2003. "Production-Sharing Update: Developments in 2002." *Industry Trade and Technology Review.* Washington, D.C.: U.S. International Trade Commission Publication No. 3534, November.

Watson, James L. 1997. *Golden Arches East: McDonald's in East Asia.* Stanford: Stanford University Press.

Wei, Shang-Jin, and Yi Wu. 2003. "The Life-and-Death Consequences of Globalization." International Monetary Fund Working Paper, June.

Westphal, Larry E. 1990. "Industrial Policy in an Export Propelled Economy: Lessons from South Korea's Experience." *Journal of Economic Perspectives* 4 (Summer): 41–59.

Winters, L. Alan, and Won Chang. 2000. "Regional Integration and Import Prices: An Empirical Investigation." *Journal of International Economics* 51 (August): 363–78.

Winters, L. Alan, Neil McCulloch, and Andrew McKay. 2004. "Trade Liberalization and Poverty: The Evidence So Far." *Journal of Economic Literature* 42, 72–115.

Wolf, Martin. 2004. *Why Globalization Works.* New Haven: Yale University Press.

World Bank. 1975. *World Tables.* Baltimore: Johns Hopkins University Press.

———. 1993. *The East Asian Miracle: Economic Growth and Public Policy.* New York: Oxford University Press.

———. 1995. *World Tables.* Baltimore: Johns Hopkins University Press.

———. 2000. *World Development Indicators, 2000.* Washington, D.C.: World Bank.

———. 2001. *Global Economic Prospects and the Developing Countries.* Washington, D.C.: World Bank.

———. 2003. *India: Sustaining Reform, Reducing Poverty.* Washington, D.C.: World Bank.

———. 2004. *Doing Business in 2004: Understanding Regulation.* Washington, D.C.: World Bank.

———. 2005. *Economic Growth in the 1990s: Learning from a Decade of Reform.* Washington, D.C.: World Bank.

———. 2007. *Doing Business, 2008.* Washington, D.C.: World Bank.

———. 2008a. *World Trade Indicators 2008: Benchmarking Policy and Performance.* Washington, D.C.: World Bank.

———. 2008b. *International Trade and Climate Change: Economic, Legal, and Institutional Perspectives.* Washington D.C.: World Bank.

World Resources Institute. 1999. World Resources. Washington, D.C.: World Resources Institute.

World Trade Organization. 1997. "Report of the Panel: EC Measures Concerning Meat and Meat Products (Hormones), Complaint by the United States." WT/DS26/R/US. Geneva: WTO, August 18.

———. 1998. *Annual Report, 1998.* Geneva: WTO.

———. 1999. *The Legal Texts: The Results of the Uruguay Round of Multilateral Trade Negotiations.* New York: Cambridge University Press.

———. 2003. *International Trade Statistics, 2003.* Geneva: WTO.

———. 2004. *Annual Report, 2004.* Geneva: WTO, June.

———. 2008a. *Annual Report, 2008.* Geneva: WTO.

———. 2008b. *Trade Policy Review: United States.* WT/TPR/S/200. Geneva: WTO, May.

Wu, Harry X. 2001. "China's Comparative Labour Productivity Performance in Manufacturing, 1952–1997 Catching Up or Falling Behind?" *China Economic Review* 12:162–89.

Yi, Kei-Mu. 2003. "Can Vertical Specialization Explain the Growth of World Trade?" *Journal of Political Economy* 112:52–102.

Yoon, Carol K. 2000. "Simple Method Found to Increase Crop Yields Vastly." *New York Times,* August 22.

Zanardi, Maurizio. 2006. "Antidumping: A Problem in International Trade." *European Journal of Political Economy* 22:591–617.

Zoellick, Robert B. 2000. "A Republican Foreign Policy." *Foreign Affairs* 79:63–78.

Index